CW00548282

DISCOVERING NORTHUMBERLAND

Books by the same author

ANGLO-SAXON NORTHUMBRIA
THE ROMANS IN NORTH BRITAIN
MEDIEVAL CASTLES OF NORTHUMBERLAND

DISCOVERING NORTHUMBERLAND

A Handbook of Local History

by

T. H. ROWLAND

Published by
FRANK GRAHAM
6, Queen's Terrace, Newcastle upon Tyne, 2

SBN 9028 3302 2

Composed in 10pt on 11pt Plantin and printed in Great Britain
by Northumberland Press Limited, Gateshead

CONTENTS

INTRODUCTION

The purpose of this handbook is to provide the ordinary reader, student or scholar with information helpful in the study of local history and the environment. It is not conceived in a narrow sense, but related to other studies. There is a suggested combination of the use of books with visual and archaeological material—a combination of study with field visits. These provide complementary and interrelated exercises and problems. History and everyday experience can be brought together, so that the past and the present illuminate each other. The pilgrim makes a similar journey through time, though circumstances are never the same. There is a complicated pattern of change and continuity, custom and reform.

Considered widely, local history is far removed from parochialism. It does not mean that a local marriage or murder is more important than a world war or famine. It does not mean that the parish council is more important than the United Nations Organization, but if people can understand the working of local communities, they are all the more likely to understand how larger communities function. They may gather some idea of interdependence, which is extremely difficult to realize in modern complex societies. Nowadays, there is a reaction towards regionalism as a result of an excessive growth of centralization. Local community spirit is fostered and developed by a sense of the past. The concept of 'understanding' is the most important to be developed. 'Racialism' would diminish if we all knew whence our ancestors came and whither they went.

Local history has another advantage: it involves participation by its students. World affairs can be studied at a great distance through books, or films, or from talks by visitors. The lecturer, or teacher, has the advantage of having chosen a particular field of study, in which few or any of his listeners can compete. In local affairs, however, they should be able to provide written, spoken and visual material first hand, so that the work itself involves immediate co-operation. Anyone can take part in this, but not necessarily produce a finished result. When a survey is completed, it is found in due course that another is necessary, to bring the information up to date. It has to be remembered that the 'expert' is needed to organize the collection, co-ordination and evaluation of material. The local study has to be put into perspective.

Archaeologically, too, all kinds of people can take part in field work —finding, plotting and recording a variety of sites and buildings. But excavation is the work of an expert just as a medical operation is the work of a skilled surgeon. Excavation is destruction; hence unskilled excavation should never be attempted. It is possible to take part in training excavations and other 'digs'. Usually these are publicized in the 'Calendar of Forthcoming Excavations' by the Council of British Archaeology. (8, St Andrew's Place, London NW1.) It is also possible to form a school society or to join an adult evening class for the pursuit of Local History or Archaeology, but it can be done individually by photography, record cards, accounts, plans and tape-recordings. The rapidity of change makes it all the more urgent for this to be done.

It is hoped that this handbook will provide some helpful suggestions and a good deal of stimulation.

PREHISTORY

Although there have been remarkable developments in the study of prehistory, and although the descent of man has been pushed back thousands of years, prehistory still tends to be regarded in this country as the unhappy prelude to the arrival of the Romans and civilization. The study of our barbarian ancestors is not considered profitable for the maturer mind. The Neolithic, or New Stone Age, in this country dates back to 3000 B.C., and there is a great deal worthy of study. This consists of careful observation of tools, weapons, pottery and armour on display in Museums. In particular the Museum of Antiquities at Newcastle University is worth a visit for here Prehistoric and Roman Antiquities can be studied in conjunction. [*Open to public 10 a.m.—5 p.m. Not Sundays and holidays. Parties by arrangement. Phone Newcastle* 21727.] There is also a fine little museum, recently reorganized, at Alnwick Castle. This is only open in summer months.

There have recently been published two books on pottery and bronze-ware in this area.

TAIT, J., *Beakers from Northumberland.* 1965.
BURGESS, C., *Bronze Age Metalwork in Northern England 1000-750 B.C.* 1968.

By an imaginative effort these objects have to be visualized in use at various prehistoric sites that should be visited.

EXCURSIONS OR FIELD VISITS

The sites recommended will only be a small selection of the most rewarding and since most of these are on private property, permission to visit has to be obtained from the tenant or landowner.

Burial places

There are very few of the massive long barrows in Northumberland and no chambered tombs. Many of these long barrows must have been robbed to provide stone for roads or field walls. The ones that survive are the Devil's Lapful (NT 641930), Bellshiel Law (NT 813013) and Monkridge (NT 913910). They are impressive in situation and size, but Bellshiel Law when excavated revealed very little—it was bounded by a *kerb* and had a cist burial at the east end. The word 'cairn' is often used for a pile of stones which may or may not be a burial place. Some piles have been made by removing stones to the boundaries of cultivated fields. This was done as far back as prehistoric times and they have become overgrown, forming mounds. Excavation has shown that some of these cairns had low retaining walls, or kerbs, of stones set upright in circular fashion. Recently a report of the excavation of one large and five small cairns at Chatton Sandyford has been published in *Archaelogia Aeliana*, 1968. It shows how these cairns were made up with small burial pits within. It was possible to date the burials—three inhumations and two cremations from carbonized material. These were of about 1700 B.C., with one a thousand years earlier. Beakers were also discovered. In lowland areas

Grooved Monolith, Duddo.

prehistoric graves are revealed as the result of ploughing. Any surface evidence has long been removed, but occasionally the plough encounters a heavy stone and this is found to be the 'lid' of a stone chest containing, perhaps, a crouched skeleton, weapons and a food beaker. [Example on display in the Hancock Museum.]

Burial sites are often found in association with settlements or fortifications, but it is difficult to prove a connection since the visible remains of the settlement are of a later period. But the presence of burial sites, standing stones and rock carvings in the neighbourhood of a settlement indicates some connection. There are more burial sites than supposed. It also has to be remembered that there were prehistoric sacred areas called 'henges'. A 'henge' consists of a circular embankment outside the ditch and gives no indication of dwellings. There are remains of stone circles—some stones have been removed, but it is possible to discern the circle. There are five stones of a circle near Duddo north of Ford, another at Goatstones (NY 845745) near Simonburn and a third at Threestone Burn (NT 212971) beyond Ilderton.

Settlements

These vary from enclosures with a ditch and fence to strongly defensible hill forts. A few selected sites will be suggested.

VISITS

Yeavering Bell (NT 928293). This is easily recognizable to the left of the road from Akeld to Kirknewton. Since it covers 13 acres with an enclosing wall, it could be called an 'oppidum' or town. Hut circles may be seen within the enclosure and there are magnificent views of the Glen Valley. The site overlooks the deserted village of Yeavering and the location of Edwin's Saxon Palace. Between the valley floor and the enclosing walls of the ancient settlement, a number of habitation sites can be distinguished on the hillside. There are a series of sites on the range of hills between Wooler and Yeavering. (NT 967283) Humbleton Hill, in particular, is worth a visit. It consists of a strong walled central fort with two enclosures attached, rather like a castle bailey. Hut circles can be picked out. There are extensive views of Wooler, the rivers Glen and Till and the mountains. In the fields to the north is a standing stone called Battle Stone. Within the area, too, are the tower at Akeld with a fine vaulted roof and the

Church of Kirknewton, which has a low vaulted chancel and an antique sculptured piece, depicting the Adoration of the Magi.

Old Bewick (NT 075225) *and Blawearie* (NT 087220)

The hill fort of Old Bewick is situated on the top of the escarpment overlooking the village. It is approached by means of a farm road leading to a derelict shepherd's house called Blawearie. Near this, overlooking the Harehope Burn, is another hill fort (Blawearie). Old Bewick is remarkable in that it is a double form hill fort, in shape not unlike a pair of spectacles. The two enclosures have double ramparts except along the cliff face. This is an area of rock carvings and tumuli. Half a mile to the north of the village on the Kirk Burn lies hidden the Norman Church with an apsidal east end. A good deal of the original masonry is distinguishable and it is perhaps the best Norman Church in the county.

Ros Castle (NT 081254). (On road from North Charlton to Chillingham.) This deserves brief mention as a site easy to visit without permission, since it is National Trust property. It involves a steep climb, but the views in all directions are rewarding—to Bamburgh, to Chillingham and to the Cheviot. It is perhaps worth remembering that this was Sir Edward Grey's favourite view. At Chillingham the herd of Wild White Cattle should be visited—these are the nearest approach we have to early native cattle. (NT 060259) Chillingham Church contains the finest sculptured monument in the county to Sir Ralph Gray and his wife, dating to the middle of the fifteenth century. Chillingham Castle, unfortunately is not accessible, but nearby Hepburn Tower is a grim reminder of Border warfare (NT 070249).

Lordenshaws (NT 055/993). Two miles south of Rothbury. This hill fort is best approached by a longish walk from the Forestburn to Rothbury Road at Garleigh, or from the Forestburn to Tosson route. If one starts at Garleigh it may be possible to pick out the remaining stones of a circle, then following westwards towards Lordenshaws, some ancient field walls and cup-marked rocks. A track leads to the East Gate of Lordenshaws which has massive stones still in position. The site is defended by a deep ditch and stone rampart. Within are the obvious remains of stone hut-circles about 30 feet in diameter. There is a subsidiary enclosure, not so strongly defended, presumably for animals. There is also a complex of enclosure walls, which can be dated to different periods, including those of a deer park. West of the enclosure can be distinguished three routes. The one to the west passes rocks, sculptured with intriguing cup and ring marks, which have not yet been satisfactorily explained. There are a number of cist burials in the neighbourhood. It is possible to walk to Tosson Burgh (NT 023006), another hill fort to the north-west, from here can be seen the sites of Witchy Neuk and Harehaugh (NY 981994 and NY 970002), overlooking the Coquet Valley and the village of Hepple.

Both the villages of Tosson and Hepple have mediaeval towers.

Witchy Neuk (NY 981994) *and Harehaugh* (NY 970002)

(Permission to visit from Hepple Whitfield Hall and the farm respectively.) Witchy Neuk is in a dominating position, but is not in fact strongly defended; Harehaugh with multiple defences is more impressive. Witchy Neuk was excavated to provide information for the *Northumberland County History* (Vol. XV), but the datable remains found were Roman. It seems however to have been a palisaded enclosure before obtaining stone walls. There are cairnfields in the neighbourhood and prehistoric trackways pass to the south towards Tosson. To the north is the Roman road from Rochester to Bridge of Aln. Harehaugh consists of a strongly defended citadel and a larger outer enclosure to the south-west. On the north it is protected by a precipitous slope; on the west the easier approach has triple defences. There are signs of burial sites in the neighbourhood and to the north is a group of standing stones in alignment known as the 'Five Kings'. There are extensive views of the Coquet Valley with excellent geographical illustrations of river meander, double courses and drumlins. Holystone Grange and the adjacent Woodhouse Pele are visible and lie along the road to Holystone.

(NT 947026) Here is Campville hill fort, close to the line of the Roman Road.

Brough Law (NT 998164) *and Greaves Ash* (NT 966164)

These are situated in the Breamish Valley beyond Ingram and have the advantage of being in the National Park area with car park and conveniences.

Immediately to the west of the car park, a steady climb will take the visitor back, through centuries of settlement from the cultivated valley floor, to the hill fort of Brough Law at a height of more than 900 feet. This is the most impressive fortification in the county and its massive fallen walls enclose the area of an acre. The extensive scatter of stone indicates the height of the walls. In places double facing of the stone work is visible, showing that there was skilled construction. There is no evidence of timber lacing, but archaelogical evidence indicates that a palisaded structure preceded the visible stone walls and there are signs of timber-type hut circles as well as those of stone. To the south of the walls appear the equivalents of stone buttresses against the hill slope. There are signs of later habitations constructed within the stonework of the fallen walls.

The Breamish valley is an area of many native settlements and fortifications, of which several can be seen from this site. It is also an area of extensive early cultivation with terraces, or lynchets, easily picked out.

Greaves Ash is chosen as a contrast to Brough Law. It lies further up the Breamish Valley in a somewhat sheltered position. It is in fact overlooked by hills on the north. There are a large number of hut circles clearly visible in two groups, both having fairly strong defences and overlooking the valley to the south. Linhope Spout, a waterfall, can be seen from the eminence to the north. Like Lordenshaws, Greaves Ash tends to get overgrown with bracken and it is better seen in early spring or late autumn. Permission to view has to be obtained from the farm where the public highway ends.

Blue Crag, Nr. Colwell (NY 944761)

This is approached by the A68 and the entry is through the gateway leading to Swinburne Quarries. Blue Crag is situated to the south of the approach lane and is easily distinguished by its precipitous northern rock face. There is a gentle slope to the south so that the settlement was sheltered from the prevailing wind. It is an impressive site. There is a stone rampart and within the enclosed space a number of hut circles are visible. The wall to the south shows a greater spread of stone that has been used for later dwellings. To the south also there is an outer enclosure on the lower slopes. The hut circles are of the Roman-British period, but excavations have given evidence of Bronze Age occupation. Some of the 'finds' are on display in the Museum of Antiquities, Newcastle. In this area, too, an investigation may be made of the line of the Roman road, Dere Street, which ran from Corbridge to Trimontium or Newstead, near Melrose. The modern road departs from the line of Dere Street, which crosses the Swin Burn a short distance to the west. Further west, in the grounds of the now derelict Swinburne Castle, is a massive standing stone with cup marks. There are several tumuli in the area and an impressive series of cultivation terraces.

Activities

(1) To make a simple survey of a site.
(2) To discover possible water supply and trace routes.
(3) To make models of huts or a complete settlement.
(4) Illustrations of prehistoric remains taken from books or from visits to museums.
(5) Experiments in Pottery and Metalwork.

Books and Periodicals

**Archaeology-Liam de Paor*. Pelican 1967.
Current Archaeology: bi-monthly: £1 per annum. 128 Barnsbury Road, London N1.
Archaeology for the Historian. D. P. Dymond, Historical Assoc.
Archaeologia Aeliana published by the Newcastle Society of Antiquities and kept in Public Libraries contains reports of local excavations.
Northumberland County History. Volumes XIV and XV.
CHILDE, V. G. *Prehistoric Communities of the British Isles*. Chambers 1949.
CLARK, J. G. D. *Archaeology and Society*. Methuen 1939.
**Prehistoric England*. Batsford 1944.
*COPLEY, G. *Going into the Past*. Phoenix House 1955.
FOX, C. *Personality of Britain*. Nat. Mus. of Wales 1947.
GRINSELL, L. V. *Ancient Burial Mounds in England*. Methuen 1936.
*GREEN, B. & SORRELL, A. *Prehistoric Britain*. Lutterworth.
*HAWKES, J. *Early Britain*. Guide. Chatto and Windus 1951.
*HAWKES, J. & C. *Prehistoric Britain*.
Ordnance Survey 1 inch, 2½ inch, 6 inch Maps.
HOGG, A. H. A. *A New List of Native Sites in Northumberland*. Proceedings of the Newcastle Society of Antiquities. XI.
*British Museum Guides to Prehistoric Antiquities.
*Ministry of Works Guide to Stonehenge.
*FEACHEM, T. *The North Britons*. Hutchinson 1965.
RICHMOND, I. A. *Roman and Native in North Britain*. Edinburgh 1958.

*JESSUP. *Age by Age*. Michael Joseph.
RIVET, A. L. *The Iron Age in North Britain.* Edinburgh 1966.
TATE, G. *Sculptured Rocks of Northumberland.* Alnwick 1885.
*THOMAS, N. *Guide to Prehistoric England.* Batsford 1960.
*THOMAS, S. *Prehistoric Britain.* Studio Vista. 1965.
TYLECOTE, R. F. *Metallurgy in Archaeology*. London 1962.
MCCORD, N. *Northumberland, History from the Air.* 1972. Frank Graham.

*Well illustrated and not so difficult to read.

THE ROMAN CENTURIES

The Romans commenced their conquest of Britain in A.D. 43. The process was helped by the fact that the country was divided into a number of tribes, some of which were ready to co-operate with the Romans. It was not till A.D. 71 that a breach came between the Romans and the Brigantes of Yorkshire, leading to destruction of Stanwick and the conquest of their territory. Agricola continued the advance and conquered Southern Scotland with the construction of forts to prevent incursions from the Highland glens. Sometime after his recall in A.D. 85 a return was made to the line of the Forth-Clyde, so that Northumberland, part of the territory of the Votadini was within the limits of the Roman province. Native fortifications within this area were dismantled and considerable trade developed. Early in the second century there was trouble and a number of northern forts were destroyed. The Romans had to withdraw.

In A.D. 122 after a visit by the Emperor Hadrian the frontier was re-established along the Tyne-Solway line—very near to Agricola's Stanegate and its forts. The Wall, which was constructed on his orders, extended some 80 Roman miles across country with milecastles every mile and turrets in between at intervals of one third of a mile. The wall-ditch and towers were first completed with foundations of the Wall. Then the Wall itself was constructed by the soldiers, but before it was completed it was found possible to reduce its width by a quarter, i.e. from about 10 feet to 7 feet 6 inches. It has been calculated that 40,000 tons of stone would be needed for a mile of wall, rising to a height of 15 feet at the rampart walk. The Cumberland length of the Wall, from the River Irthing, was first built of turf and later of stone. The main forts were at first behind the Wall, but they were moved up, to override the Wall itself. There was a military way to connect these camps and finally the Vallum was constructed. This was to define the military zone and prevent intruders from the South. It could also be used to control traffic through the Roman frontier. The Vallum was a large flat-bottomed ditch 20 feet wide and 10 feet deep with mounds of upcast on either side of the cutting at distances of 30 feet. These mounds were 20 feet wide and 5 feet high. The only crossings of the Vallum were at the forts and the milecastles.

Hadrian's Wall, after A.D. 144, was superseded by the Wall of Antoninus along the Forth-Clyde Isthmus. It was not abandoned completely, although the Vallum was partly filled in. The Antonine Wall suffered destruction in a revolt of A.D. 155, but it was rebuilt and maintained till A.D. 180. There was further trouble for the Romans in the early years of the third century and Hadrian's Wall was badly damaged. It was restored by Caracalla, son of Severus, and is sometimes known as the Wall of Severus. For nearly two hundred years this was the Roman frontier, though the area of the Votadini beyond the Wall received Roman support and protection with troops stationed in forts like Risingham and Rochester. There was a system of signal stations, from as far as Newstead, to give warning of attack. Groups of 'exploratores' or scouts helped to provide information and keep control. The visible remains in the area are mostly military, but roads can also be traced and their relationship to various sites. It also has to be remembered that there were civilian settlements adjacent to the forts. Corbridge was important as a commercial centre as well as a military base. Some of the products of Roman civilization are on display in the Museum of Antiquities, Newcastle and also in the Museums at Corbridge, Chesters, Housesteads and Carlisle.

ROMAN SITES

EXCURSIONS OR FIELD VISITS

Ideally all parts of the Wall are worth visiting, but there are various factors besides time that enter into consideration, namely the size of the party in relation to the visible remains and more important the problem of safe parking. Unfortunately the Military Road is one of the worst for traffic, being comparatively narrow for motor vehicles and undulating with little opportunity for safe parking. The greater part of the Wall area should be designated as a recreational and tourist area. The best way to visit the Wall is on foot.

For convenience places to visit or notice will be given in order from east to west. [Refer to *O.S. Map of the Roman Wall.*]

South Shields Roman Fort (NZ 365679)

South Shields Fort is in fact further north than Newcastle (Pons Aelii in Roman times) and an essential part of the Roman supply system. It also has to be remembered that Rome was a great naval power—a most eloquent reminder of this, even from a photograph, is the vessel excavated from the Lake of Nemi in Italy and destroyed by the Germans, at the end of World War II. In Newcastle we have reminders of Roman ships from inscriptions on stone and on coins.

South Shields (Arbeia) served the double purpose of guarding the mouth of the Tyne and providing supplies for Roman troops, who manned the Wall, or engaged in protracted campaigns beyond. There may well have been an Agricolan fort, but there was certainly one in Hadrian's time and this was rebuilt in the time of Severus with a large number of store-houses. Visible remains are parts of the west wall and gate, the foundations of granaries, the Headquarters buildings, water supply and barrack blocks. There is a small museum on the site, and the items are very well displayed. Two of the best Roman tomb-stones in the north are at South Shields. [To Victor and to Regina. Replicas in Newcastle Museum.]

Guidebook by I. Richmond to South Shields

Obviously South Shields could be combined for excursion purposes with the Saxon remains at Jarrow and Monkwearmouth. The areas of Roman forts at Wallsend, Newcastle and Benwell have been built over and the Wall itself has been used as a quarry. The sites of Wallsend and Newcastle overlooking the Tyne could provide interesting experiments in archaeological detection. Also the strategic situation could be considered since there was an extension of the Wall to Wallsend—it was not the original east terminus. The Military Road from Newcastle occupies the line of the Wall for nearly 20 miles, but it is possible to pick out the Wall-ditch to the north of the Wall and the Vallum to the south.

Benwell (NZ 216647) 2¼ miles West of Newcastle

Here can be seen the small temple of Antenociticus and the causeway across the Vallum leading to the fort. The gateway is the only one still in existence and here can be seen a section across the Vallum.

East Denton (NZ 198655)

Here may be seen Turret 7B with the broad wall of 10 Roman feet in width on either side of it.

Heddon on the Wall (NZ 137669)

Here a length of the Wall is preserved by the Ministry of Works. It consists of the broad wall (9 feet 7 inches) on a flagstone foundation (10 feet 7 inches). The Wall-ditch is plainly visible to the north and the Vallum, cut through the rock, to the south. Roman stone was used for the original Church of Heddon in Saxon times.

Rudchester

The fort is situated at the junction of the Military Road and the Stamfordham Road. The grass covered outlines of the walls can be seen, especially to the south. A Mithraeum here was excavated and the remains are in the Museum of Antiquities, Newcastle. [The construction of the Military Road after 1745 could be an interesting project. The Survey is available.]

Wallhouses (NZ 039685)

In this neighbourhood a very distinct two mile length of the Wall-ditch can be seen and, in the fields to the south of the farm, the Vallum fillings at 45 yard intervals are also visible.

Portgate (Junction of A68 and B6318)

At this point the Roman road from Corbridge passed through the Wall, slightly to the east of the present crossroads. It is possible to halt near here and view the line of the Roman road to the north. Both the Wall-ditch (to the west) and the Vallum (to the east) can be seen.

Also visible is the site of the site of the Roman camp at Halton Chesters and the medieval tower, embodying Roman stone.

CORBRIDGE. This is a good centre with complete facilities.

The Roman town (Corstopitum) is some three miles by road from the Portgate and a mile to the west of Corbridge. Here the Roman roads of Dere Street and Stanegate met. Corstopitum was one of the early Agricolan forts on the Stanegate and constructed originally in timber. There was a former British settlement on the site, which was chosen as a convenient river crossing. The fort was re-aligned and altered in size, before it was reconstructed in stone. Here again there were several periods and Corstopitum is a series of forts superimposed. This can be sorted out from the printed guide and from the plans on display in the Museum. The Museum contains a great deal of Roman material—inscribed stones, military equipment, tools, pottery and glassware. On the exposed site can be seen the granaries, barrack-blocks, temples, the aqueduct with water troughs, and workshops. Some unfinished work shows Roman building methods. Only part of the area is uncovered for there was a large civilian settlement. The military bath-house near Red House Burn has been excavated, but covered again with earth. There is a model of the Roman bridge in the Museum. Excavations take place here almost every year, providing further information.

Corbridge of the post-Roman period provides a visit in itself. There are porch, tower and west end of a Saxon Church, built in Roman stone. The tower arch is an obvious transfer. The church shows other stages of building. There is a vicar's pele-tower in the churchyard and within the town a number of fine old houses. It is well documented in a complete volume of the *Northumberland County History*.

Returning to the Military Road and still travelling westwards both the Wall-ditch and Vallum can again be seen. After passing the site of Oswald's victory at Heavenfield, a length of the wall can be seen at *Planetrees* (NY 931696)—it is an example of narrow wall on broad foundation. The next place of interest is *Brunton Turret*, which is approached by turning left at the crossroads from B6318 to A6079. The turret is signposted and reached by a path over the fields. This is a good example of a turret and again shows narrow Wall on broad foundation.

CHESTERS (NY 912701). [Complete facilities. Guide by E. Birley.]

Chesters is reached by turning to the left at Chollerford. This is perhaps the most attractive of the Roman forts on account of its riverside situation and the fact that the visible remains are understandable as a unity. The gateways have been excavated and exposed, also one section of the barracks and stables. The principia is open to view and by the river the military bath-house. It is interesting to work out the various stages of Roman ablutions. The abutments of the bridge carrying the Wall over the river are visible, but better investigated by taking a path from the George Hotel by the old railway on the other side of the river. Here too was a Roman mill. There is another fine collection of Roman remains in the Museum. In passing, the country house of Chesters and its stables are worthy of notice. Beyond Chesters there are two possible routes. The first is to keep to the river by turning to the left beyond Chesters, following B6319 to Fourstones and then taking the line of the Stanegate, passing Newborough, Settlingstones and eventually to Chesterholm.

Chesterholm (NY 771663), also called Vindolanda (Guide R. Birley)

This was originally an Agricolan fort on the Stanegate and abandoned by Hadrian. It was reoccupied later and rebuilt under Severus. There was a further rebuilding under Constantius Chlorus, the remains of this fort being those now visible. The interest is the site itself, the layout of the fort and the illustration of the way in which a wall can emerge by excavation from a grass grown bank. There was also a civilian settlement here. Chesterholm (Vindolanda) is being systematically excavated under the direction of Mr Robin Birley and presents exciting prospects.

There is a milestone in position to the east of the fort. It also may be worth considering that the area has a considerable amount of industrial archaeology with evidence of coal mining and limestone quarrying. The interesting mine at Settlingstones has been closed after a working life of 300 years. From Chesterholm the route is back to the Wall, which will have been observed at its magnificent best (weather permitting) from the Stanegate.

The other route is to follow the Military Road from Chesters and two miles west of the fort, the road leaves the Wall, revealing a considerable stretch of it to the north in the area of Black Carts. The Vallum and the ditch also emerge. It is possible to park near Limestone Corner and see the Vallum cut through solid rock. The ditch on the other side was not completed and huge blocks of stone lie there neglected over the centuries by later wall and roadbuilders. The Wall ditch westwards is in excellent condition and the full extent of the Vallum is revealed towards Carrawburgh farm.

Carrawburgh (NY 858710). There is now a car park provided.

The outline of the fort is plainly visible, but the main place of interest is the Temple of Mithras, preserved by the Ministry of Works. A dry summer and the shrinking peat revealed the tops of three altars and the site was excavated. A full report can be read in *Archaeologia Aeliana XXIX* 1951 or in *Recent Archaeological Excavations in Britain* Ed. R. Bruce Mitford. The remains are housed in a reconstructed temple in the Museum of Antiquities at Newcastle. The Museum should be visited as a part of any Roman Wall study, since it contains a full length representation of the Wall with models of the forts, milecastles and turrets. Near Carrawburgh fort, too, was Coventina's Well, where more than 13,000 coins were discovered.

About a mile and a half to the west, at Shield on the Wall (NY 726668), the Military Road crosses the Vallum. The road now becomes completely separated from the Wall, which follows the higher line of Whin Sill. Here is the best Roman Wall country and a car or bus becomes a base for exploration on foot. This means stout shoes or boots and full protective clothing. Walks have to be carefully planned, allowing plenty of time to reach and return from the Wall as well as adequate time for inspection of sites.

Housesteads (NY 790688)

This is an obvious centre, providing parking and other facilities. There is also a Museum which is sometimes useful for shelter. The fort itself is some distance from the road in an elevated situation. There is a great deal to explore there with the Knag Burn gateway to the east and a milecastle (No. 37) to the west. A feature not evident at other forts are the Roman latrines and the vicus or civilian settlement to the south with the site of a double murder. The official guide book is by Professor E. Birley.

Walks along the Wall *Vindolanda* (see 21 as Chesterholm)

1. Sewingshields (NY 809702) to Housesteads (NY 790688) (Car Park).

2. Housesteads to Winshields (NY 751676) (Car park).

This can be shortened by coming out from Milking Gap (NY 771680), where there was a native settlement, to the main road.

3. From Winshields westwards. Winshields is reached from Twice Brewed and the Wall can be explored as far as Cawfields Quarry where there is another parking place. This is potentially dangerous, for the deep quarry is water filled and at one point the wall ends abruptly at the quarry edge. Though this is fenced off careful supervision of children is needed.

4. From Cawfields (NY 716667) eastwards. At Cawfields there is a fine stretch of the Wall and a very good milecastle. There is a way out to the main road between Cawfields and Winshields from another farm called Shield on the Wall, but there is no suitable parking place.

Observations can be made on the structure and thickness of the Wall, the siting of the turrets and milecastles, the Vallum that lies at some distance to the south and any lines of approach to the Wall from the north. The views over the countryside in both directions are most impressive. Near Winshields the highest part of the Wall is 1,230 feet above sea level. Returning to the Military Road there is a complex of fortifications near the Haltwhistle Burn. Westwards Walltown Crags are well worth a visit, but the fort of Carvoran has little to offer.

There is a good deal in the Gilsland area (NY 632662).

1. Poltross Burn Milecastle which is approached through the station yard of Gilsland.

2. A length of the Wall in what was formerly the vicarage garden, now a guest house.

3. There is a long stretch of the Wall excavated from a tree covered bank by the Ministry of Works. This goes as far as (NY 628664) Willowford Bridge. Here the situation is very similar to Chesters with the bridge abutment, a tower and evidence of a mill. These can be seen very dramatically from the cliff face on the other side of the River Irthing.

Birdoswald (NY 615663) (Cumberland)

This is the next ford westwards from Gilsland, overlooking the horseshoe bend of the river. Burnswark in Scotland is visible from here. The fort is on private land and payment is required.

[Apply to J. Baxter, Birdoswald, Gilsland, Carlisle.]

The perimeter of the camp and the gateways are visible, but the interest here is that the turf wall and the stone wall can both be seen on different alignments. This continues from Harrow's Scar

(Milecastle 49) to Wall Bowers (Milecastle 51). The wall, narrow on narrow foundation is worth following towards the river and milecastle 49 to get the view of Willowford Bridge. Westwards before reaching Wall Bowers from a lane marked Lanerton, which has to be walked, the sods of the turf wall can be seen in section as they were originally placed.

This is beyond the limits of Northumberland's Wall, but a county boundary is not the logical limit. Carlisle can be regarded as main terminus in Cumberland and should be visited. But Roman remains could be combined with visits to the castle, cathedral and Tullie House Museum. *Bewcastle* to the north of Gilsland was an important Roman outpost fort. There is also a castle and church in the area, the churchyard containing a fine Saxon Cross.

At Over Denton behind the Wall, the chancel arch of the church is made of Roman stones. There was a Roman fort in the area.

Whitley Castle to the south is another impressive Roman fort overlooking the Maiden's Way. It has multiple lines of defence.

Roman Roads

Tracing and recording Roman Roads is one of a number of possible projects. They could be surveyed in connection with other types of roads and trackways. A new road can be a modification of an older one. The Stanegate has already been mentioned.

Stanegate

At Corstopitum West Gate excavations showed the road to be 22 feet wide and from here it turned southwards to negotiate a steep-sided valley. Its course can be followed westwards for some distance, then there is no sign until the northern slope of Warden Hill, where it was again excavated. It continues to Fourstones and there is covered by the existing road until it approaches Chesterholm. At Seatsides it crosses the Twice Brewed Road and then passes over the Military Road near the fort on Haltwhistle Burn. From here it continues to Carvoran, a Stanegate fort almost on the Wall and, crossing the Gilsland road north of Greenhead, proceeds to Upper Denton (fort). After this the alignment is to Old Brampton and Stanwix. There is still a good deal to be done in detecting the Stanegate by a combination of the study of air photographs and field walks.

Dere Street

Another important Roman Road is Dere Street. With the help of I. Margary's book on Roman Roads, it can be traced both north and south of Corbridge. North of the Wall it can be combined with a look at Roman outposts and Marching camps.

Dere Street leaves Corbridge Roman Station through the fields and does not join the present road till some distance north of modern Corbridge. It passes Stagshaw Common and reaches the Portgate, where it crosses the Military Road. To the north at Bewclay, where there is a toll house, a branch road known as Devil's or Cobb's Causeway leaves to the east. From this point, Dere Street can be seen stretching miles in a straight line northwards. After passing the five roads near Colwell, the Roman Road and later turnpike part company. The Roman Road goes towards Swinburne, while the modern road makes a deviation. But they rejoin and next part company near Fourlaws. Here was a Roman signalling station, which was used to maintain contact between the outpost forts and the Wall. The rectangle of a Roman camp can be picked out to the west of Fourlaws farm. This area shows signs of intensive iron working from Roman times to the present century. The Roman Road does not join the modern road again till West Woodburn has been passed. It led to the fort of Risingham, which overlooks the Rede, a mile to the west of Woodburn. It is a most impressive place and deserves detailed study. A number of sculptured stones from here can be seen in the Museum of Antiquities. [Photograph also.] An aerial view of the site can be obtained from the rising ground to the north, where the roads rejoin. There is another Roman Marching camp to the west of the road. The roads again diverge near Corsenside and rejoin, to part company again near Troughend, the Roman Road passing through Dunn's Houses. There is another camp at Dargues and yet others at Blakehope. The roads again diverge near Elishaw and the Roman Road crosses to the east of A68, making for High Rochester, another Roman outpost fort. This again is well worth a visit and two huge stone balls ornamenting the entrance of old School house indicate the importance of Roman artillery. The massive ballista, mounted on platforms for defence to north and west, could hurl these projectiles for some 250 yards. The fort was founded by Agricola and thrice rebuilt in stone. The multiple ditch system was associated with artillery. There is an impressive west gateway and considerable remains of walls. Within the enclosure is a medieval tower and a farmstead of later date. Eastwards a branch road leaves to join with Devil's Causeway at Learchild.

To the north there are several camps beyond the present Otterburn Camp and a careful check should be made whether there is firing on the range. These are the Redesdale Camp, Bellshiel, Silloans, Sillsburn and Featherwood. The modern army road follows the line of Dere Street. At Middle Golden Pot (the base of a Cross) the Roman Road is called Gemmel's Path and reaches the Border of England and Scotland at Coquethead. Here is situated a remarkable collection of Roman military works known as Chew Green (NT 789084). These

Outer Golden Pot, Chew Green.

were related to troop movements. A marching camp for a legion was succeeded by a half acre permanent fort. There was another marching camp, succeeded by a 5 acre labour camp for the construction of a fort with wagon parks. It was obviously of great importance for convoys, troops and supplies. On the Pennine Way, it is most easily accessible on foot.

To the Romans this was no border post, but a halting stage on the way to the fort of Trimontium (Newstead) near Melrose 50 miles from Corbridge. Chew Green, like other Roman sites, can be most profitably studied from an aerial photograph.

The Devil's Causeway is another Roman road that lends itself to field work. It is detected by an agger or raised mound, bounded by ditches and, though the areas through which it passes have been much subjected to the plough, it is quite often visible. Detection is assisted by O.S. maps and Maclauchlan's Survey made for the Duke of Northumberland in 1864. [Also Margary—*Roman Roads in Britain*.] The road leaves Dere Street at Bewclay and is first detected near Shellbraes Farm and then to the east of Ryal. It is very easily picked out where it crosses the Kirkheaton road at the entrance to Boghall and again there are traces near Brandywell. It is visible again at Bradford Edgehouse before crossing A696 and there is a very good section on the approach lane to East Shaftoe. The Prehistoric tumulus and standing stone, called the Poind and his man, are very close to it. The agger has recently been a little obscured by ploughing but is easily detectable. The road passes between the native sites at Shaftoe and those of Huckhoe and Slate Hill. There are rectangular enclosures at Bolam Low House and Angerton. The road can be traced to the east of the farmhouse of Marlish and then at its crossing of the Hartburn west of Hartburn village. It is near the site of a Roman settlement detected by air photography. Thornton Moor is crossed and the road proceeds east of Netherwitton towards Todburn. It can be clearly seen in the field to the west of the drive to the farm called Todburn Moor. For a considerable distance it is almost parallel to the line of pylons and slightly to their west. The Coquet is crossed near Thistleyhaugh, half a mile west of Weldon Bridge, and the road continues west of Longframlington to approach the A697 near Beesom Farm. The Roman Road almost follows the present road to the milestone at Gate burn. Here the A697 turns eastwards to take the lower land, while the old coach way and the Roman Road continue separately to the west. Devil's Causeway crosses A697 about a mile south of Newmoor House and B634 (the Alnwick road) about a mile eastwards from the same hostelry. A section of the Roman Road was excavated here for the County History. It continues west of Edlingham to the fort of Learchild, where another Roman Road came in from Rochester, 19 miles to the west. Devil's Causeway recrosses the main road at Bridge of Aln and continues to the east of Glanton. They rejoin at Powburn and continue on a joint course for 2 miles as far as Percy's Cross. There is an impressive earthwork at Crawley, overlooking the Breamish near Powburn. Here is a Pele Tower within an earthwork, possibly used by the Romans. The course of the road can be checked at East Lilburn, at Newton Farm and west of Fowberry. From East Horton it follows closely the present road to Lowick and beyond this the line to Berwick cannot be traced.

In a similar way the east-west route can be followed from Rochester via Dykehead, Stewartshiels, Branshaw, North Yardhope, Campville, west of Holystone, east of Sharperton, slightly north of High Trewhitt, near Kiln House and Dancing Hall. From an enclosure east of the Callaly road, the Roman Road is plainly visible cutting across the plough rigs at almost right angles. The western approach to Callaly is called Street Way and the roads coincide from South Lodge to

Lover's Lane. When the present road turns north towards Whittingham, the Roman Road continues directly eastwards to Thrunton and reaches the fort of Learchild a mile south of Bridge of Aln.

Roman roads provide a fascinating study in communications and obviously—*place names.*

Roman Wall and Frontier

Books

Archaeologia Aeliana—the yearly publication of the Newcastle Society of Antiquities—contains up to date excavation reports.

BIRLEY, A. R. *Life in Roman Britain.* Batsford 1964.

Hadrian's Wall. H.M.S.O. 1963. 5/6. [The best general guide, well illustrated.]

BIRLEY, E. *Research on Hadrian's Wall.* 1961.

BRUCE, J. C. *Handbook to the Roman Wall* (latest Ed.).

BURN, A. R. *Agricola and Roman Britain.* E.U.P. 1953. [Much more than a short biography.]

British Museum, Guide to Antiquities of Roman Britain.

COLLINGWOOD, R. G. *Roman Britain.* O.U.P.

Centenary Pilgrimage to Hadrian's Wall. 1949, also 1970.

HARRISON, D. *Along Hadrian's Wall.* Cassell 1962.

Jackdaw on Hadrian's Wall.

JESSUP. *Age by Age.*

MOTHERSOLE, J. *The Saxon Shore and Hadrian's Wall.*

Map of Hadrian's Wall. Ordnance Survey. 1964.

MARGARY, I. *Roman Roads in Britain.* John Baker 1967.

Ministry of Works Guides to Housesteads, Corbridge, Chesters. Also Northern England.

QUENNELL, M. *Everyday Things in Roman Britain.* Batsford.

RICHMOND, I. A. *Roman Britain.* Collins.

Roman Britain. Penguin 1963.

Romans in Redesdale Vol. XV County History.

Introduction to Pevsner. *Building of Northumberland.*

Ed. *Roman and Native in North Britain.* 1958.

South Shields Guide. 1963.

'Temple of Mithras at Carrawburgh.' *Archaeologia Aeliana.* 1951. (Also in *Recent Excavations*—Ed. Bruce Mitford.)

SORRELL, A. and FOX, A. *Roman Britain.* Lutterworth.

SORRELL, A. *Living History.* Batsford.

TACITUS. *Agricola and Germanic* (Penguin translation).

WILSON, D. R. *Roman Frontiers of Britain.* Heinemann.

Regional Archaeology. 1967.

ROWLAND, T. H. *The Romans in North Britain.* F. Graham.
DOBSON, B. and BREEZE, D. *The Army of Hadrian's Wall.* Frank Graham 1973.
BIRLEY, R. *Hadrian's Wall. Guide to Central Sector.* Frank Graham 1972.
BIRLEY, R. *Vindolanda.* Guide 1973. Frank Graham.

PLACE NAMES

Place names, which can be associated with personal names, not only provide a fascinating study in themselves, but also information for local history. Places were named by people and many of these names are prehistoric. It will be found, for example, that many river-names and landscape features date back to time immemorial. A map of Britain shows that a large proportion of British or Celtic names have survived in the north and the west. Waves of invaders at various times tended to push back the 'natives' into the hills of the remoter parts. In Northumberland there is a strong survival of Celtic hill and river names.

Britain was conquered by the Romans, who made their impression on the country. They created our town sites and sometimes the Roman name survives, as 'London' itself. The expression 'cester' or 'chester' is derived from the Latin 'castra' meaning fort or camp. The Roman name of the fort was not remembered, but 'Rudchester' results from a person Rudd (probably Saxon) taking over the site of the Roman 'chester'. Words like Hetchester or 'Chesters' are reminders of the pre-Saxon sites. The word 'Street' is derived from the Latin 'strata'. The Romans had similar sounding words—'Porta'—a door or gate and Portus—a harbour. To make things more difficult one Saxon leader had the name of 'Porta'. Portsmouth was his landing place: Portchester was the Roman site. Guesswork can be completely misleading. Place names have to be checked for derivations and for earlier spellings. The interpretation depends on the earliest recorded evidence of the site. The basic book for this is E. Ekwall. *The Concise Oxford Dictionary of English Place Names* (1960 Edition).

Place names are important evidence for the settlements of the Anglo-Saxons. The name 'England' or 'Angle-land' is not strictly accurate to describe this country until these settlers had arrived. Nor is 'Scotland' accurate for the country to the north till after the Scots had arrived from Ireland. Many of our shires are derived from early

Anglo-Saxon Kingdoms. E.g. ESSEX was the kingdom of the 'East Saxons'. Northumberland was the remaining Anglian part of a much larger kingdom, stretching from the Humber to the Firth of Forth. The Saxons lived in villages. Words such as 'tun', 'ham', 'botl', 'hahl' are terms for their settlements. There is a personal name like 'Bedla' and 'Bedlington' is the place where his group or community settled. Bebside is literally 'Bebba's seat'; Bothal is 'Bota's hall'; Backworth is 'Bacca's worth'; Bamburgh is 'Bebba's burgh' and Bavington is 'the tun of Baba's people'. There are considerable number of 'ingham's and 'ington's. But Ashington was not one of these. It was 'Essendun' or 'the vale overgrown with ash-trees'.

Place names may describe the features or vegetation of a particular site. 'Akeld' means 'oak slope' and 'Acomb' is the plural 'oaks'. 'Bitchfield' was a 'beechfield'. Branton and Brandon were the same as Broomhill, 'the hill covered with broom'. Angerton means 'grazing farm' and 'Callaly' 'pasture for the calves'. Hartford was where the deer crossed the 'merry' or 'gentle' river called 'Blyth'. Beal, Bewick and Bickerton all have associations with 'bees'. Blagdon was the 'black valley', but Birtley was the 'bright-leah'. Both Nun-riding and Newton Underwood indicate clearances in the forest.

There seem to be few Scandinavian place names, but there are indications of the Norman Conquest. 'Newcastle' got its name from the new castle built in the time of William the Conqueror, but Benwell remained 'within the (Roman) Wall'. Sea-ton (the settlement overlooking the sea) acquired a Norman lord de la Val (of the Valley) and so became Seaton Delaval. Bellister and Bellasis were both 'fine sites' in Norman French. Blanchland, too, shows French influence. But care is needed about Cambois—this is not French as might appear, but British for 'bay'. In course of time things change a good deal. 'Ancroft' is no longer the 'lonely croft', but a village. A remote farmstead nowadays, may retain the name of a village that has disappeared completely. [Names on signposts can be amusing. Near Gilsland a signpost points to Moscow and Spadeadam (a rocket testing area). In Gilsland there is 'Mumps' Hall.]

Place names can be used within a town or village. A house or field may take the name of a person. A wood or plantation may be named after the man who was responsible for the setting of the trees. Field names are important and from these can be obtained a complete plan of the village. Their names may indicate features of sectors of the land, their uses or the persons who owned them. Old features—standing stones, dykes and marshes, can be sorted out in the same way. Old routes and meeting places can be discovered from names. There are 'carriers' ways' and 'salters' ways': there are drove roads and watering-places. There are all kinds of words for enclosures—croft, close, yard, fold or pen. Position, size and shape of fields can be indicated from names—the West ridge or Westfield, the 10 or 20 acres, the Long Close. There may still be remembered 'glebe' land or 'the demesne', belonging to the Church and the Lord of the Manor respectively. [Farm names also provide information. 'Make me rich' may be a name given to a rather poor farm. 'Minorca' relates to events of the early eighteenth century. 'Tempe' shows a classical interest on the part of the landowner.]

Personal Names

These are an essential part of our English language and are derived from a multiplicity of sources. It is rather strange to look at the names of heroes in the Celtic histories and genealogies—Cadwallon, Gruffyd, Bleddyn, Caradog, Condidan, Farinmail, and compare them with Roman names such as Julius, Claudius, Quintus, Antonius, and Victor. Old English names include Aethelberht, Aelfhere, Aethelbald, Aethelheard, Aethelwig, Aethelweard, Aethelwine, Aethelwulf. There were Cadda, Mul, Moll, Eata, Offa and Bosa. Edwin, Alfred, Edmund, Edward and Edgar are recognizable, but Ida, Lilla, Duduc, and Cissa strangely enough were men. Aelle was son of Yffe and Yware was a sacristan; Putta was a bishop and so was Heca. The Danes increased the variety with Eshric, Aethelwold, Guthrum, Anlaf, Raegnald, Thored and Sweyn. The favourite Norman names were William, Robert, Henry, Ralph, Roger, Geoffrey, Hugh, and Philip. Others were adopted from the Bible. Female names show a similar variety and popular names vary like fashions.

Family or surnames are added in due course. These are to distinguish persons with like Christian or fore-names. Harold, who became King of England in 1066, was Harold Godwinson. In the Anglo-Saxon Chronicle there are Eadred, son of Eadwulf; Raegrald, Guthfrithson; Sigeberht, son of Sigensilf and Swein Estrithson. The additional name was an indication of family pride or a distinction from others with the same Christian or fore-name. In the post-Norman period emerge many of our common surnames— Robert'son, Rob'son, William'son, Thom'son, John'son, Jack'son, Robin'son, and Adam'-son. But the Christian name often becomes a surname unaltered—Allan or Allen, James, Herbert, Gilbert. In Johns and Jones (which is derived from Johns) the possessive is implied.

Personal characteristics are another source of surnames—Black, White and Dark: Large and Little: Small and Strong: Good and

Godley. Godfrey was 'God fearing'. Denoting places of origin are Green (of the green), Hill (of the hill), Vale (of the vale): possibly the same are Wood, Marsh and Forest. A large number of places become surnames—Morpeth, Swinburne, Middleton, Selby, Mitford, Craster and Cresswell. The implication is that these names would be applied to those who had left the areas of their origin. There would be no advantage in calling all the inhabitants of a place by the place name. John was known as 'the Scot' when he entered England.

Occupations provide yet another source of surnames. Obviously there would be no sense in regarding all persons who took part in agriculture in the Middle Ages as 'farmers'. 'Farm' was a legal expression rather than an agricultural occupation. But if 'smith' is considered, this is an entirely different matter. Among villagers mostly concerned with agriculture, the term 'smith' was a distinction. Each village would have a 'smith' and the smiths would multiply with their sons taking their names. Some might become Smithson, but most would remain Smiths and this becomes the most common name in England. (12 columns in the Newcastle Directory, Jones scarcely 3, but Robsons nearly 8 and Taylors are strongly represented with 7.) Some of the occupational names are fairly obvious such as Cooper, Miller, Sadler, Butcher, Sawyer, Potter, Tyler, Slater, Carpenter, Woodman, Shepherd, Horseman and Butler. Many others can be sorted out. In the Middle Ages the clergy were literate and did the writing. Our word 'clerk' is derived from cleric. In those days only a small minority could write, now the great majority can and the task of 'clerks' is performed by typists. It is suggested that these factors could be studied together.

1. The place names of an area.
2. The surnames of an area with some statistical analysis.
   (a) The numbers of each name.
   (b) Occupational analysis.
   (c) Where did these people come from and when?

It can be established the number of generations a family has lived in a particular neighbourhood.

3. *Family histories.*

Usually family trees have been established (even made up) for the leading families in an area. It was often important to have this information for purposes of inheritance. There is no reason why this type of research should not be attempted by anyone who has the necessary advice. The Americans spend a great deal of time trying to establish family origins in this country. 'Mayflower' descendants are very select.

Tracing of family history can be done initially by enquiring among older members of the family and establishing various connections. In

Reconstruction of the *Mansio* or Inn at Vindolanda.

Four Altars found at Vindolanda.

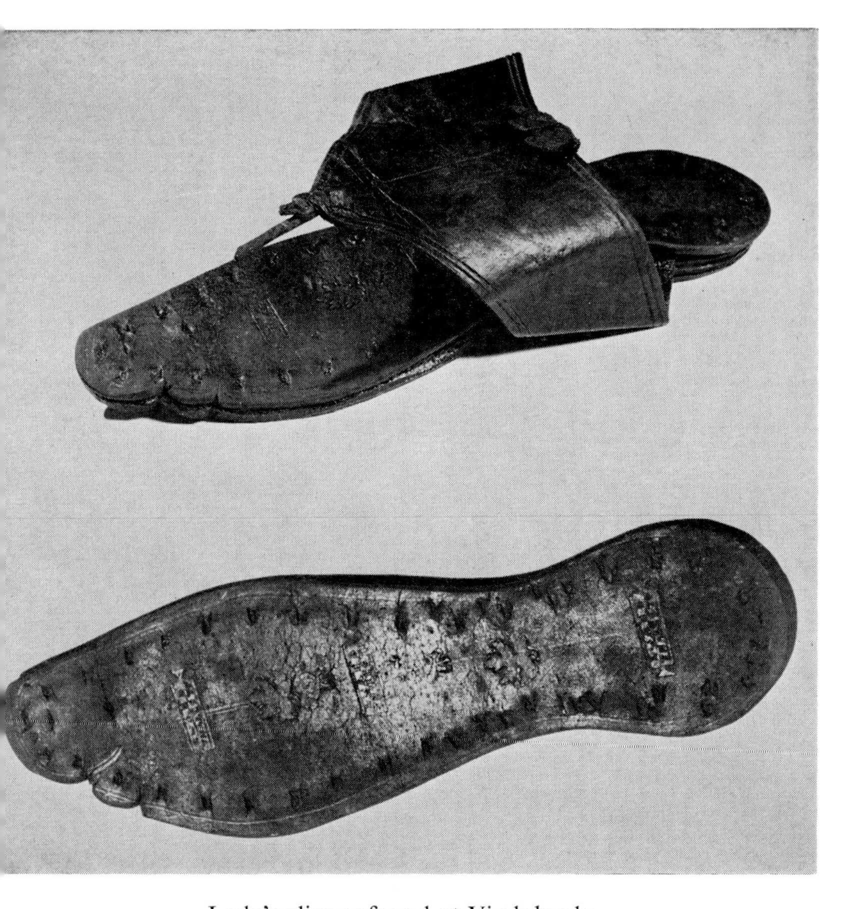

Lady's slipper found at Vindolanda.
The stamps on the sole are very rare. The maker is L(ucius) AEB(utivs) THALES, son of Titus.

the last century a good deal of family information was collected and names of the family were inscribed in the household Bible. Old books can provide information i.e. that a book belonged to a person at a particular school or college at a given date. Small libraries were built up in the same way—by handing on possessions. Compulsory Civil Registration of Births, Marriages and Deaths did not come about till the beginning of the reign of Queen Victoria in 1837. Before this information has to be obtained from the Parish Registers. A priest of the Church of England from 1537 was required by law to keep such records of his parishioners. Comparatively few have survived from that time, but a number of churches have records dating from the reign of Charles II. The incumbent expected payments at baptism, marriage and death. In the reign of Charles II he had to certify that a corpse was properly buried 'in wool' for the benefit of that trade. Nonconformists were included in the same records, although they might keep their own separate accounts. Family research can be directed towards various parts of the county or even of the country. Some families will be discovered to have descended from Dutch or French Protestant refugees in the sixteenth or seventeenth centuries.

A certain amount of information can be obtained from tombstones, but obviously these memorials imply a certain amount of wealth. Information can be obtained from other sources.

1. Registers of Schools and Colleges.

2. Registers of admissions to Guilds and Crafts. Particulars about apprenticeship.

3. Directories compiled during the nineteenth century and after. These give information on each village and town. A large number of people are listed with their occupations.

4. Old Newspapers provide information and larger libraries have files of back numbers.

5. Correspondence and Accounts. Some people kept very detailed accounts.

6. Legal documents concerning property. Wills and Inventories. Lawsuits.

Family matters can provide a very wide field of study. Old people, in particular, can provide a fund of valuable information about their own and other families.

In the field of fiction may be strongly recommended:—

GALSWORTHY, J. *The Forsyte Saga.*

WALPOLE, H. *The Herries Chronicle.*

Books

Place Names

CAMERON, K. *English Place Names*. Batsford 1961.

EKWALL, E. *The Concise Oxford Dictionary of Place Names*. 1960

MAWER. *Place names of Northumberland and Durham*. C.U.P. 1920.

REANEY, R. H. *The Origin of English Place Names*. Routledge 1960.

WAINWRIGHT, F. T. *Archaeology, Place Names and History*. Routledge 1962.

WATSON, GODFREY. *Goodwife Hot*. Oriel Press 1970.

Christian Names

The Pan Book of Boys' Names (Paperback).

The Pan Book of Girls' Names (Paperback).

WITHYCOMBE, E. G. *The Oxford Dictionary of English Christian Names*. 1950.

PARTRIDGE, E. *Name Your Child*. Evans 1968. 3/6.

WEEKLEY, E. *Jack and Jill*. London 1948.

Surnames

Penguin Dictionary of Surnames.

HASSALL, A. L. *History through Surnames*. Blackwell.

REANEY, P. H. *A Dictionary of British Surnames*. O.U.P. 1950.

HUGHES, J. P. *How you got your name*. Dent 1963.

WEEKLEY, E. *The Romance of Names*. 1922. *Surnames*. 1922.

Genealogy, Northumberland

HEDLEY, W. P. *Families of Northumberland Vol. I and II.*

General

WAGNER, A. R. *English Ancestry*. O.U.P. 1966. 5/-.

PINE, L. C. *Trace Your Ancestors*. Evans 1966. 5/-.

They came with the Conqueror. Evans 1966. 5/-.

CAMP, A. J. *Tracing Your Ancestors*. Foyle 1964.

WAGNER, A. R. *English Genealogy*. Oxford 1960.

HAMILTON EDWARDS, G. *In Search of Ancestry*. M. Joseph 1966.

Heraldry

Heraldry is a rather more specialized interest, but it can be of importance locally, when heraldic shields are imposed upon buildings and monuments. It can help in the dating of buildings and in establishing connections between different areas owned by the same family.

Guilds and Companies were also granted coats of arms. The Smiths of Newcastle had on their shield, three silver hammers. The crest showed a phoenix, burning and renewing herself—symbolic of metalwork. Their Motto 'By hammer and hand, all arts do stand'. In the Middle Ages, these devices were of the greatest importance since most people were illiterate. Emblems were 'advertisements' in the earlier, stricter sense of giving 'a warning'. For a craft it was an indication that only members of the guild could take part in a craft and it was a sign of quality in workmanship. For some people it could be a 'warning' in another sense. In feudal times, the barons and knights had the special function of doing military service for king and country. They also took part in tournaments for practice, sporting and display purposes. There was 'unofficial warfare' between rival families when royal authority was weak. Since the baron or knight was clad from head to foot in chain mail, or later in plate armour, and since his face was not visible, it was an advantage to have some ready form of recognition. Hence the importance of the device and the coat of arms. Quick recognition was a matter of life and death. It was as important to those in authority as the registration of motor vehicles at the present day.

As a study heraldry is as interesting to the artist as the historian and lends itself to the work of display. There is no reason why people should not invent their own 'devices', as well as tracing their families. Heraldry is important in connection with the study of church monuments and memorials.

Books

Boutell's Heraldry revised by C. W. Scott-Giles and J. P. Brooke-Litte. Warne (Revised 1950).

ST JOHN HOPE, W. H. *A Grammar of English Heraldry*. C.U.P. 1953.

PINE, L. G. *Story of Heraldry*. Country Life Observer's Book of Heraldry. Warne.

There is a good deal of local heraldry in *Archaeologia Aeliana*.

THE ANGLO-SAXON PERIOD

During nearly four centuries of imperial rule, the Romans had brought order and unity to Britain. Their departure after A.D. 400 was followed by a long period of conflict between the inhabitants themselves and with Anglo-Saxon invaders. It was not until about A.D. 450 that the Anglo-Saxons began to settle. The process of settlement can be traced by means of their pagan cemeteries and by place names. The new village settlements have Anglo-Saxon names and a number of shires (or counties) were once separate Angle or Saxon Kingdoms.

Place names have been mentioned, but here the material remains have to be considered. Unfortunately most of these have disappeared, since the Anglo-Saxons were primarily builders in timber. Buildings in stone are comparatively few.

At Yeavering Edwin's palace has to be imagined: on Bamburgh's rock Ida's fort has been covered by later structures and at Lindisfarne the remains of the Priory are subsequent to the Norman Conquest. However in the structure of Lindisfarne Parish Church are remains of early masonry and in the Ministry of Works Museum, not only some fine Saxon carving, but a replica of the famous Lindisfarne Gospels. A certain similarity will be seen in the patterns of both media. One of the most impressive stones may represent the sack of Lindisfarne by the Vikings. The church at Ebbs' Nook near Beadnell has been covered over and one at Wooden near Alnmouth has not been located, but there is a considerable amount of Anglo-Saxon architecture in some existing Northumberland churches. It is, of course, obvious that visits should be made to the Durham churches as detailed in the *History Field Studies in the Durham Area.* These include Jarrow, Monkwearmouth, Escomb and especially Durham, where the relics of St Cuthbert remain together with a collection of Anglo-Saxon crosses and fragments from various parts of the diocese of Durham. Lindisfarne came under the control of Durham after the Norman Conquest.

It is suggested that visits to the Anglo-Saxon sites should be combined with consideration of other remains, i.e. Saxon and Norman together or the study of a particular area.

Churches with Saxon Masonry

Bywell, situated on the Tyne, probably gets its name from the bend in the river. It has two churches adjacent to each other, dedicated to St Andrew and St Peter respectively and both containing Saxon architecture. Bywell itself is an example of a small medieval town that has become 'deserted'. Bywell St Peter's (NZ 049614) in spite of its Norman looking tower is the older church. The present tower overlies an earlier one and early Saxon masonry can be detected in the north wall of the nave and in the angle of the nave and chancel, shown by the quoins. There are also round headed windows in the

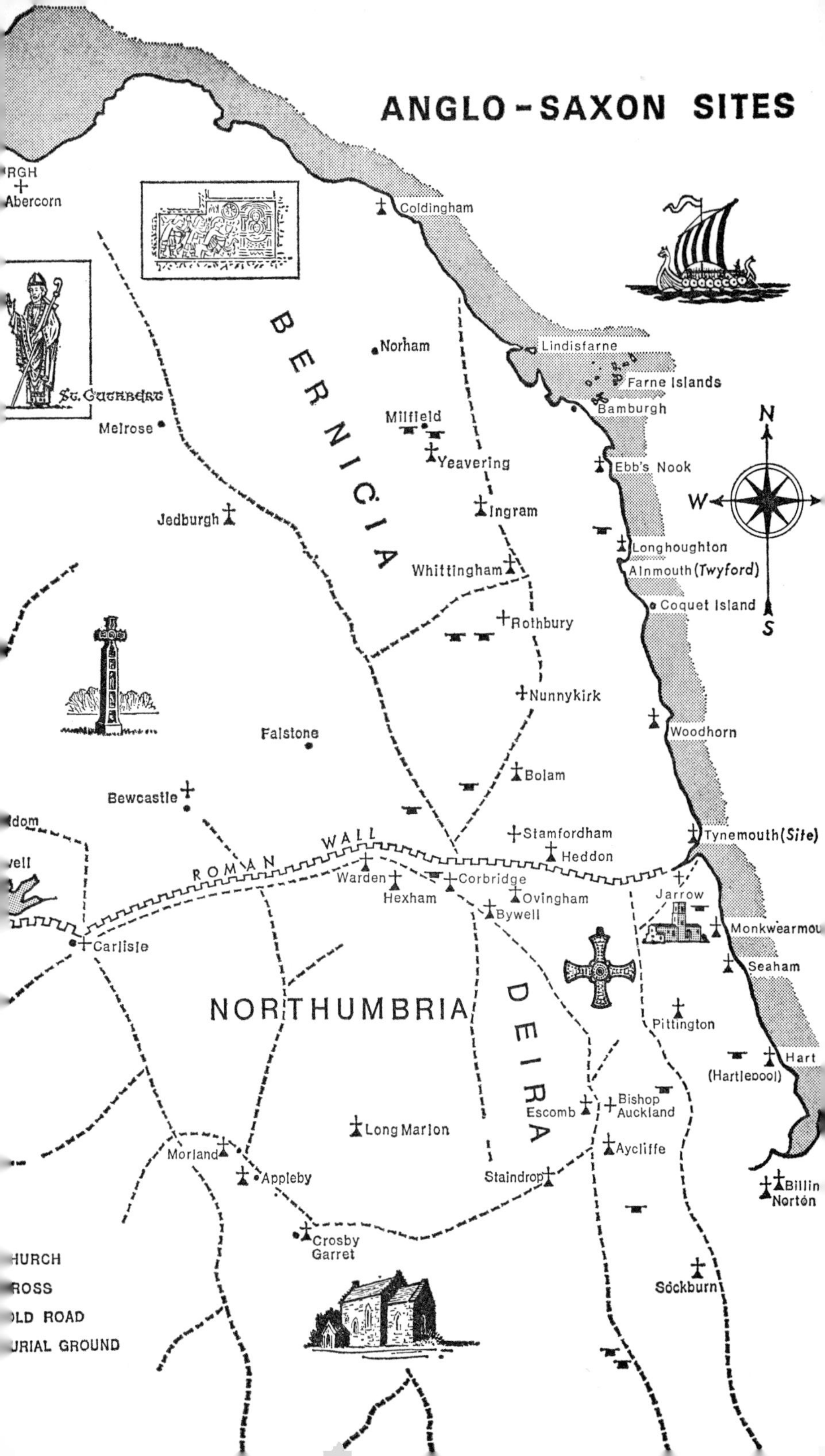
ANGLO-SAXON SITES
RGH
Abercorn
Coldingham
St. Cuthbert
BERNICIA
Norham
Lindisfarne
Farne Islands
Bamburgh
Melrose
Milfield
Yeavering
Ebb's Nook
N
W
S
Jedburgh
Ingram
Longhoughton
Alnmouth (Twyford)
Whittingham
Coquet Island
Rothbury
Nunnykirk
Woodhorn
Falstone
Bolam
Bewcastle
dom
Tynemouth (Site)
Stamfordham
WALL
Heddon
ROMAN
vell
Warden
Corbridge
Jarrow
Hexham
Ovingham
Bywell
Monkwearmou
Carlisle
Seaham
NORTHUMBRIA
DEIRA
Pittington
Hart
(Hartlepool)
Bishop Auckland
Escomb
Long Marton
Aycliffe
Morland
Staindrop
Appleby
Billin
Norton
Crosby Garret
HURCH
ROSS
OLD ROAD
URIAL GROUND
Sockburn

north wall of the nave and signs of a blocked door. A date of the early eighth century has been suggested for this construction. Bywell St Andrew (NZ 048615) has a very fine west tower of the Anglo-Saxon period. Though the lower courses may be earlier, the main part of the tower is eleventh century.

The characteristics of the Tower are that it is tall and almost square with massive masonry and small windows. The belfry stage above the string course is more elaborate. Saxon churches tended to be tall and comparatively narrow.

Warden Church (NY 914665), two miles beyond Hexham and situated at the junction of the North Tyne and South Tyne, has the same type of tower and there is a castle mound in the vicinity. The church tower could be Norman because Saxon styles persisted.

Ovingham (NZ 085637), overlooking the Tyne a little to the east of Bywell, has a very similar tower and could be combined in a visit. So could *Corbridge* and *Hexham.*

Corbridge (NY 988644). The church is dedicated to St Andrew and the earliest parts are the west porch and the nave walls. The west porch (eighth century) was converted into a tall tower, at present more than 60 feet high and the greater part of this dates back to A.D. 1000. The long and short work of the tower is obvious and the quoins of the nave can be distinguished. The arched entrance to the west porch has been blocked with masonry and windows inserted. The Tower arch within the church is obviously built (not very expertly) with Roman stones from Corbridge. As at Ovingham the later thirteenth century work is most impressive, partly by contrast with the simpler Saxon architecture.

At Hexham Priory Church (NY 935641) the Saxon remains are mostly underground. Wilfrid's magnificent church was built towards the end of the seventh century in Roman style and with Roman stone. It was lavishly ornamented, so that the present remains are a grim contrast. These consist of the crypt with its stairs and cells. Here saintly relics were kept for the edification and consolation of pilgrims. An inscribed Roman stone shows the erasure of Geta's name, during the reign of Caracalla. This stone like others probably came from Corstopitum.

[Permission to visit the Crypt has to be obtained from the Verger and numbers obviously have to be limited for a particular viewing.]

Bishop Wilfrid's throne is situated in the chancel.

Heddon on the Wall (NZ 135669) has a church to St Andrew and Anglo-Saxon work is visible at the south-east quoin in the angle of the aisle and chancel.

Other churches which may well contain Anglo-Saxon work are Edlingham (south-west quoin of nave), Ingram (west wall of nave), Longhoughton (possibly the chancel arch), and Woodhorn (the nave walls with simple round headed windows). Two churches which deserve special mention are Bolam and Whittingham, in villages of Saxon origin, which have had a very different history.

Bolam (NZ 093826) has evidence of an early native earthwork and a later 'castle'. It was (1305) once a flourishing places with 200 houses, but these have been reduced to a scattered few. The church, however, has survived German bombs and its tall square tower stands proudly amongst the trees. This is the main Anglo-Saxon feature, though it is comparatively late in date—eleventh century. It may well represent the Saxon style of building within the Norman period. The Saxon part stands to a height of 55 feet, with a cornice and parapet that are modern. There is also herringbone work at the upper level.

The quoins are of characteristic long and short work. The windows at the base have been altered—the older Saxon windows can be seen inside the tower—similar to those of the second storey. At the third storey are double belfry windows on each face of the tower. The two lights of each window are separated by a founded, bulbous shaft carrying a corbelled stone to the thickness of the wall. The quoins of the west wall of the nave can also be seen. The Tower arch is Norman and so is the chancel arch, the east end of the Norman church being apsidal. Additions to the church in the thirteenth century and later have made it more spacious without destroying its unity. There is a mutilated effigy of a fourteenth-century knight in south-east chapel.

This church is very good for a general visit, since it has many fine tombstones in the churchyard as well as a wealth of detail within the church.

Whittingham (71 NU 066119) presents something of a contrast, since it has survived as a population centre. The old coach road passes through the village and it possesses a restored medieval tower. The church could easily be ignored as 'Victorian restoration', since the tower carries four incongruous pinnacles. But a closer examination reveals a good deal of Anglo-Saxon work, namely the lower half of the tower and the west wall of the nave of the narrow early church. Taylor claims that the lowest six feet of this work, which is of side alternate construction, is of an earlier period than the other Saxon work on the Tower. The quoins are of very fine quality. Some Saxon work has been detected at the east end of the nave. The dimensions of Tower and nave are very similar to those at Corbridge and elsewhere. It has been suggested that 'Whittingham' was the 'Twyford' of a seventh-century synod.

Anglo-Saxon Crosses

During the period that followed the Conversion of the English to Christianity, Northumbria provided scholars, artists and sculptors, whose work was not surpassed in quality anywhere in Europe. This is especially so in sculpture and some scholars were inclined to regard the work as medieval. But the Bewcastle Cross has the name of Aldfrith, a Northumbrian sub-king who ruled no later than 664, enscribed upon it. The writing may be doubtful but the cross can be dated to the late seventh century and there is much more of the same school of sculpture. The crosses had special religious significance and were fairly common. They showed biblical figures carved in relief with decorative motifs of vine scrolls, leaves and chequered patterns. Some have bird and animal figures. There are full sized crosses at Bewcastle (Cumberland) and Ruthwell (Dumfries). Acca's Cross from Hexham is at Durham, but there are numerous fragments in both museums and churches that are interesting to study in detail. Places where these stones or fragments have been discovered are—

Alnham
Alnmouth
Bewcastle (Cumberland)
Birtley
Bywell
Edlingham
Falstone
Hexham
Lindisfarne
Nunnykirk
Ovingham
Rothbury
Simonburn
Warkworth
Woodhorn

Books

Anglo-Saxon Chronicle. Everyman Edition 1960.
Bede-Ecclesiastical History translated L. Sherley Price. Penguin.
HUNTER BLAIR, P. *Introduction to Anglo-Saxon England*. C.U.P. 1965.
BROOKE, C. *Saxon and Norman Kings*. Collins Fontana.
DAVIDSON, H. *The Golden Age of Northumbria*. Longmans 1965.
DUCKETT, E. *Anglo-Saxon Saints and Scholars*. Macmillan 1947.
FISHER, E. A. *Introduction to Anglo-Saxon Architecture and Sculpture*. Faber 1959.

HAMILTON, T. and SORRELL, A. *Saxon England.* Lutterworth.
BRUCE MITFORD, R. *Recent Archaeological Discoveries.* Sutton Hoo.
PEVSNER, N. *Buildings of Northumberland.* Penguin 1957.
QUENNELL. *History of Everyday Things in Roman, Saxon and Norman Times.*
TAYLOR, H. M. & J. *Anglo-Saxon Architecture.* C.U.P. 1965.
WEBB, J. F. *Lives of the Saints.* Penguin 1965.
WEST, T. H. *Architecture in England.* E.U.P. 1965.
WHITELOCK, D. *Beginnings of Anglo-Saxon Society.* Penguin.
WRIGHT, D. *Translation of Beowulf.* Penguin 1957.
WILSON, D. M. *The Anglo Saxons.* Thames & Hudson 1960.
ROWLAND, T. H. *Anglo-Saxon Northumbria.* Frank Graham 1972.

THE MEDIEVAL PERIOD

The term 'Middle Ages' is sometimes used rather vaguely. Here it is intended to cover the four centuries that followed the Norman Conquest. This left a very definite impression and the material remains of the Conquest are easy to recognize. Northumberland was not easily added to the English Kingdom and the revolt of 1069 led to devastation, so that the county was not included in the Domesday Survey of 1085. This is unfortunate, since Domesday is a most valuable source of information in other parts of the country. The effects of the Norman Conquest can be seen in language. Besides the English dialects, there was Latin for the clerics and Norman French for the new landed aristocracy. This leads to a multiplication of terminology. An example is the using of French terms for 'meats', whereas the English name is kept for the animal. The pig provides 'porc' (French for pig), the sheep—'mouton' and the ox—'boeuf'. Many terms are duplicated such as 'shire' and 'county', 'little' and 'petty', 'great' and 'grand'. French terms apply in matters of law and administration, but also in arms, armour and fortification.

The other signs of the conquerors were the division of estates and the establishment of castles. Also the Church was re-organized: there was a good deal of church building, from parish churches to cathedrals like Durham. There was also a great monastic revival, which resulted in the building or rebuilding of some very large establishments.

VISITS

It is perhaps best to visit Norman buildings together where this is possible. It has to be remembered that the process of building went on for a century, so that both churches and castles will show various periods of building. The first stage of castle building was work that had to be completed rapidly, if the Normans were to survive in the land which they had conquered. The first castles were of earth and timber: they are generally known by the term 'motte and bailey'. Wherever possible the Normans made use of a natural site, that could be conveniently adapted to defence.

The best example in Northumberland is at Elsdon and the castle survives in its early state, because the Umfravilles transferred their headquarters to Harbottle.

Elsdon Castle dominates the village and the old crossing of the burn. It consists of a huge circular mound to the south, separated from the bailey or courtyard by a very deep ditch. The bailey is semi-circular in shape, the narrow dimension being near to the mound and the wider away from it. The distance from the motte to the outer ditch of the bailey was 100 yards roughly. This was usual and a bigger area was obtained by widening the sector enclosed. This could be covered by firing arrows from the height of the motte. The ditches and ramparts on the north and east are very striking. On the west the steepness of the slope made them unnecessary. The approach to the castle is by a lane to the farm on the site, where permission to view can be obtained. Elsdon Castle dates back to about 1080 and the site was probably used in prehistoric times.

Harbottle Castle, begun in 1157 is seven miles to the north and can only be seen in passing. This too was a motte and bailey type of castle.

Norham on Tweed has both a Norman church and castle. The church is dedicated to St Cuthbert and was connected with the Bishopric of Durham. The best surviving Norman work is the chancel, not including the east-end, which is a later addition. The Norman part of the nave consists of five bays with large circular piers like Durham. There is a zig-zag frieze above the arches. The chancel is wide and spacious. The five round-headed Norman windows are easily recognizable on the south side, half way up the wall, between stone pilasters. On the south side is decoration, but not on the north. There are Anglo-Saxon remains within the church.

Norham is a village with a green and its cross is still in position.

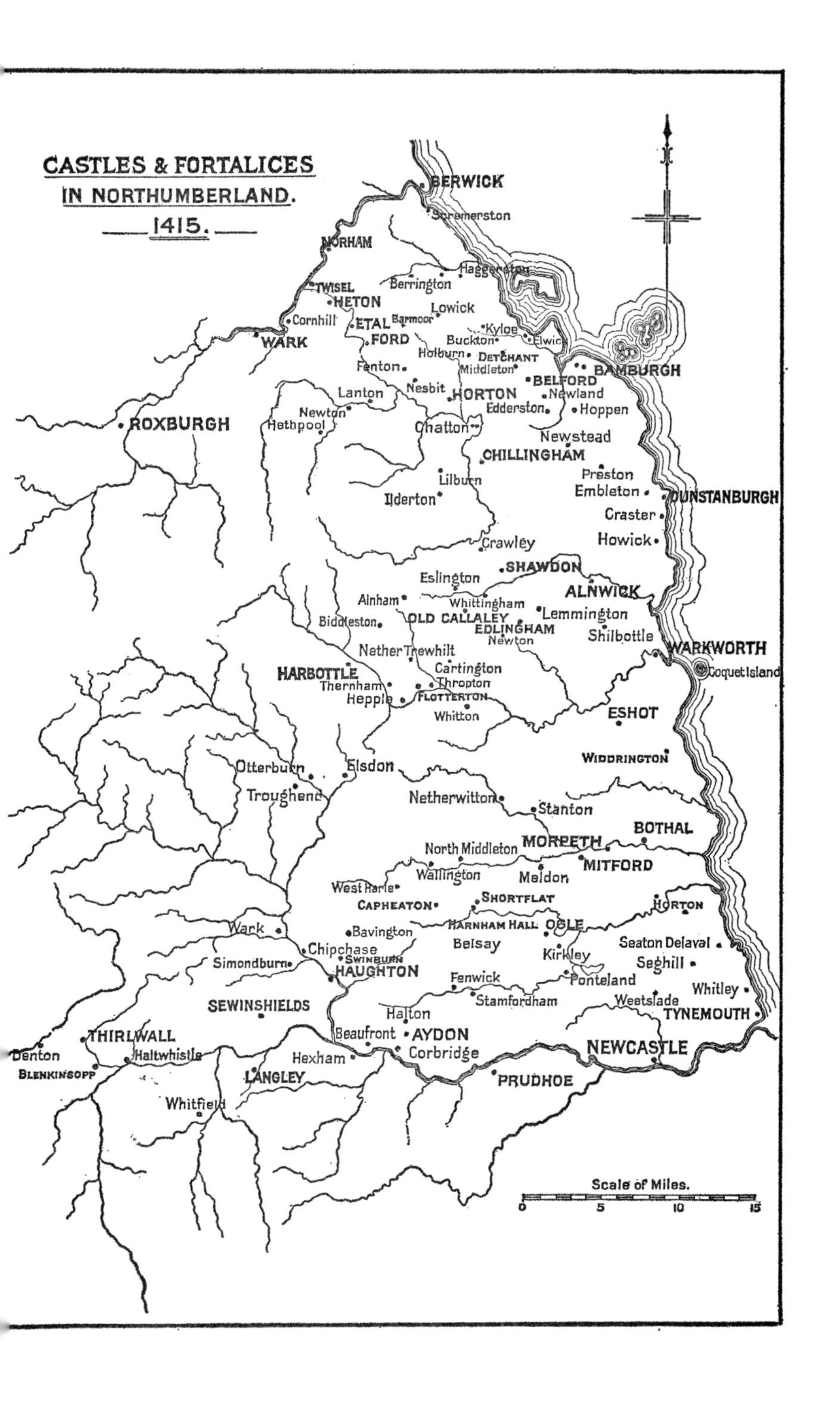
CASTLES & FORTALICES
IN NORTHUMBERLAND.
1415.
BERWICK
Scremerston
NORHAM
Haggerston
Berrington
TWISEL
HETON
Lowick
Cornhill
ETAL
Barmoor
Kyloe
WARK
FORD
Buckton
Elwick
Holburn
DETCHANT
Fenton
Middleton
BELFORD
BAMBURGH
Lanton
Nesbit
HORTON
Newland
Newton
Hethpool
Edderston
Hoppen
ROXBURGH
Chatton
Newstead
CHILLINGHAM
Preston
Lilburn
Embleton
DUNSTANBURGH
Ilderton
Craster
Howick
Crawley
SHAWDON
Eslington
ALNWICK
Alnham
Whittingham
Lemmington
Biddleston
OLD CALLALEY
EDLINGHAM
Shilbottle
Newton
WARKWORTH
Nether Trewhilt
Coquet Island
HARBOTTLE
Cartington
Thernham
Thropton
Hepple
FLOTTERTON
Whitton
ESHOT
WIDDRINGTON
Otterburn
Elsdon
Troughend
Netherwitton
Stanton
BOTHAL
North Middleton
MORPETH
MITFORD
Wallington
Meldon
West Harle
CAPHEATON
SHORTFLAT
HORTON
Wark
Bavington
HARNHAM HALL
OGLE
Seaton Delaval
Chipchase
Belsay
Kirkley
SWINBURN
Simondburn
Seghill
HAUGHTON
Fenwick
Ponteland
Whitley
Stamfordham
SEWINSHIELDS
Weetslade
Halton
TYNEMOUTH
THIRLWALL
Beaufront
AYDON
Denton
Haltwhistle
Hexham
Corbridge
NEWCASTLE
BLENKINSOPP
LANGLEY
PRUDHOE
Whitfield
Scale of Miles.
0
5
10
15

It is dominated by the castle, which dates back to the time of Bishop Flambard (1121). Norham was head of the shire of that name and also of Holy Island, both areas belonging to Durham and defence was necessary against the Scots. The castle controlled the crossing of the Tweed and its position was very strong. Flambard's Castle was a 'motte and bailey' type. The motte is situated in the northern angle

Norham Castle from the West.

of the site between the Tweed and a ravine. South of this is the bailey with deep ditches and beyond this is a larger enclosure, probably for cattle. The motte would carry a timber tower and palisade. There would be a timber palisade also, on the rampart surrounding the bailey, and timber buildings within. It was taken by the Scots in 1138. After 1157 Bishop Hugh de Puisnet built a very strong tower or keep, a great deal of which still stands together with the south-east section of the curtain wall. Norham was subject to many sieges and was reputed to be the most dangerous place in the north. It was twice captured by the Scots in 1327 and again in 1513 before the battle of Flodden. Norham illustrates the art of fortification over a period of four centuries, including modifications in the age of gunpowder. [Keep = 84 feet × 60 feet × 90 feet high.]

Another castle was built in the reign of Henry I at Wark on Tweed by Walter L'Espec. This was 'motte and bailey', but it was destroyed by King David of Scotland in 1138. It was rebuilt in the reign of Henry II, after 1158, probably with a shell keep on top of the original motte. It was important into the sixteenth century, but visible remains are few and information waits upon excavation.

Bamburgh calls for attention as another important Norman place. It had a long history as a fortified site before the Normans took over. The massive outcrop of the Whin Sill stands up to a height of 150 feet, dominating the village and overlooking the sea. It was a natural defensive site and fortified by King Ida in the sixth century. It was the chief town of Northumberland until Norman times, when it became a royal stronghold. The whole area on top of the rock (not unlike the Acropolis of Athens) was within the defences and there was no motte. The keep is much the same date as Norham. It was built after Henry II had recovered the earldom of Northumberland from King William of Scotland. The dimensions of the keep are 69 feet × 61½ feet × 60 feet. It is tunnel vaulted and the entrance was at ground floor level, which was unusual. It has square turrets at the angles and buttresses to strengthen the walls.

The castle has been subject to much modification and alteration up to and including the nineteenth century. It was completely restored by Lord Armstrong at great cost.

The castle has three baileys—the west bailey had the original entrance, while the east bailey has the present entrance with medieval barbican and gatehouse. There are the remains of a twelfth-century chapel in the east bailey and the vaults of the medieval cellars underneath the hall. The castle is open to the public.

Bamburgh is a very suitable place for a village study, since in addition to the castle there is a church with several architectural periods, the earliest being Norman. The houses are clustered round the village green and the fine house near the church belonged to Dorothy Forster. Both the museum and churchyard are associated with another famous woman of the north—Grace Darling. There was a Benedictine Friary to the south of the village. The area has possibilities for the study of Industrial Archaeology, including landscape, industry, agriculture, communications and population changes.

Prudhoe provides yet another early Northumberland castle. It was the head of a barony and belonged to the Umfravilles who held the liberty of Elsdon. Here on a natural mound to the south of the Tyne, was constructed a motte and bailey type of castle at the beginning of the reign of Henry I. A deep ditch was excavated to cut off the site from the high ground to the south. The motte was to the west on the prepared site and the bailey on the east. After 1174 when the castle had twice defied the Scots, it was largely rebuilt in stone with a curtain wall surrounding the defended area and with a strong gate-house. The keep is similar to that of Newcastle, but smaller. Its dimensions are 44 feet by 41 feet, with an extension eastwards to cover the entrance. It has suffered later modifications and the old entrance is now concealed. The enclosure contained other buildings. The gatehouse was altered in the thirteenth century to admit a chapel above the entrance. In the early fourteenth century, in face of danger from the Scots, the entrance was further strengthened by the construction of a barbican on the south of the moat. The approach is the most arresting of any of the castles. There was formerly a drawbridge, but no portcullis. Probably of the thirteenth century are the round towers at the west end of the castle. The one on the north remains, but the south-west one has been reduced to foundations. Also in the fourteenth century, there was a pale-yard or enclosure to the south of the castle, later converted into a garden. At the end of the fourteenth century Prudhoe came into the hands of the Percy family, who also held Alnwick and Warkworth. There was a sixteenth-century house within the walls and yet another constructed in Georgian style. Prudhoe Castle is in the hands of the Ministry of Works, undergoing repairs at present. It can be safely asserted that it will be open to the public. The site itself is worth a careful study to see why it was chosen and retained. The owners of Prudhoe in the early thirteenth century brought about a premature end to the building of Nafferton Castle, which lies two miles to the north.

Warkworth is at present day a village, but it can be regarded a very fine example of a medieval town. These old towns were comparatively small and all kinds of factors affected development. There were communications, trade and the question of security. A castle or a monastery might be the original cause of a settlement or they might add to the development of an area. Kings and nobles did in fact create new towns by granting to each a free market, some form of self government and plots of land for settlement. Warkworth presents an ideal natural site. There is a tongue of land almost surrounded by the river, which protects the whole area on the north—the direction of danger. The River Coquet was a means of access since it is tidal in this area. The bridge was the only means of crossing the river and was controlled by a defensive tower. The south end of the site is dominated by the castle, which has the river to the east, north and west. Thus the whole area was defended and the castle could control both the town and its communications. The one main street comes in to the east of the castle and straight down to the market place in the centre of the town. The market was held in the open air under a cross to encourage just dealings. The market was the essence

WARKWORTH BRIDGE, co. NORTHUMBERLAND.

of the town or borough and strangers had to pay for the privilege of trading. South of the market place is the church of St Lawrence, one of the finest in the county. It is basically Norman and has a long nave with chancel. The north wall of the nave with flat buttresses and round-headed windows is almost completely Norman. The west wall is Norman and the tower comparatively early. The spire is later, but the chancel is twelfth century and contains some very fine vaulting, similar to that of Durham. The south aisle is very late medieval and obscures the Norman elements of the church. Within the church is a carved fragment of Saxon stone and the impressive effigy of a fourteenth-century knight. The road turns at right angles from the market place to approach the bridge tower. On either side of the street are the frontages of eighteenth-century or nineteenth-century houses, which have taken the places of earlier dwellings, but the settlement pattern is obvious. There are long strips of territory called burgages, running from either side of the street towards the river, providing a good deal of garden space, room for extensions or rear access. In this way the medieval pattern is preserved and can be plainly distinguished either on an aerial photograph or from the north windows of the keep of the castle. This is now in the custody of the Ministry of Works and open to the public daily.

The castle is worth a detailed study, since the structure covers several centuries. The perimeter should be walked completely to get the 'feeling' of the site. On the western side is the steep fall to the River Coquet, with a pathway, leading to the hermit's cave. On the north is the keep on top of the original motte or mound. On the east the ditch and rampart of the bailey can be seen and on the south is the main entrance. Originally the bailey would have a timbered palisade, but probably after 1174 came the first rebuilding in stone by Roger, son of Richard and by his son, Robert. Robert did a good deal of rebuilding and the strengthening of the curtain walls, keep, gatehouse and frontal towers, overlooking the deep moat to the south. The polygonal turrets were a development of the thirteenth century and were proved to be more effective for counter attack against besiegers. Like round turrets they had the advantage of being stronger, more economical to build and reduced the amount of 'dead ground' that had to be covered. Presumably Warkworth had a drawbridge and there is evidence of a portcullis. The loopholes show how the entrance and the base of the walls could be covered with archery fire. Above the entrance can be seen machicolation, which was permanent and the 'put holes' into which timber hoardings could be fixed. The gatehouse has guard-chambers and a vaulted passage with gates at either end, where attackers could be trapped and eliminated. On the western side of the bailey are the chapel and great hall. These were modified over a period of time. On the eastern side of the bailey are the stables and various offices. The outer bailey is divided from the inner bailey by the foundations of a collegiate church, dating from about 1400. The inner bailey is approached by means of a tunnel and in the restricted space between the church and keep are the remains of a brew-house. The keep shows very dramatically how a building or area could be modified to meet the demands of a differing age, when space was restricted. It is basically the solid square keep with storage space in the lower levels, but it has been modified to meet the conflicting demands of bodily comfort and defence. Each of the four corners has been bevelled and to each side has been added a polygonal turret. These four towers meet in the centre providing a series of four apartments at each level and the square of the keep is thus

~Roman Bridge at Corbridge~

Medieval Bridge at Corbridge.

Aerial View, Housesteads, looking west along the wall from the fort.

Scene from Trojan's Column.

Reconstruction of a Saxon Hall.

divided into another separate series of four apartments at each level. In the centre is a square turret rising far above the summit of the keep and providing both a watch tower and a well for channelling down the light. Within the keep are ingeniously arranged hall, kitchen quarters, chapel and various private apartments with the full range of stores below. There is increasing window space on each floor and these show that ecclesiastical and domestic architecture are not to be strongly differentiated. Reconstructed in the early fifteenth century, Warkworth Castle was intended to meet the double demands of the proud and powerful family of Percies—powerful enough to challenge Henry IV. The keep duplicated all the buildings of the outer bailey, but it was not intended as a last line of defence. It provided comfort and privacy for the owners, with a complete view of fortress, river, town, port and deer park. It could be supplied from the sea and could be used in the same way as Dunstanburgh. It was provided with portholes for guns and was the favourite residence of the Earls of Northumberland till 1670.

Warkworth requires a prolonged visit, or preferably, several.

The Ministry of Works provide a boat to take small parties to the Hermitage up the river. Again this is something superior to the ordinary cell. This is a little chapel and house carved out of the rock in the fourteenth century. The house contains a small kitchen, dining-room and solar as well as the chapel which has carved vaulting. The occupant had his own garden facilities and fish directly from the river. It is not certain whether this would be the residence of a strict anchorite or a priest. However it adds another dimension to Warkworth.

Books

SIMPSON, W. D. *Castles in Britain.* Batsford 1966.
Castles from the Air. Country Life 1949.
Exploring Castles. Country Life 1957.
ST J. O'NEIL, B. H. *Castles.* H.M.S.O. 1953.
BROWN, R. A. *Medieval Castles.* Batsford 1954. (Also paperback.)
TOY, S. *Castles.*
ST JOSEPH, J. K. *Castles in Northumberland from the Air. Archaeologia Aeliana.* 1950.
HUNTER BLAIR, C. H. *Early Castles of Northumberland. Archaeologia Aeliana.* 1944.
Warkworth. H.M.S.O. Guide.
Norham. H.M.S.O. Guide.
GRAHAM, F. *Bamburgh.* 1962. *Warkworth.* 1971.
PEVSNER, N. *Buildings of Northumberland.* Penguin.

ROWLAND, T. H. *Medieval Castles of Northumberland.* 1969.
BATES, C. J. *Border Holds.* 1891.
HUGILL, R. *Castles and Peles of the English Border.* F. Graham 1970.

MORPETH

Morpeth is another town that can be used to illustrate a number of periods of development. It is surrounded by native sites and enclosures of indeterminate date on the higher ground above the Wansbeck, but its recorded history dates from Norman times. It may well have been that there was a number of scattered farmsteads with a small concentration of people near the river crossing. The attention of the Norman conquerors is shown by the construction of a 'motte and bailey' castle dominating the area and still giving an extensive view of the borough. This is Ha' Hill within Carlisle Park and not to be confused with the present castle. This lies a little to the south-west across the Church Burn and consists of fourteenth-century gatehouse tower with a curtain wall. The courthouse is sometimes mistaken for the castle, since it is built in medieval style with battlements and a central entrance. It dates from 1822 and the architect was Dobson. This is situated to the east of Carlisle Park.

There were several factors that helped the development of Morpeth. It was the head of a Barony and the De Merlays were often resident. (The later lords were often non-resident.) In 1138 a Cistercian Abbey was established at Newminster and this became a place of very considerable importance. Eventually there was the advantage of a bridge from the late thirteenth century. The Wansbeck could be forded at numerous places, but there was always the advantage of a safe and certain crossing, which the bridge provided. This was maintained by the crafts of the borough. These, by a Charter of King John, had some form of self-government. They took tolls to maintain the bridge and established a Chantry Chapel of All Saints for the benefit of their members and travellers. This building also provided space for a school and was the original grammar school. The ecclesiastical structure of the building can be traced. The present footbridge lies across the piers of the old medieval bridge. The arches were demolished in the last century after the magnificent Telford Bridge had been constructed in 1831.

The development of the town in this direction left the Parish Church of St Mary's somewhat apart from the main population centre. Later development was still further northwards along 'Newgate Street' so that in the 1840s when a new church was needed, it was built here —St James's. Strangely enough this is perhaps the best example of Norman architecture in Northumberland, although it is nineteenth century. The church, by Benjamin Ferry, is a replica of a Norman Sicilian Church and so gives the complete plan. Various features of this church can be picked out in parts of earlier churches in the county—the tower for example is strangely reminiscent of Hexham. The other contribution of this church was that St Mary's was able to maintain its medieval form with its fine Jesse window. St Mary's is one of the best churches in the county for detailed study and the churchyard contains a fine collection of tomb-stones.

From St Mary's, too, the common fields can be studied, still with distinctive ridge and furrow, showing very plainly on the parts appropriated by the golf course.

Newminster Abbey, to the west of Morpeth, and originally sited between Morpeth and Mitford for purposes of seclusion, has been overrun by the town in the sense that most of the stone has been carted off to provide material for walls and houses. Decorated stones are found in many a Morpeth garden and capitals have been converted into chimney tops. The layout of the abbey can be seen from the footpath leading up the hill from the newly built house. Permission has to be obtained to go on to the site.

Within Morpeth itself the outlines of the old burgages can still be seen with some of the old yards. There are no houses in Morpeth earlier than the late seventeenth century, though fragments and foundations of earlier buildings may well be embodied in houses still existing.

Other interesting features are the Town Hall—a restoration of the original Vanlurgh façade—and the bell tower, from which curfew is rung. At one time this served as a gaol.

The cattle market has been transferred from its old site to the area of the railway station, but on Wednesday Morpeth still presents something of the old throng. The medieval origins of the borough are not completely submerged by modern development and it presents an interesting problem in town planning.

Suggested studies could be:

1. The medieval plan.
2. Communications including the railway and the modern motorway.
3. Provision for the various religious denominations.

4. Public utilities—gas, water and sanitation.
5. Educational establishments.
6. Public Houses.

References

Official Guide to Morpeth.
Directories.
Hodgson's *History of Northumberland.* Part II, Vol. II. Frank Graham reprint.
Woodman Collection of documents and papers at the County Records Office Gosforth.
County Library Headquarters, Morpeth.

ALNWICK

Alnwick in its development shows the very close connection there has always been of the castle and the community. The castle now presents aspects of culture and paternalism, rather than the crude domination of the Norman Keep. Yet realities were stark enough, and the original castle (a motte and bailey) guarded the passage of the Aln in one direction and overlooked the town in the other. The view that the traveller obtains from the north with the trees and terraced slopes is the work of Capability Brown in the eighteenth century. Originally the motte, which is easily visible, separated the east and west baileys. The timberwork was replaced by stone in the middle of the twelfth century and there was a shell keep on the mound. At the end of the thirteenth century, in the time of the Scottish Wars of Edward I, the castle was greatly strengthened with semi-circular towers before the shell keep. The curtain wall was rebuilt and provided with towers, but most important is the barbican protecting the gatehouse. There were two gateways and two drawbridges. The recessed entrance is covered by square towers and these are connected by walls to the corresponding inner polygonal towers. All are battlemented and now decorated with figures.

The entrance to the buildings on the motte is strongly defended and most impressive. For a period Alnwick was somewhat neglected by the Percies, who preferred Warkworth. However in the eighteenth century the castle was extensively rebuilt and again in the nineteenth century, without obscuring the most important medieval features. So Alnwick Castle presents the full story of the castle over nearly nine centuries and is still inhabited. It is open to the public in summer months. Within the castle is a very fine library and in a mural tower, a small archaeological museum.

After leaving the castle, it is worth walking north to the Lion Bridge, for a general view. Then, on returning, turn right along Walkergate to see the remains of St Mary's Chantry and on reaching B6346, it is possible to take a look at the ruins of Alnwick Abbey in the Park. It was founded in 1147 for Premonstratensian Canons, but only the gatehouse remains and the site. At the top of the hill, returning to Alnwick, is St Michael's Church. This is a large and perhaps a rather unusual church for Northumberland—comparatively rich and elaborate. Northumberland churches in the later Middle Ages tended to be simple, austere and defensive, reflecting the disorder and poverty of the area. Alnwick Church is mainly fourteenth century and fifteenth century, and in spite of being perpendicular in style, tends to have a solid appearance. The tower is heavily buttressed and both the nave and chancel have been widened. There is some very fine decorated work on the

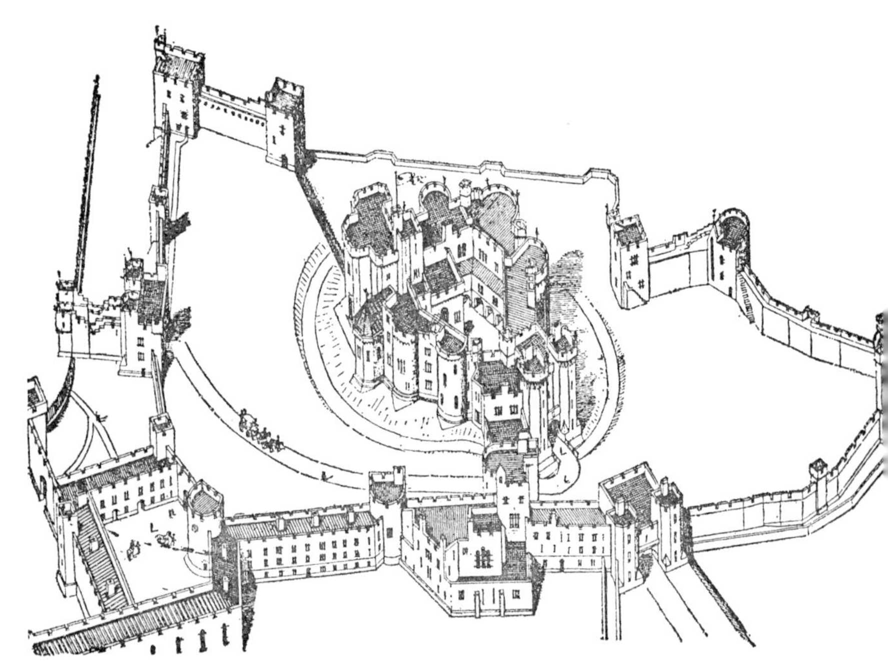

capitals of the piers of the chancel chapels and this is matched by artistic modern wood carving, which shows the tradition of craftsmanship. The churchyard contains a full and varied collection of tomb-stones.

The town lies to the south of the castle area and can be studied separately. It is possible to pick out the limits of the medieval town, with the Hotspur Gate on the southern limit still in position. The gatehouse has polygonal towers and was connected with the town walls of the fifteenth century. The Market Place is central within the intramural area and the streets speak for themselves—Bondgate Within and Without, Clayport, Narrowgate and Pottergate. Near the castle is Bailiffgate. The castle has had its influence on the buildings of the town as well as the parkland of the north of the area. Alnwick is a town of antique character and this should be preserved. The western approaches to the town show that this can be done without the clash of old and new. Development in the nineteenth century and later has been on the southern approaches. This includes the railway station, recently closed to traffic. At one time it was connected with Wooler.

Books

TATE. *History of Alnwick.*
CONZEN. *Alnwick.* Geog. Association 1960.
GRAHAM. *Alnwick, History and Guide.* 1973.
DAVISON. *Historical View of Alnwick.* Frank Graham reprint.

NEWCASTLE

Newcastle upon Tyne must also be treated in the first instance as a medieval town. Although the site was recognized by the Romans as a place for a bridge and fort, the real development comes with the Normans and the siting of a 'New Castle' to guard against incursions from the debateable land to the north. It controlled the obvious route from north to south and would naturally develop as a port and a market. A bridge can impose limits to shipping. The Tyne was the the southern limit to Newcastle and the bridge was its focal point. The earliest routes radiate from it and the growth pattern was outwards from this base.

The original castle was of the motte and bailey type. The enclosure had as its southern limit the steep slope to the river; on the east and west ravines cut by streams: the northerly limit was the point of the Black Gate. The motte was in the south-east corner, not where the keep is. Robert, son of William the Conqueror (1080) restored the bridge and built the first castle in timber. After the rebellion of 1095 it remained in royal hands, and it may well be that from this time there was building in stone—the gateway and some of the surrounding walls. In Stephen's reign the castle was held by Earl Henry, son of the King of Scotland. It was recovered by Henry II. It was surrounded by a new stone wall with the postern and great new gate.

Then by 1178 the huge, strong rectangular keep was constructed. The cost was something like £1,000 and it was built by Maurice, the Mason, who has been identified by Maurice the Engineer, later responsible for Dover. A cross wall divided the castle enclosure into north and south baileys with the keep and hall in the north bailey. The keep dominated the entire area and it has to be remembered that a lot of the medieval buildings would be small and situated at a lower-level. The keep, which is open to the public, should be studied in detail as a fine example of military architecture, but combining some residential comforts. The entrance was on the second floor, the basement was used for stores and the chapel contains some fine Norman vaulting. A view from the top of the keep indicates the strategic value of the site and explains something of the growth of the town. The development is shown by the churches of St Nicholas, St John and St Andrew. The latter has suggestions of Norman architecture. St Nicholas and St John are mainly of the fourteenth and fifteenth century. All Saints, which is eighteenth century, was constructed on the site of an older church. Street names are eloquent—Pilgrim Street for example. Nun Street is a reminder of a Benedictine Nunnery. The Friars, who are evident from early thirteenth century, favoured towns as opposed to secluded places. The building of the Dominicans or Black Friars still remains. There were Grey Friars and White Friars as well as Austin Friars. So Newcastle was well provided for, religiously.

The town became very prosperous through shipping and trade.

The castle together with the town walls, which date back to the middle of the thirteenth century, gave security in spite of the Scottish Wars. The Black Gate which dates to 1247 increased the strength of the castle. It now houses a number of interesting relics of old Newcastle.

The town received the customs of the free burghs of Scotland in the time of David I and by the end of the twelfth century was able to purchase a charter of incorporation.

Newcastle remained very much within the confines of the walls till the seventeenth century, though there were changes within, resulting from religious changes and changes in the ownership of property. The locations of the markets can be traced and the use of the High Bridge and Low Bridge over the Lort Burn. Considerable stretches of the old walls and remains of the mural towers can be discovered. These were used as meeting places for the ancient crafts. There is also the Guildhall near the castle and the development of the Quayside.

Spede's Map of Northumberland (1610) gives an excellent picture of Northumberland and Newcastle at the beginning of the seventeenth century. The map of Newcastle shows the pattern of the town within the walls.

The walls and gates can still be studied on the site and a perambulation provokes interesting reflections on the outward development of the town. The problem of communications is apparent. At every stage one sees the conflict now, not of Scot and English, Royalist and Parliamentarian, but the claims of the past and the conflicting needs of the present. The city plan should preserve the various periods of its evolution.

For those who require it, the City provides the service of experienced guides. [Information from the Central Library.]

Museums

Black Gate and Keep. Open—On Monday afternoons only. Tuesday-Saturday 10 a.m.-5 p.m. (earlier closing in winter).

The Laing Art Gallery displays armour/weapons/pottery/clothes besides pictures. Open—Weekdays 10 a.m.-6 p.m. Sundays 2.30-5.30 p.m.

Books

The Official Guide: Guide to the Castle.

MIDDLEBROOK, S. *Newcastle upon Tyne: Its Growth and Achievement.* Published 1950.

This book is essential to the study of Newcastle. It has recently been revised by the author and a re-issue is available.

GREY, W. *Chorographia. Newcastle in 1649.* Reprint by F. Graham.

BOURNE, H. *History of Newcastle 1736.*

BRAND, J. *History and Antiquities of Newcastle 1789.*

CHARLETON, J. *A History of Newcastle upon Tyne 1888.*

SYKES, J. *Local Records.* 4 Vols.

DIBDIN, T. *Newcastle in 1836.* Reprinted by F. Graham.

Map of Newcastle 1736. Reprinted from Bourne by F. Graham.

Map of Newcastle 1789. Reprinted from Brand by F. Graham.

OLIVER, T. *A New Picture of Newcastle upon Tyne. 1831.* Reprint Frank Graham.

GRAHAM, F. *The Sandhill, 1972.* *Historic Newcastle. 1970.*

The Castle and Town Walls of Newcastle. 1972.

DOUGAN, D. *Newcastle Past and Present. 1971.*

Northumberland and Durham a Century Ago. F. Graham.

The Old Prints preserve in picture form some of the oldest relics of Newcastle, that have now disappeared.

FELTON

Felton, on the A1 midway between Morpeth and Alnwick, can also be regarded as a medieval town. The medieval bridge here over the Coquet explains its existence as an important thoroughfare with a need for shops and hostelries. It is essentially a single street settlement with the river front effecting a cross structure. The old bridge, now confined to foot-traffic, can be studied at leisure and is a vantage point for considering the settlement pattern with burgages. The church is situated on higher ground to the west and changes in structure may well reflect growth of population in the thirteenth century. From the exterior it appears small and squat. The characteristic bell cote may well be medieval, but the interior astonishes from size and poses a number of architectural problems. Hamilton Thompson suggested that the church must date back to the early twelfth century. It was aisleless and the second arch of the south arcade was the original doorway. The porch doorway was embedded in the wall of the south aisle. The chancel with lancet windows was thirteenth century with the roof level raised in the nineteenth century. There is a chapel to the west of the porch and the north aisle has five arches of the fourteenth century. At thc cast end of the south aisle is a very fine monolithic window head (i.e. cut from one piece of stone). It is curvilinear in style and its width of 77 inches makes it the largest one yet known in Northumberland.

The monuments include the broken effigy of a priest.

Felton had burgage tenements and a market from 1200 (the reign of John). The Northern barons did homage to Alexander of Scotland at Felton, after John had revoked Magna Carta.

This is the site of Old Felton, which is merely a farm.

MEDIEVAL TOWNS AND MODERN DEVELOPMENTS

Medieval towns provide studies of wide and general interest. The extent of change can be surprising, especially with the onset of the

Industrial Revolution which is associated with increasing population. Change and decay have been continuous factors. A list of towns in Northumberland paying the lay subsidy in 1296, gives some idea of their size from the point of view of population. In Newcastle 297 persons paid the tax, Corbridge 77, Alnwick and Newbiggin both 49. Chatton and Alwinton each had 40 taxpayers, Morpeth 35 and Wooler 34. North Sunderland and Doddington each had 30; Bamburgh and Alnmouth 28. Rothbury had 24. Hexham, belonging to the Archbishop of York, was not included. These figures have to be multiplied several times to arrive at the full population. One has to consider the factors that made for the growth or decay of the town over a number of centuries.

The first is its strategic position in relation to travel, trade or defence. A bridge tended to channel traffic and then a castle might provide the means of defence.

A second factor was the interest or residence of the lord, whether King or baron. His occasional or permanent presence was of the greatest importance and he could provide the privileges of a market and some form of self-government. Beresford in his book on medieval towns shows that ten new towns were planted in Northumberland in the later Middle Ages. Alnmouth developed as a port for Alnwick: Warenmouth served a similar purpose for Bamburgh. A further factor in the medieval period was the extent of religious provision. Churches with Saints and their relics could attract pilgrims and monasteries provided accommodation for travellers. Far more persons travelled around in those times than is commonly supposed, from the King downwards. It was of great advantage to him to visit various parts of the country, periodically, to make use of the produce of these areas. Barons with scattered estates did the same. Masons and builders travelled too, so did pedlars and story tellers.

War was another factor in the development of a town and this could work both ways. It could cause devastation or stimulate trade and industries in an area as did the Scottish wars of Edward I. Places like Bywell and Bolam were flourishing centres: now they are regarded almost as 'deserted' villages.

Hexham is a town with many possibilities. It provides the best monastery in the county for detailed study. Once the seat of a Bishop, Hexham became a liberty of the Archbishop of York. It has a medieval prison and a moot hall which was the medieval castle. The grammar school goes back to medieval times and was refounded in the reign of Elizabeth I. The old plan of the town can be determined and its history is well documented in the *Northumberland County History*

(Vols. III and IV). Hexham was an old market town and possessed the old craft guilds. The glove making industry was still flourishing in the nineteenth century. The town was affected by the development of the Military Road in the middle of the eighteenth century, and of the Newcastle-Carlisle railway nearly a century later.

Corbridge, among many other things, provides material for the study of the open fields associated with a small town.

Tynemouth, associated with North Shields, had a monastery together with a castle which became part of the system of medieval defences. It was connected with St Alban's Abbey and provided a 'Siberia' for refractory southern monks. One prior of Tynemouth, Prior de la Mare, was transferred to St Alban's in 1349. After the Dissolution of the monasteries, Tynemouth became royal property and was developed in the sixteenth century as part of the coastal defences. Tynemouth is also associated with ships, trade and smuggling.

Berwick could be regarded almost as a small kingdom. It was once the most flourishing port in Scotland, till seized by the English during the Border Wars. It changed hands several times, not always to the benefit of the inhabitants. It continued to have a military emphasis and in the reign of Elizabeth I was protected by defence works that would compare with the best in Europe at that time. It remains a port and communications centre. Provision for different forms of religion here could be considered. A church was built in Cromwell's time.

PORTS

The development of ports is another consideration. The tendency has been to concentrate trade on a few large ports for purposes of efficiency. But in the past a large number of ports were needed to supply and take products from small localities. The sea and rivers provided the best means of travel and transport. There were large numbers of comparatively small boats plying up and down rivers and coastways between the small ports. Keels were used for loading the colliers and there were numerous fishing boats. The lading bills of the harbour of Seaton Sluice give evidence of a large number of small cargoes.

Ports that provide interesting studies include Alnmouth, where the river changed its course in the last century. It developed in medieval times and received a great stimulus in the eighteenth century with the improvements in agriculture and especially corn growing, which was helped by new techniques and governmental finance. There were Corn Laws to encourage the export of corn. Alnmouth was the terminus of a Turnpike road, leading from Hexham by way of Rothbury. There were large granaries at Alnmouth as well as other coastal termini. Trade has declined and Alnmouth, a fairly important medieval town has become a small pleasant holiday resort.

The small port of Seaton Sluice was flourishing too in the eighteenth century, but it has been overtaken and swallowed by the port of Blyth, which with improvements in the nineteenth century and later could take and build much larger ships. Blyth and Whitley Bay both boroughs at the present day, are essentially nineteenth century developments. Whitley Bay submerges Cullercoats and shares Seaton Sluice with Blyth.

Other ports deserving detailed study are Amble, Craster and Newbiggin. Although no longer a coal port, Amble still retains its coal staithes and railway approaches. The harbour works are of considerable interest and from the quays, quantities of barley are now exported. There is still a limited amount of fishing from the port. Craster has the interest of a small port redeveloped in the last century. Plans and particulars of improvements can be seen in the County Record Office. Newbiggin suffers badly from coastal erosion.

It is noticeable that there was considerable ship building in ports from Blyth to Berwick and boat building still goes on. There is no mention of this in a recently published book on *Shipbuilding in the North-East*.

The smaller ports have great possibilities for development as leisure centres with emphasis on boating and sailing. They present excellent opportunities for local studies, when all kinds of factors—historical, geographical, economic and social can be considered.

The Old and New Towns can be considered together. Places that received 'new creations' in the Middle Ages, have in modern times moved on to a third stage with an urban population far greater than ever previously visualized. There is a process of urban growth and decay. Certain areas have to be developed industrially; clearances have to be made for new roadways: derelict areas come under demolition. There are areas termed urban 'fallow' (i.e. awaiting development) that are interesting to record before changes take place.

Industries change also and with them different techniques develop in factory or workshop. These also can be recorded together with the housing and transport related to them. The requirements of different forms of transport can be indicated—the horse, the ship, the railway, the motor car and the aeroplane.

Beresford gives as 'new' towns in *Medieval Northumberland.*

Alnmouth by 1147
Felton c. 1200
Mitford 1100-57
Morpeth 1199-1239
Newborough 1221
Newcastle 1080-1130
Newton in Warkworth 1249
North Shields 1225
Warenmouth 1247

(This does not preclude an earlier settlement in the same neighbourhood.)

Modern new towns are Killingworth and Cramlington, but other towns have extended enormously and the medieval nucleus may be difficult to discover. It is interesting to study urban development and to plot the housing and industrial developments of different periods. This can be done partly by the study of maps and partly by looking at buildings in their location. The increasing height of buildings has to be considered as well as the extending area. Materials and styles help to determine dates and street names often give evidence of the period of development.

Books

BANKS, F. R. *Old English Towns*. Batsford.
BERESFORD, M. *New Towns in the Middle Ages*. Lutterworth.
BERESFORD, M. & DR ST JOSEPH. *Medieval England (from the Air)*. Cambridge.
BURNS, W. *New Towns for Old*. Leonard Hill.
Newcastle, a study in Planning. Leonard Hill.
BCC. *People in Towns*.
BRADLEY, J. *People and Places*. Intertext Books.
OSMOND. *Towns*. Batsford.
SHARP, T. *English Panorama*. Architectural Press.
Town and Townscape. J. Murry.
H.M.S.O. *Historic Towns: Preservation and change*.

Some books on individual places.

N.C.H. = *Northumberland County History* in 15 Volumes, printed from 1893-1940.

The area from Newbiggin across country to Elsdon was not included. It was covered by Hodgson.

Alnmouth. *N.C.H.* Vol. II.

Alnwick. TATE, G. *History of the Borough, Castle and Barony of Alnwick.* 1886-9.
Amble. MCANDREWS, T. L.
Berwick. SCOTT, J. 1888.
Walls of Berwick. MCIVOR, I. H.M.S.O. 1968.
Blyth. BALDWIN, C. *Blyth Harbour Commission.* 1929.
Bamburgh. *N.C.H.* Vol. I.
Bywell. *N.C.H.* Vol. VI.
Bedlington in "North Durham". RAINE, J. 1852.
Corbridge. DIXON, S. F. *History.* 1912. *N.C.H.* Vol. X.
Cramlington. *N.C.H.* Vol. IX; *1968 Booklet on centenary of the Church.*
Felton. *N.C.H.* Vol. VII.
Hexham (& Shire). *N.C.H.* Vols. II & IV; HEWITT, J. *Handbook to Hexham 1879*; B and P Club, Hexham 1947; RIDLEY, J. *The Hexham Chronicle 1862*; WRIGHT, A. B. *An Essay towards the History of Hexham.*
Morpeth. HODGSON, J. *History of Northumberland* Part II. Vol. 2. This includes Mitford and Newbiggin.
Newburn. *N.C.H.* Vol. XIII.
Ponteland. *N.C.H.* Vol. XII.
Rothbury. *N.C.H.* Vol. XV.
Tynemouth. *N.C.H.* Vol. VIII.
Warkworth. *N.C.H.* Vol. V.
Wallsend. RICHARDSON, W. *History 1923*; *N.C.H.* Vol. XIII.
Wooler. HALL, *Guide to Wooler 1895*; *N.C.H.* Vol. XI.
GRAHAM, F. *Berwick, History and Guide. 1972.*
DAVISON, W. *Historical View of Alnwick, 1822.* Frank Graham Reprint 1973.
FULLER, J. *History of Berwick, 1799.* Frank Graham Reprint 1973.
HODGSON, J. *History of Morpeth, 1832.* Frank Graham Reprint 1973.

THE VILLAGE

Villages are characteristic English settlements and it is often possible to trace their origins and development. They combine elements of change and continuity which are understandable, because the community is limited in size. There is a tendency to conservatism which

By Courtesy of British Museum.

Lindisfarne Gospels, *c.* A.D. 700 Cruciform page at beginning of St. Matthew's Gospel. The finest piece of decoration in the book.

FORD CASTLE, 1887.

Gateway, Morpeth Castle

Arms on Sergeants Mace.

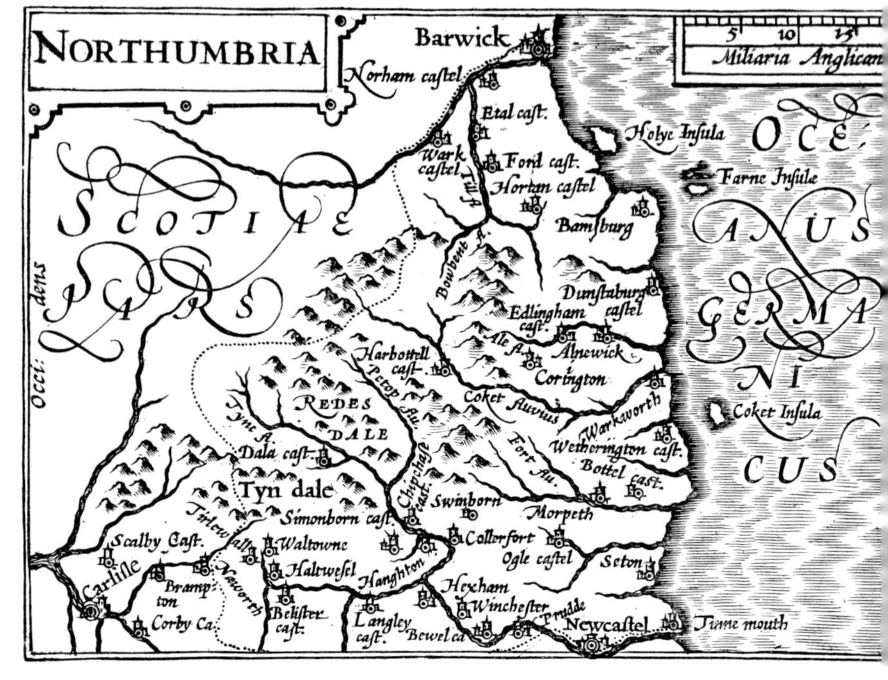

Miniature Speed Map. A.D. 1650

PHILIP DE ULECOTE'S CASTLE, NAFFERTON.

has the advantage of preserving things of the past, yet converting them to a present use. Buildings are adapted to other purposes and not knocked down. Older enclosures and lines of demarcation will be used. The medieval fish pond may be retained for the use of ducks and geese and cattle. Belts of trees can be retained for the purposes of shelter and old routes are kept. The old house may be used for workers storage or animals when a new house has been built on the site. The carriage house is easily adapted for the use of a car and a tractor will repose in any shed.

The village has to be considered basically in connection with farming and agriculture, for this was the main occupation although there were allied and subsidiary industries like milling. The life of the village reflects the progress and prosperity of agriculture. The cultivation of crops requires a larger number of labourers than the keeping of animals. During the twelfth and thirteenth centuries there was a very considerable development of agriculture, assisted by a milder climate and enterprising landowners. The plough was taken to the limits of tillage in hill country and marginal land produced corn. Long contour terraces or lynchets seen in the neighbourhood of Hethpool and Ingram, may well be the result of medieval ploughing. At the beginning and end of a fine day, shown up by the low rays of the sloping sun, the ridge and furrow pattern is quite plain. Late autumn and early spring when the cover of vegetation has been removed, are best times for viewing the cultivation pattern.

Medieval ploughing can often be picked out by the S shaped rigs that are the result of using teams of oxen. These required a wide headland for turning the plough. Since the same pieces were ploughed in the same way for centuries, the old field patterns became fossilized and only today with heavy mechanical equipment are they being obliterated. The modern tractor can climb up slopes in ploughing, that animals had to plough along the contours. Even so, the old pattern may persist. Eighteenth-century horse ploughing was much more regular and the straight rigs can be seen fitting into an enclosure with wall or hedge. The plough extended its range during the Napoleonic Wars, but before this agriculture had receded a good deal. The changes were periodic and varied from area to area.

The fourteenth century saw very considerable changes in agriculture and the settlement pattern. The country as a whole was badly affected by visitations of the plague called the Black Death. In 1348-9 there was a particularly bad epidemic and another in 1361-2. It has been conservatively estimated that a third of the entire population *was* wiped out, though this varied with the area and it is likely that Northumberland was not so severely affected. It happened too that there was murrain among the cattle and these animals not only provided food but did the work of ploughing and carting. There was a shortage of labour and also a shortage of draught animals. Agriculture declined—large areas were described as waste. Tenements were not taken up and landowners could not work them. The general result was an increase of sheep and cattle rearing. In upland areas in particular the sheep became more profitable. Cistercian monasteries had extensive sheep granges. In the north, too, the Scottish invasions tended to make agriculture a hazardous business. The farmer not only had to contend with weather, but marauders who waited till harvest time before they made their depredations. Some northerners emigrated to other parts, but others remained. The tendency to shrinking population was offset by the necessity of having to keep large numbers of men for frontier defence. The Percies used the situation in the fourteenth century to extend their estates enormously and were able to acquire royal money to enable them to man the defences. In the fifteenth century the reduced Percy Estates were not nearly so prosperous. It has been estimated that the revenue from them declined by a third, while prices went up. Two mills were tenanted, but another was not. The Earls of Northumberland tended to rely on fees from farms and entry fines, rather than working their lands directly. The causes of depopulation tended to be economic decline, rather than the dramatic results of either the plague or the Scots. The damages of a Scottish raid could easily be repaired and population in certain villages tended to decline when not so many men were needed for frontier defence. Examples of 'deserted' villages tend to appear in the sixteenth century and later. The enclosure movement in Northumberland tended to be prolonged and a great deal was done before the eighteenth century.

Deserted villages were at one time regarded as a figment of the poet's imagination. Two of the best known pictures of the village in the eighteenth century are from Gray's 'Elegy written in a Country Churchyard' or from Goldsmith's 'Deserted village'. Goldsmith was thought to be relying on his childhood memories of Ireland. But within the last twenty years 'Deserted Villages' have become a study in themselves. The starting point was Professor Beresford's valuable book on the subject. He listed several hundred deserted villages county by county with mention of a score in Northumberland. Since that time the number of possibilities in this county has risen to something like 200, although a number of these have not been investigated. Very few have been excavated since the deserted village site can occupy many acres. Some villages have disappeared and returned. Two examples here are Seaton Delaval and Newsham, both obliterated in the late sixteenth century, but have since returned as colliery villages. Colliery villages in turn can suffer decline when the colliery closes. In the area mentioned the old villages of High and Low Horton have disappeared, together with Old Bebside. Very often a farmstead retains the name of what was once a village. Plessey Hall overlooking the Blyth is now a farm, with some signs of a medieval moat. The village of Plessey has disappeared; this was the result of the closure of the pits in the neighbourhood in the early nineteenth century. Mining has a longer history than supposed and the county is pock-marked with old bell pits. Mining provided an additional form of employment and some of these areas were being worked in the late sixteenth century.

The evidence for villages that have been deserted consist of the tax returns at the end of the thirteenth century and later. Poll tax returns may also provide evidence of population at a particular date. Following these in the sixteenth century are the muster rolls, which give particulars of the number of fighting men, mounted and otherwise, that could be expected at the fixed assembly points. Very often the numbers were deficient—the place had decayed or lay waste and there were not the able bodied men available. One finds a place that was then expected to provide 10 or 20 men, reduced to a single farmstead. Old maps also provide evidence of the incidence of villages or places of settlement. On Spede's map of Northumberland, published in the reign of James I, can be found the names of villages which no longer exist.

Villages can be completely deserted, or shrunken and decayed. Grass grown hummocks in a field that do not fit a cultivation pattern or have been avoided by the plough may indicate the foundations of the buried houses of a deserted village. Some of the stones to surface level may have been removed to construct barns or field walls.

The pattern of the medieval village can often be picked out with sunken ways indicating the approach routes. The traffic had to confine itself to certain channels which were deepened by the impact of many feet. The village green is indicated by an open space, square or triangular. On each side are ranged the houses of the former inhabitants. There are a series of squares within squares. The larger square is the croft and the smaller square, the toft and house, of the villager. Each villager had a little enclosure near his house as well as his share of common pasture and grazing on the green. Beyond the village can be detected the ridge and furrow pattern of the open fields. Other features that may show up are the ruins of the tower or house of the lord—though this may have been replaced by the single farmhouse that takes over the site. There may be evidence of fish ponds which were essential in the Middle Ages. Sometimes can be detected on the green the walls of the 'pound', where stray animals were imprisoned until the owner paid a fine. There may be signs of the base of a windmill or it may be possible to trace the broken course of a mill-race from higher up the stream to the point where it came into contact with the mill wheel. From the deserted village it is possible to get a fossilized plan, though there was not a sudden catastrophe. Sometimes the owner of the land cleared the old village site and had a new estate village constructed in another area more convenient for himself and not obtruding on his view. The mounds of derelict houses can be traced under the turf and trees of a place like Bolam. The trees are obviously subsequent to the cultivation pattern of the fields and the small square enclosures that were once tofts and crofts.

It is not unknown for a church to stand isolated in the trees, away from any habitation except a local farm or hall. This is often the sign of a deserted village.

It is fascinating to survey or map out one of these sites and then, from the records, to attempt to discover when and why it was abandoned. Sometimes a boundary stone will also be its gravestone—the stone bearing the initials of those who enclosed the land and the date of the enclosure.

A very good example of this is the deserted village of West Whelpington, which is being systematically excavated in advance of quarrying. It is approached by turning westwards from the Newcastle Otterburn road at Knowsgate, near the new motel. The site is a rocky escarpment overlooking the Wansbeck and is approached by the quarry entrance. A considerable part has already been quarried, but there remains a number of ruined houses on either side of the old street. Although the situation seems exposed, the village was sheltered by the fact that the land falls eastwards and the houses lay under the wind. The open fields can be seen on each side. The houses of various types that have been excavated range from medieval to the late seventeenth century. The village was deserted by the middle of the eighteenth century as can be shown from documentary and other evidence.

In 1552 West Whelpington and Ray provided four men for the nightly watch. Ray, Hawick and Sweethope in the same neighbourhood are also deserted villages. Hodgson, who was vicar of Kirkwhelpington, wrote in his *History* (1827) that West Whelpington was an example of Goldsmith's 'Deserted Village'. Names of local families of West Whelpington were included in his parish registers till 1715. Hodgson also noticed that as well as the ruins of houses, there was a pele tower with a barmkin. An old man told him that a Mr Stote, for whom he once worked, was responsible for putting out 15 farmers, but not in his life-time. He always knew the site as deserted, but there are a series of boundary stones to the west, which run from Ferneyrigg to the summit of the Wannies. They are marked with the date 1736. There are the initials on one side of the stones M.M. (Mark Milburn) and on the other—W.B. T.J.S. These could be Stote and Blackett. This presents a number of unresolved problems. If this is the likely date, why?

Was there anything to do with the 1715 rebellion? It is known that some of the older families were financially embarrassed and the Blacketts were acquiring considerable property for exploitation. It seems that the enclosure and depopulation of this area was not the result of a desire for agricultural improvement, but for a clearance of surplus population. The old rig and furrow may indicate a reversion to pasture.

Obviously here and elsewhere there is a need to examine estate records in connection with field patterns and boundaries. Enclosures of several dates will be found and the boundary stones of 1736 have been embodied in walls of a later date.

Excavation of West Whelpington—Archaeologia Aeliana 1962. pp. 189-225. Complete up to date report in A.A. 1970.

There is another deserted village site at Welton which has been scheduled by the Ministry of Works as an ancient monument. This is just south of the Roman Wall and very near the Whittledean waterworks (B6309 crosses B6318 [O.S. 78 NZ 063674]. Welton was held in the Middle Ages by a family of that name and then Walter de Middleton by marriage. It was recovered by the Weltons. On the site are signs of the house that preceded the fourteenth-century tower. To these have been added an early seventeenth-century hall which obscures the older structure. This has the initials W.W. (Welton) and the date 1614. In 1694 Michael Welton sold the land to Sir William Blackett.

In 1538 15 men with horse and harness were expected to appear at the musters together with 26 unmounted men. This is a very considerable number and one is tempted to think of this as a collecting centre, since there exist only two farms with cottages. But a casual glance will show that the whole of the area between the two farms, with an axis east-west was once inhabited. It is possible to pick out the line of the street with houses and enclosures. To the south can be seen the ridges and furrows of the open fields. The time of the desertion is not known, but the indications are that in the seventeenth century it was developed as a large unit, rather than a collection of small freeholders or tenants. There is no precise dating for these things, but the decline in the numbers of men needed for defence is an important factor.

Another site mentioned by Hodgson as deserted is the area of the Middletons, lying between the present village of Middleton and Wallington. The road from Scotsgap to Bolam bisects the old village [South Middleton. O.S. NZ 053840], which is immediately south of the Wansbeck. Middleton Hall lies to the east and Scarlet Hall to the west. Humps and hollows in the fields denote the old houses, enclosures and roads. There is very distinct ridge and furrow both to the north and south of the old village. Bolam itself can be recorded as a deserted village. The parkland has covered, but not obliterated the old village and the ridge and furrow of the fields.

There are many others, but once the form and pattern are realized, they are easy to pick out. By far the best way of discovering and studying deserted villages is the use of the air photograph. These can be studied in connection with the O.S. maps and maps of an earlier date.

The Assessments for the 1296 Subsidy have been edited by Dr. C. Fraser and published by the Newcastle Society of Antiquities. These are presented in a readable way and it is possible to discover the number of people in a village who were taxable. Names are also given and so information is obtained on surnames, place names and occupations.

In the sixteenth century the local musters give some idea of the number of able bodied men in an area and in the late seventeenth century hearth tax returns can supply the number of inhabited houses. From 1801 census returns are available, but before this parish registers can be studied for purposes of assessing the population.

F. R. BANKS' *English Villages*, pp. 195-202 (Batsford) considers Bamburgh, Blanchland, Corbridge, Elsdon, Etal, Holy Island, Mitford, Norham, Warkworth and Whalton as deserving special mention.]

Walls and Hedges

These were the means of effecting enclosures. Northumberland has used both of these methods, though in the present century many miles of hedge and wall are not being maintained. They are still available for study and can help to interpret the changing pattern of the landscape.

Walls are in areas where the stone is readly available and the type of walling may depend on local geology. But history has its effect too and both prehistoric cairns and camps have provided material for field walls. Quern stones have been included. The abandoned Roman Wall and camps have provided quarries for farmsteads and field walls. Castles and derelict stone houses have provided their quota and so walls may be of good building stone. Limestone has also been used for field walls. Some of the stone was burnt to provide lime and the better sections were used for building walls. The debris of the slate quarries (the slate was required for roofing) has provided material for field walls with characteristically thin courses. Some of the walls of the deserted villages are from river boulders and stones that impeded ploughing. Having being transferred to the perimeter of a patch of land they could be used for walling. Some of these walls have provided the basis for hedges. Field walls can be examined to discover the type of stone and its fashioning. There may be local variations of structure. The dimensions have to be noticed—the broad base and the pronounced batter, with often heavy capstones. There are courses of alternating larger and smaller stones. Gateways and stiles may be included with small traps to allow the passing of sheep. Walls can be seen to be of two periods on one base or alternatively later walls can take a completely new line. The old boundaries might be kept with different divisions within and there may be walls of three or four different periods in the same area.

Hedges contrast with walls in that they appear changing and not so durable. They tend to be in the lowland areas, but hedges can be found in exposed places in hill country. They have the advantage of providing shelters as well as barriers and should be maintained for this reason. Hawthorn was the most common hedgerow plant, though gorse might be retained as part of a perimeter fence. Other shrubs and trees introduce themselves or may be introduced by birds. The number of different types of bushes within a hedgerow helps to indicate its age. Other factors are of course the strength and size of the stools (butts) of the plants or indications of how often they have been layered or plashed. Hedges that have been allowed to grow wild give evidence of a hoary old age and become the places of prolific animal, bird and insect life.

Some hedges on parish boundaries may go back 1,000 years but others are the result of different periods of enclosure. There was a good deal in the eighteenth century, but also earlier. Between 1489 and 1624 there were numerous Parliamentary Acts against private enclosure and in 1517-8, 1548, 1566 and 1607 there were Inquisitions to see if the provisions of the Acts had been carried out. Very often they were not and this is the evidence of a prevalent but piecemeal practice. Later by contrast Acts of Parliament were obtained to bring about enclosure.

The study of hedgerows can help to elucidate this process, but in addition provides interesting field work for naturalists. There can be the recording of miles of hedging, the types of plants, the period of growth, the attention the hedges have received and their present purpose. [Indications are that miles of hedging increased from the Middle Ages to the mid-nineteenth century and have rapidly declined since 1940 with the increase of mechanization.]

Hedgerows can also be associated with a study of animal and bird life.

Copies of proforma for a hedgerow survey can be obtained from Dr Max Hooper, the Nature Conservancy, Monks Wood Experimental Station, Abbots Ripton, Huntingdon.

Village and Parish

The village can be studied as a living entity—a community that has been subjected to various pressures through the ages. The village varies, but the parish had its boundaries fixed originally for ecclesiastical reasons and it became in time a unit for civil administration. The area of a parish may include several villages and hamlets, together with a number of scattered farmsteads. These very farmsteads may be the remainders of old villages. Village and farmsteads may have to be studied in conjunction with each other, or two villages together in order to achieve a viable (reasonable) unit.

The name of the village will have significance and indicate the date of settlement, probably Anglo-Saxon. Then the boundaries have to be discovered. There are various ways of doing this and folk memory or tradition can be an important factor. In some areas the custom of riding the bounds or beating the bounds is still carried out. There are also traditional landmarks—a standing stone, a syke, an old mound, the margin of a moss or the banks of a stream. In hill country the boundary can be a ridge, since on either side the villagers appropriated the marginal land until the limits were reached. These villages and farms tend to have land called 'in bye' near the dwellings or village and 'out bye', the rougher grazing that stretches to the summit of the hills. Sometimes only the lowland pastures are enclosed. Names of hamlets and farms may give evidence of clearings of forest, marsh or waste.

Sometimes there are boundary stones to delimit villages or estates. There can be found the double bank and ditch, with a sunken road between, marking the margins of two areas. The old terriers or estate maps sometimes describe limits that can be followed on foot in the field. In certain areas a whole series of these divisions needs to be sorted out. Some idea of sequence may be given by one wall or bank superseding another. Hedges may have been planted on the top of turfed dykes. Plantations or clumps of trees give further evidence. Areas of common land have to be checked and now these have to be rapidly registered if they are to be preserved. Through the ages common lands have been continuously encroached upon and intruders (squatters) remained when occupation went unquestioned.

The farm and field boundaries have to be considered within the limits of village or parish.

The situation of the village will depend on a number of natural factors including water supply, shelter, security and the availability of exploitable farm land. Further development depends upon other resources and communications.

The pattern or plan of the village will indicate both elements of natural growth and deliberate location. There is at one extreme the completely haphazard growth of a shapeless village and at the other the entirely planned estate village. Most villages are within these extremes and among many variations, several forms can be determined.

(1) The green village, where the houses are grouped about a triangular or rectangular green space.

(2) The 'round village' where the houses are grouped about a central feature such as the church.

(3) The street village in which the houses are ranged on either side of a broad way.

(4) The shapeless village which merely occupies an area. It can be the result of sudden industrial growth e.g. mining.

There is another general distinction between the 'nucleated' and the 'scattered' types of village.

The size and shape of the village may explain a good deal of its story. For example Longwitton was a colliery area for two centuries. The last mine closed at the time of nationalization and the last line of colliery cottages have now disappeared. The village stretches some two miles with few houses and long gaps. Other villages have been reduced in size and some have been swallowed by expanding towns. The general tendency has been that people of Northumberland, instead of looking north to the hills and routes to be defended, have turned towards the area of Tyneside as a place of great concentration of wealth.

Communications or lack of them had a great effect on the life of the village. This can be seen especially in the matter of building. Until less than a century ago areas depended on local materials for building. Transport was difficult and expensive, so that only special materials were brought to Newcastle as ballast, but strange products had to overcome local prejudice. The principal building material from pre-Roman times to the later nineteenth century was stone, which was quarried in huge quantities for both building and road making. Very often a gash or pit in local rock shows the source of building material. Sometimes the 'quarry' is an earlier building. Local limestone was used for the making of cement. Timber was used for roof structures. These factors make Northumberland houses difficult to date. In other parts of the country brick, timber and cob were used over long periods, exhibiting different styles of building.

The earliest surviving dwellings are the castles and towers. These had their influence on the earliest buildings that were strictly domestic in purpose. A number of towers date to the early seventeenth century. Perhaps the earliest dated domestic building is Bradford Hall adjacent to the site of a deserted village. This, now used as a barn, has a fire-place dated 1567. The old Black Heddon Hall is dated 1611. There are very few genuine early timbered buildings and these are in Newcastle in the Sandhill area. (Bessie Surtees House seventeenth century.) The front or façade is of timber and the rest of the house of brick or stone. Such houses depended on domestic peace and the protection of town walls. Timber structures would not have survived the border raiding period. It is quite possible that the basements and lower parts of stone houses are comparatively early, with the superstructure of a later date. Two periods of building may be detected, though the style and stonework do not differ. However differences can be seen in the addition of wings or an irregular roofline, showing alterations. The roof of a house is the part that is least durable, because of the decay of supporting timbers and the effects of fire. After a fire—the shell of the house would remain and restoration would apply to the roof and the interior. The burning of a thatched house could be confined to roof only, involving the removal of burning straw. Straw, heather and turves could provide cover for peasant houses over a period of several centuries. For great houses, castles and churches, lead and stone slates were used. Pantiles came into fashion at the end of the seventeenth century, but local slate continued in use into the nineteenth century and local tileries were in production for a long period. There are quite a lot of local tilesheds and brickworks.

Some brick was used in the seventeenth century, but much more in the eighteenth century when rich red brick was regarded as very attractive. A number of houses acquire the title of 'Red House' as a result of construction in red brick and tiles as opposed to the local grey stone. The early bricks tended to be comparatively thin i.e. 2 inches, but during the later part of the eighteenth century were increased in thickness on account of a governmental brick tax. It was assessed per 1,000 bricks, so that increasing the thickness of bricks could save considerably in the cost of the construction of a house. There are different styles in brick building as well as in stone that are indicative of the period. Usually there is a little time lag before a particular style reaches the north. It could however be immediate through the efforts of local aristocracy. An example of this is Sir John Vanburgh's construction of Seaton Delaval. The eighteenth century is the period of regular Georgian symmetry and proportion. The same style applies to both town and country houses. There are similarities in both brick and stone.

Windows and doorways can also help with dating. The early windows tend to be small, within a stone surround. Glass was very expensive and the panes tended to be small and diamond-shaped. Their size increased but they still tended to be small well into the eighteenth century. Another development of the late seventeenth century and later was the sash window which takes the place of the casement. The glazing bars of the older windows tended to be thicker. External shutters or bars could provide extra protection against thieves.

The incidence of window tax is another factor that can be used to date houses. It was first imposed in 1697 for the purpose of restoring the currency. The rate of the tax depended on the number of windows (below 7 were exempt) and it was a rough and ready method of imposing a tax upon wealth. But it provoked evasion by extending the size of windows and when the tax was assessed on window lights it was evaded by the blocking of windows. It can be indicated that a house with deliberately blocked windows may date back to the seventeenth century. But there were actual blockings in the eighteenth century especially when Pitt further increased window tax during the Napoleonic Wars (1797). Fielding mentions blocked windows as if it were a common practice. It has to be remembered that quite a number of what appear to be blocked windows are 'blind' or 'dummy' windows, included in the building to keep the symmetry and regular pattern of fenestration. These were painted to look like real windows and if the illusion is properly maintained, it is almost impossible to detect. This can be a feature of houses constructed during the period of window tax, which was not abolished until the year of the Great Exhibition 1851.

The size, number and position of chimneys is another dating feature of houses. The increasing use of coal as a fuel meant the enclosing of the fire place. It also provided the problem of sweeping, for which small boys were generally employed.

Some houses are dated with the initials of those who were responsible for the building. The date, however, may be that of a restoration of a house and not the first buildings (foundation).

Maps, plans and prints may indicate that certain buildings were there at a given time. All kinds of changes can take place. A stone building can be surrounded by a shell of brick. A timber building can loose its framework behind a wall of brick. On the other hand a brick building can receive a bogus exterior of timber and plaster. Some stone or brick buildings can be covered with plaster, stucco or colour wash, so that the original appearance is lost. But all kinds of external features—spout heads, fire marks and old blocked windows can provide evidence of an earlier date. It is possible to find farm houses of three different periods on one site.

Another feature is the increasing number of storeys to a house.

(1) There can be the single storey farm-house or cottage.

(2) The loft can be converted into sleeping quarters reached by a wooden ladder.

(3) A second storey can be added.

(4) Dormer windows can be inserted.

(5) Larger houses can have a third storey added to provide quarters for servants.

(6) Various additions can furnish evidence of dating. Sometimes an old house receives a new frontage and a look at the rear indicates a building of a much older period.

(7) Different sizes of brick within the same building or a mixture of brick and stone may suggest several periods of construction. There may be a mixture of roofing materials.

(8) Evidence of an external chimney or stair.

(9) Different stages in stonework are:

Rubble = undressed stone; Freestone = easily worked.

1. Dry stone walling.
2. Shaped quoin stones and rubble.
3. Coursed rubble.
4. Dressed rubble.
5. Ashlar or specially cut facing stone.

(10) Information may be obtained from records and accounts.

(a) scheme and contract for building.

(b) details of repairs carried out.

(c) Inventories often detail furniture and effects as they were located room by room. From this can be obtained the arrangement of the house at a particular time.

(11) The flooring may be of interest. Older floors were of trampled clay or flagstones. Upper floors could be of plaster above brushwood.

(12) There may be features such as cellars for storage and ovens for baking bread. Kitchens and other offices may be added. Associated with building are the various craftsmen of the area—bricklayers and stone masons; joiners and carpenters.

(13) Other changes are that several small dwellings can be converted into one large house and alternatively a large house can be converted into a number of separate establishments.

(14) A house with a narrow street frontage, may extend longitudinally down the tenement or burgage.

There is a need to survey and record the domestic buildings of Northumberland in both town and country.

Mrs Finberg in her book *Exploring Villages* (1958), inaccurately sums up as follows:

p. 120 ... 1 'centuries had to pass before men could live in peace in the northern counties. No unfortified house would survive a Scotch raid, *and no unfortified houses more than about two hundred years old remain in Northumberland and Cumberland.* The rich man had his castle and the well to do their "pele", a massive two storey building, with the merest slits for windows and heavily fortified doors. The cattle were driven into the ground floor during a raid and the women and children of the small community took refuge above while the men would do what they could to save the undefended houses and barns, the sheep and crops. They were still living this precarious existence in the fifteenth and sixteenth centuries when many of the "peles" now used as barns were built. "Peles" are recognized by their massive walls, the doorways showing the sockets of heavy bars and iron grills: they usually have no chimney. These belonged to the yeoman farmers, the rather more handsome structures built by gentlemen often form part of a modern house. Hardly any better illustration of the blessings of peace could be found than a comparison of these gloomy refuges with the house of a Kentish yeoman of the same period with its high wide hall, light and comfortable chambers at each end and a graceful chimney stack.'

Books

Investigation of Smaller Domestic Buildings. Council for British Archaeology.

ADDY, S. O. *The Evolution of the English House.*

ATKINSON, T. D. *Local Style in English Architecture.* Batsford.

BARFOOT, A. *Homes in Britain.* Batsford.

BARLEY, M. W. *The English Farmhouse and Cottage.* Routledge 1963.
The House and Home. Vista Books 1963.

BRIGGS, M. *The English Farmhouse.*

CLIFTON, TAYLOR, A. *The Pattern of English Building.* Batsford.

GLOAG, J. *The Englishman's Castle.* Eyre and Spottiswoode.

GOTCH, Y. A. *The Growth of the English House.*

HENDERSON, A. *The Family House in England.* Phoenix.

INNOCENT, C. F. *The Development of English Building Construction.*
OLIVER, B. *Farmhouses and Cottages.* Batsford.
TRENT, C. *England in Brick and Stone.* Blond.
VALE, E. *How to look at Old Buildings.* Batsford.
WOOD, M. *The Medieval English House.* Phoenix.
YARWOOD, D. *Architecture of England.* Batsford.

THE BIG HOUSE, HALL, OR MANSION

Very often the village was dominated by the castle or tower. In the long period of border warfare and raiding in Northumberland, the big house had to be fortified. This necessity persisted to the Union of the Crowns in 1603, but before this James VI of Scotland and Elizabeth I of England had long tried to limit border lawlessness. Habitations of the more important people were castles or towers with more modern comforts, including a little more light and ornamentation. Larger windows are admitted at the higher levels. In the sixteenth century a number of 'bastle' houses were built rectangular in plan with

The Blackbird Inn, Ponteland.

a central tower on the south side to take the entrance and stairway with small rooms. Examples of this are at Doddington (now ruinous), Whitton Shields and Stanton (near Netherwitton) and Coupland (near Wooler).

There is very little recognizable sixteenth-century domestic architecture in Northumberland and one exception is Bradford near Belsay, close to the river Blyth and connected with a 'deserted' village. The Hall, with a misleading metal roof is now used as a barn, but careful observation of blocked windows and doorways reveals the sixteenth-century house. But conclusive is the evidence of the great vaulted fire place, inscribed with the initials G.O. and the date '1567'. The property belonged to the Ogle family and pride in the building is so displayed. Still near the river Blyth and to the east of Belsay-Otterburn road, is situated Harnham Hall. The building is on top of a rocky hill, which was completely surrounded by a stone wall. The hall overlooks the northern escarpment and consists of a medieval tower to which an early seventeenth-century house has been added. This is in front of the tower, which is only seen from the north.

Scarcely a mile away on lower land is Shortflatt. The original tower dates back to the early fourteenth century (licence to crenellate 1305). This had other buildings attached but in the late sixteenth century or early seventeenth century had the eastwards extension of a country house with a massive chimney. The house was extended beyond the chimney and finally domestic offices were added to the north at a still later date. The tower which has been opened with doors and windows, is made to fit architecturally with the rest of the building. But the whole is the work of three or four periods.

Alterations were made at Ford Castle in the late sixteenth century and at Chillingham in the early seventeenth century. At Chipchase in 1621 Cuthbert Heron constructed a fine Jacobean mansion to the east of the medieval tower, probably replacing another extension. The Middletons of Belsay added a wing to the north-west of Belsay Castle. The portico, dated 1614, carries the arms of the family and the new building blocked the entrance to the old castle. Here the old tower dominates the later building. Additions to Welton Tower are of the same date (1614). Here William of Welton built himself an L-shaped country house to the south of the medieval tower. This house was also extended at a later period.

At Mitford a tower with entrance portico was built at the south entrance of the second castle. It carries the Mitford arms and is dated 1637. Probably it was added to a manor house already in existence and all the building is not of this date. This site was abandoned for the hall, built some distance to the west, by Dobson

Fair at Elsdon

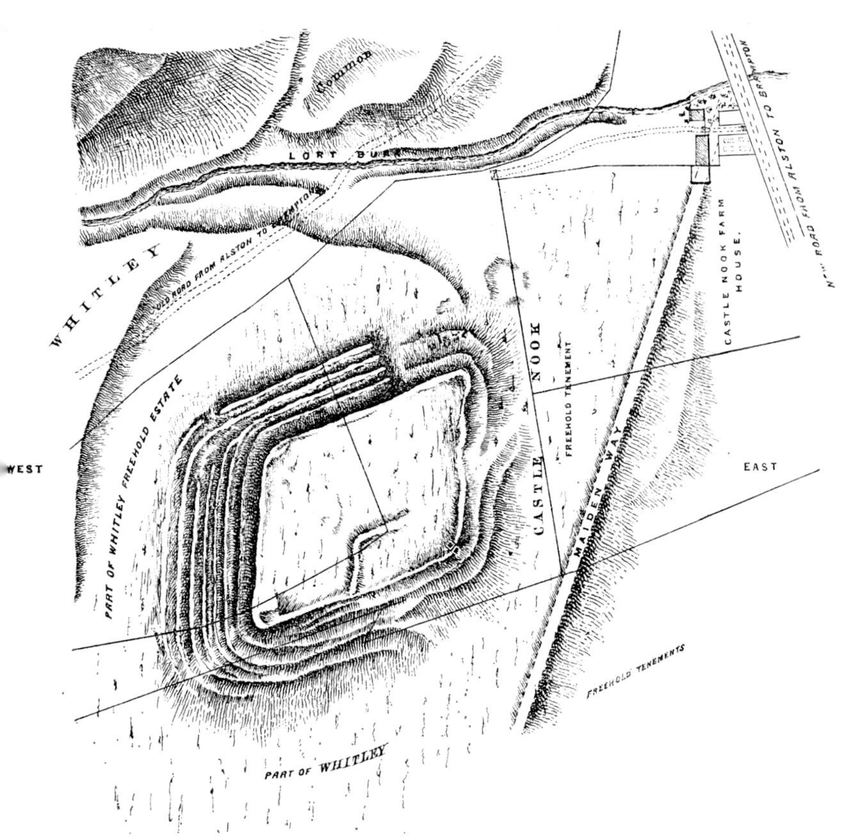

ROMAN STATION at WHITLEY in NORTHUMBERLAND

SIMONBURN CHURCH AND RECTORY, North[d]

Published March 1825, by W. Davison Alnwick.

Opposite page. Aerial view of Bamburgh.

Bridge at Wallington

Bellasis Bridge

in the early nineteenth century. A number of country houses show these stages in evolution—the fortified tower, the additional country mansion of the sixteenth-seventeenth century and further additions in the eighteenth century. Sometimes a ninteenth-century wing or tower was added, enormously increasing the size of the house, but adding to the problems of heating and service. This was no great problem when both coal and servants were cheap.

Sometimes the earlier constructions were obscured or completely obliterated. Sometimes the old hall was abandoned and a new hall was constructed at some considerable distance and the names survive. It can become confusing when New Deanham is a house 300 years old and little altered, while Old Deanham is a house which is less than half this age. At Blackheddon, the old hall, dated 1611, is a farmhouse, while the newer hall of the nineteenth century is on the other side of the road.

There was a good deal of rebuilding in the river valleys in the seventeenth century, particularly after the Restoration (1660). Robert Trollope, a Newcastle architect, who remodelled the Guildhall, becomes a well-known name at this period and did work for patrons in both town and country. He was responsible for designing a hall for the Swinburnes of Capheaton. It could be almost described as an architectural frolic. The transactions are available as to the size and layout of the house, but a mere plan would give no idea of the elaborate ornamentation of the exterior. At a time when the names of Inigo Jones and Sir Christopher Wren stood for architectural propriety, Trollope with an exuberant name went his own way. The style of Capheaton could be described as rustic baroque. It has banded pilasters, ornamental window frames and a south doorway with carved vines twisting round its columns. The door head is also decorated and on either side are rustic garlands in stone. There is a wealth of mixed ornament. In this type of building the former vaulted basement becomes a cellar. There are similarities at Bockenfield (to the north of Morpeth) and Swarland Old Hall (between Felton and Longframlington), once the home of the Northumbrian Haselriggs.

Much more severe in appearance and dating to the end of the seventeenth century is Netherwitton Hall. This was a border tower and evidence of this is still visible on the north side. Cromwell's troops stayed at Netherwitton in 1650 and the home of the Thorntons was redesigned at a later date. The hall has three storeys and the windows have three types of pediment. The building is surmounted by a balustrade at roof level.

Similar to Netherwitton in style is Callaly Castle. Here the former tower is completely submerged in the new west wing. The house added to the east end of the old tower was remodelled by Trollope about 1676. It consisted of five bays with three storeys and the windows have three types of pediment as at Netherwitton. Callaly received additions in the eighteenth and nineteenth centuries, mainly to the north and east. In considering dating factors, mullioned windows tended to persist later in the north and from 1697 Window Tax was imposed. This tended not to affect the larger houses so much, but the taxing of window lights may well have helped to reduce the number of mullioned windows.

In the late seventeenth and eighteenth centuries the vicarage tends to emerge as a country house and a good example is Bywell dated 1698. At Simonburn the old tower of the rector was replaced by a house in 1666 and this in turn was replaced by a five-bayed, three-storeyed Georgian house of 1725. It had a hipped roof and very pronounced quoins with a regular window arrangement. There is an early eighteenth-century house of brick at Higham Dykes, north of Ponteland. Halton Tower, a medieval structure of Roman stone received the addition of a five-bay house to the east. The tower dominates the house to the extent that from the distance it looks like a church. Another such building is West Bitchfield. Here a seventeenth-century house was added to the east of the tower and alterations were made in the early eighteenth century. There is a sundial with date 1712 over the south door, which dates to the latter period. The house is of six bays with extensive additions to the north.

There was a great deal of building in the eighteenth century, but the most spectacular and exciting architectural piece was at Seaton Delaval. Here the remains of a castle with seventeenth-century additions were completely swept away. Admiral George Delaval decided to redeem the family estate and rebuilt the house. He chose as his architect a man who was also a dramatist. Vanburgh was descended from a Dutch family that took refuge in England to escape the Duke of Alva's religious persecution in the sixteenth century and he was well acquainted with continental architecture—he knew Versailles and was responsible for the building of Blenheim Palace for the Duke of Marlborough as well as Castle Howard in Yorkshire for the Earl of Carlisle. Seaton Delaval is considered to be his finest piece of work, though an effort of the imagination is needed to overcome the effects of a century of neglect and the encroachment of smoke laden areas in either direction. It was in its heyday for a period covering a century and a true representation of the spirit of the north in the same way as Bamburgh, Dunstanburgh or Warkworth. This is no longer defensive, but dramatic—the scene for great events in the eighteenth century. It was an expression of culture, but maintained from the profits of the land, of coal, of glass and shipping. The Delaval family provided great entertainment and Seaton Delaval induced other great families to build.

It has the plan of a Palladian Villa, but appears much more robust. There is a central block containing the hall and the main apartments. This faces north and south overlooking the sea in each direction. The southern aspect with a portico of Ionic columns appears more mellow and approaches the gardens. The north entrance is flanked by massive columns and each of the four angles of the main building has a polygonal tower. To the east and west at right angles to the central building are colonnades flanking the stables on one side of the office and kitchen ranges on the other. This provides a courtyard with an open front or more appropriately a stage. It suited the spirit of the owners, even if it were not entirely suitable to the climate. However, avenues of trees in time provided some shelter and the owners did not intend to spend all their time in the north. Vanburgh is regarded as an essentially Baroque style of architect, but this is individual—nothing else is quite like it. Admiral Delaval gave him the opportunity, but neither architect or patron saw the completed work.

Admiral Delaval was responsible for the beginning of another very fine eighteenth-century house at Bavington, now the home of the Shaftoe family. This is more compact and restrained in style. It consists of seven bays and two and a half storeys. The window surrounds show the influence of Gibbs. Newmoor Hall, near Swarland, is built in the same style. But speaking generally the traditional Georgian style was adopted in Northumberland as elsewhere. The main difference was that Northumberland buildings were still mainly of stone and so the rich coloured brickwork with contrasting stone for the quoins is unusual. In fact brickwork is so unusual that the term 'Red House' could be used to distinguish the structure. Seaton Delaval had brick for the internal partition walls, but not externally. At Humshaugh there is a Georgian house of red brick extending to five bays with stone quoins and lintels above the windows. Yet another attractive red brick house is situated south of Warkworth at Morwick.

The eighteenth-century houses are too many to mention in any detail. This was the period of confiscation and development. A number of old families lost their lands and other families—the Delavals, Whites, Ridleys, and Blacketts became more prosperous. Agriculture provided profits for the development of industry and in turn the profits of trade and industry affected agriculture. The big families had town houses and country houses. They were in close contact with

London as a centre of influence in architecture and the arts. They were able to employ Italian plaster craftsmen for the decoration of their interiors: they were able to collect pictures, silver, and other works of art. The Adam family provided designs for all parts of the country. But most important of all was the house in its setting—its association with the landscape. This is so 'natural' that we take it for granted. The countryside, however, in spite of arguments about Art and Nature, is the combined product of natural influences on the works of Man. Our English landscape was made in the eighteenth century—the making or renewal of divisions by hedge, wall or ha-ha; the pattern of the cultivated fields; the growth of parks and plantations; the emergence of lakes and country houses.

It was said of Wren 'If you require a monument, look around.' ('Si Monumentum Requiris, Circumspice.') The same could be the epitaph of Capability Brown, who has no monument at Kirkharle, in the church of the village of his birth. Many landscape effects are the results of his influence, if not directly attributable to him. Lancelot Brown could quickly see the 'capabilities' of an area for development in landscape fashion and only a minimum of modification was necessary. Others could carry his recommendations into effect. The new contours appeared natural and the trees planted singly or in groups never had the effect of regimentation. The garden escaped from formality—the lawns extended harmoniously towards the meadows and parkland. The scattered trees, protected at first, provided animals with shelter and the ha-ha prevented their intrusion on lawns and gardens, without interrupting the vista. Capability Brown was responsible for landscaping at Alnwick and at Rothley. The artificial lake at Rothley was his and he was probably responsible for the modification of Codger's Castle. A plan exists of a central block for an arsenal against the '45. This was never built or has since disappeared. Brown also had a hand in laying out the gardens of Wallington Hall, though there have been modifications since.

The rugged area to the north of Wallington was developed with the walled enclosure or a park, the planting of trees and the planning of rustic gardens. From Rothley Castle, another folly, magnificent views are obtained in all directions. This was the work of the Blacketts. Landscaping often involved the removal of shrunken villages. People were provided with other accommodation in estate villages and might find employment on the estate or in its associated industries. Cambo village was entirely rebuilt to a plan with terraces of accommodation for estate workers. The development of the large estate in the eighteenth century could alter the entire area. Since the materials for building were mainly local, quarries would be developed for building stone and road making material. Local slate might be used for roofing and some local timber. Local brickwork and tileries would also be developed. For building, iron smelting and agriculture large quantities of limestone were needed; this involved kilns for lime-burning and the development of local coal pits to provide burning material, when timber supplies tended to become exhausted. There were settlements in connection with these works and these tended to be temporary.

The emphasis at Wallington Hall is mainly eighteenth century and the very fine building to the north was designed as a chapel. Wallington has the advantage of a particularly fine guide book written by the late Sir Charles Trevelyan. This has the virtue of being both informative and readable—a Trevelyan trait. Blagdon, too, now has an eighteenth-century emphasis and was constructed in plain classical style in two periods. It was much extended in the nineteenth century because of the needs of a growing family. In 1944 it was damaged by fire and reduced to something like the original size. Sir Edwin and Robert Lutyens were responsible for changes both to the house and gardens. The Ridley family have long been concerned with both agriculture and industry in the neighbourhood.

Eslington Hall, the property of the Earls of Ravensworth, is mainly an early eighteenth-century house in classical style. Like Blagdon with an exterior comparatively simple, a great deal of attention was devoted to interior decoration. The setting was of the greatest importance with gardens and terraces. There was a large area of parkland and the vistas were provided not for the passer by, but for the invited visitor who arrived by coach and then was able to survey the entire scene from the great house or garden.

Other notable eighteenth-century houses are Shawdon Hall and Wylam Close House, showing the influence of Adam. At Howick Hall William Newton made use of Ionic columns for the south front.

The contrasting Gothic Revival is shown partly in landscape effects and follies. The Delavals altered the southern aspect of Ford completely by adding artificial towers, a rusticated entrance with mock portcullis and loopholes. Alterations were made at Craster, but the greatest enthusiast was the Duke of Northumberland. Not only was Alnwick 'landscaped' but the interior of the castle was completely altered by Robert Adam. This was again altered a century later, but within the extensive estates all kinds of embellishments were added. There was the observatory perched on Ratcleugh cliff, Brizlee Tower was erected in the park and the Lion Bridge below the castle. Alnwick Abbey ruins and Hulne Priory were made into pleasances (pleasure places). Kielder Castle was built in the more remote parts as a

Hunting Lodge and the Pottergate Tower was erected in Alnwick itself.

Most extravagant of all was the Folly of Sir Francis Blake at Twizell. This was not intentionally a folly. It was to be a magnificent residence in a spectacular position overlooking the Till and its beautiful arched bridge. Twizell Castle though carried to a height of five storeys was never completed and the rich well fashioned masonry is now hidden among the trees. There is evidence of four round corner towers and to the north in the fields are indications of garden enclosures. The work went on during the period of the Napoleonic wars, but agricultural prosperity was not able to save Sir Francis from bankruptcy.

Other country houses affected by the Gothic Revival are not very far from Ford—namely Barmoor Castle and Fowberry Tower.

There was a contrasting development of classical style architecture. The emphasis in the eighteenth century had been Roman and Italian, but in the early nineteenth century there was a great enthusiasm for Greece. This was shared by writers, poets, politicians, architects and their patrons.

Sir William Middleton of Belsay married a wealthy heiress, Miss Monck, and their son took her family name. He was able to go on a combined honeymoon and Grand Tour lasting several years. Though the Peace of Amiens between Napoleon and Britain (1802) did not last, Sir Charles was not deterred and spent a great deal of his time in Greece, then under Turkish rule, and Sicily. Everywhere he went, he noted, sketched and collected all things Greek (1804-6). Afterwards at Belsay he built a new hall. 'The new mansion house stands on a dry knoll to the south-east of the old castle and partly occupies the site of the late chapel of Belsay. It is a square of about 104 feet. The external architecture is of the Doric style. Two tiers of lights appear on the east, south and west fronts, around which a Doric entablature of great beauty is continued. The entrance front is on the east and has two fluted columns of 4 feet 11 inches in diameter and 29 feet in height. The entrance hall is 29 feet long by 21 broad and wholly of polished stone; and opens into the staircase hall, which is also of polished stone and is surrounded within by a gallery six feet broad and supported by 12 Ionic columns and four double pilasters, one at each corner. A similar arrangement of columns and pilasters also supports the dome which lights the staircase. The dining and drawing-rooms are each 31 feet long by 23 broad; and the library, which has been placed between them is 45 feet 9 inches long by 31 feet broad. The cellars are partly underground on three sides and cut out of rock, arched over with stone; and the attic chambers are lighted in the upper part of the walls of the staircase, excepting on the north, where the windows of all the four floors of the house are seen. The kitchens, stables and other offices, are to the north; and they and the whole of this beautiful and unique structure are not more remarkable for the simplicity and elegance of their parts than the fineness and solidity of their masonry, which is calculated to continue them to remote generations as a splendid monument of the architectural skill of their designer and proprietor.' [Hodgson pp. 365-6 Part II Vol. I.] The building is also a monument to the skilled craftsmen who completed the work. The stone has a mellow beauty and the whole area was landscaped. The quarry for building stone was converted into an ornamental rock garden with many shrubs and imported plants, Belsay itself was rebuilt as a planned village. At Bolam, Mr Horsley was converting the bog into an ornamental lake and planting trees in the neighbourhood. 150 years later the influence of the 'big house' is evident. Belsay Hall is now empty, but should be preserved as one of the great architectural pieces of the county.

Cresswell Hall, the work of the architect John Shaw and built for the Baker Cresswells in the Grecian style, has been demolished and only the stables remain. This mansion aroused Hodgson's enthusiasm and he regarded it as the best building of that period—its date 1821-5. Like a number of other fine buildings of the period the basis of the wealth that provided them was coal. In the same area of Cresswell good roads were constructed and some very fine farm buildings were set up in good quality stone.

William Stokoe, who was responsible for the Moot Hall, Newcastle, in 1810 was also the architect for Hartford House on the Blyth, built for Mr Burdon. Hodgson, again, was enthusiastic about it and remarked on the beauty of the building in its setting. John Dobson, the architect partly responsible for the rebuilding of Newcastle in the early nineteenth century was much in demand as an architect of country houses. His patrons had property in town and country, combining the wealth of farming and of industry.

There is a tendency to find John Dobson, like Capability Brown, everywhere. In places where he did not built entirely anew, he was responsible for modifications. Among his many works are three on the Wansbeck—Mitford Hall (1823), Longhirst Hall (1828) and Meldon Park (1832). These are built in the Greek classical style with strong similarity, but with differences in detail. Dobson had a great liking for the Greek portico. At Mitford the columns are Doric, at Meldon, Ionic, and at Longhirst, Corinthian. The new mansion was accompanied by modifications to the landscape and the planting of trees that have now achieved their full glory. Dobson was also responsible for rebuilding Nunnykirk Hall in classical style (1825).

He was versatile and was prepared to provide for other tastes. In the Victorian period there was a tendency to the grandiose and the Gothic. Beaufront Castle by Dobson might be described as the 'Belvoir' of the north. Its proud towers overlook the Tyne to the north-west of Corbridge. Dobson was also responsible for the building of Lilburn Tower in Tudor style for the Collingwoods. Matfen Hall (1828-32) built by Rickman for Sir Edward Blackett is a mixture of both Gothic and Tudor styles.

The impression given is one of enormous size and complexity. It required a whole army of servants. Here again the changes involved the entire area over a period of time—landscaping and the development of a new estate village immediately north of the hall. The first church here was built in early English style with a magnificent spire. The other side of the story is the development of local works—brickyards, quarries and kilns. The big house had determined the development of the area.

It was a centre of power as well as wealth. The squire or lord was responsible for local government, together with the parson and a few other prominent figures. They were responsible for the keeping of public order and preserving property: they promoted the development of turnpikes and schools. They were also concerned about the welfare of the villagers, including the maintenance of the place of worship or the development of a library. All these things can be seen in the Matfen or Mitford estate papers. The repression and depression of the lower orders was not an entirely accurate picture. There was concern about their welfare. Many persons were resident within the big house or were provided with adjacent but separate accommodation. There was a strict hierarchy among both the male and female employees. The stables, offices, laundry, pantries, wine cellars and stores give some idea of their occupations and tasks. Very often their apartments were near their particular work, or in the big house on the top floor. There was a system of wires and bells for communication.

During the nineteenth century there was an increase in the size of big houses and when a new house was not built extensive wings were added. The additions might include the addition of a chapel and a large tower for observation and display. It was considered good for servants to have to carry things over long distances and to have plenty of tasks to occupy their time. There was no need to be overcrowded and numerous guests had to be accommodated as well as large families.

The big house provides all kinds of avenues for investigation.

(1) What did various members of the family do? One continued to help manage the estate, another might become a naval or military officer; the law might attract one, medicine another. Yet another might take up scholarly pursuits or enter the church. Politics for a time might prove attractive. The daughters of the family were expected to marry well. Each family had its rakes and those given to racing and gambling. The family had to have some members with financial acumen to survive.

(2) What about members of the household? Domestic service was a form of apprenticeship and there were various grades. A village girl could emerge as a polite, well mannered, well spoken young woman, well trained in domestic matters and not confined to ever-lasting service in the same household, but probably obtaining her own. The boys might be trained in various skills in and out of the household. It was not unusual for some to enlist in the army for a spell and on their return (if fortunate enough to do so) take up occupations of gamekeepers, horsemen and estate workers.

(3) It is of interest to study the accepted dress of a period and the attire that was considered suitable for a particular occupation or appropriate to social status. It was possible to assess a person from his bearing or what he was wearing. This is practically impossible in our time, nor does speech always provide a criterion. One has to imagine the kind of persons that lived in particular apartments at a particular period. Rooms can be decorated and furnished with period pieces. This is as necessary to the understanding of history as to the performance of plays. What kind of pictures would hang on the walls? Things Victorian are a valuable part of the antique business nowadays.

(4) Another problem to consider is whether there is any correlation between dress and the heating system of a house. Fires, fire places, baths and the heating of water provide fascinating problems. There are also things unmentionable in polite society that could be investigated.

(5) Kitchens, ovens, cellars, larders and pantries can be explored with the help of Mrs Beeton's book on *Household Management*.

(6) Lighting is another important factor. In the middle of the twentieth century we are used to effective and even penetrating light. Perhaps this makes us less superstitious. Our predecessors lived by the guttering light of a candle in hours of darkness. Candles were often home made and account for a whole number of expressions that have entered into the English language. One candle made a little pool of light and several were needed to light a small room—

hundreds for a large hall. Both paraffin and gas lights provided an element of fitfulness. How were they to be lit? Arnold Bennett takes 500 words to say 'Rachel lit the gas' and it illustrates the length of the process. Now with an imperious pull at a switch a small child can say 'Let there be light' and it exposes the area. There are no dark corners of a room.

(7) Water now is 'laid on' except in very remote parts of the country. In former times water had to be pumped and carried. The well, pump or pant might be some distance away and this had the effect of limiting supply. Water could be more than 'once' used. Baths were rationed by difficulties of water supply.

(8) From this follows the problem of drainage, a matter that was often neglected. Even the great houses were deficient in this respect. Sanitation was one of the greatest problems of the nineteenth century.

The tendency has been for houses of very great or very small size to disappear. Most of the one or two roomed cottages have gone and many of the big houses have been demolished or are doomed to decay. This is the result of social developments and an army of persons that found employment in the private sector are now public employees. It becomes difficult to run the big house unless it has been turned into a public institution. A number of big houses have become offices for the National Coal Board, others may have become hospitals or convalescent homes. Some have become Adult Education centres and others have become parts of a University. More of them should be used for public purposes rather than permitting decay. Northumberland still needs a Museum and could do with a residential centre for Adult Education purposes only. Such places are important to the study of the environment and in times of change they are necessary reminders of the past—not to be admired or condemned, but available for consideration.

'Three score years was this temple in building', is a general reminder that it is much easier to destroy than to construct. There has been a good deal of mindless destruction.

Books

COUNTRY HOUSES

DUTTON, R. *The English Country House*. Batsford.
English Interiors. Batsford.

HUSSEY, C. *English Country Houses open to the public*. Country Life.

GRAHAM, F. *Northumberland and Durham 100 years ago.*
There is an annual publication of Castles and Country Houses open to the Public. [Index Publications.] This includes National Trust, Department of the Environment and private residences. It gives details of opening times which may vary from year to year.
WILKES, L. *Tyneside Portraits. 1972.*
SACHAVERELL SITWELL. *British Architects and Craftsmen* [includes Vanburgh]. Batsford.
Guide to Alnwick Castle.
Guide to Seaton Delaval Hall.
Guide to Holy Island Castle.
Sir Charles Trevelyan's Guide to Wallington.
SHARP, THOMAS. *Northumberland and Durham.* Shell Guide.
PEVSNER, N. *Buildings of Northumberland.* Penguin.
Country Life Book of English Country Houses (contains Belsay).
WOOD, M. *The Medieval House.* Phoenix.
Reference to *Northumberland Country History* (15 Vols.); works of Hutchinson, Mackenzie and Hodgson.

GARDENS

DUTTON, R. *The English Garden.* Batsford.
HADFIELD, M. *The Art of the Garden.* Dutton Vista.
HYAMS, E. *The English Garden.* Thomas & Hudson.

LANDSCAPE

FLEURE, H. J. *Natural History of Man in Britain.* Collins.
HOSKINS, W. G. *Making of the English Landscape.* Hodder & Stoughton.
MANLEY, G. *Climate and the British Scene.* Collins.
STROUD, D. *Capability Brown.* Country Life.
STAMP, DUDLEY. *Britains Structure and Scenery.* Collins.
Man and the Land. Collins.
STAMP, DUDLEY with HOSKINS, W. G. *Common Lands in England and Wales.* Collins.

PLACES OPEN TO THE PUBLIC

(1) Castles & Countryhouses
Alnwick Castle (Duke of Northumberland)
Bamburgh (Lord Armstrong)
Brinkburn (Department of the Environment)
Callaly (Major Browne)
Cragside (Lord Armstrong)
Dunstanburgh (Department of the Environment)
Harnham Hall (Mr Wake—by permission)
Howick (Lord Howick)
Holy Island (National Trust)

Langley (Mr Bates—by permission) (Medieval Banquets)
Norham (Department of the Environment)
Seaton Delaval. (Lord Hastings) (Medieval Banquets)
Wallington (National Trust)
Walton (Manor House) (Mr Norton)
Warkworth (Department of the Environment)

(2) Gardens open to the Public under Gardens Scheme

Blagdon (Viscount Ridley)
Carrycoats (Lt. Col. Burn)
Coupland (Mrs Aitchison)
Chesters (Major and Mrs Benson)
Dissington Garden House (Judge Wilkes)
Eglingham Hall (Mrs Bewicke)
Etal (Lord Joicey)
Falloden (Lt. Col. Bridgeman)
Guyzance (Lady Milburn)
Hallington (Mr Fairbairn)
Lilburn (Sir E. Collingwood)
Low Angerton (Commander Lestock Reid)
Meldon Park (Col. Cookson)
Newborough Lodge (Mrs Newall)
Newton Hall, on the Moor (Capt. Widdrington)
Preston Tower (Major Baker Cresswell)
Slaley Hall (Mrs Priestman)

CHURCHES

The churches of Northumberland reflect the tormented history of the county with its emphasis on warfare in the medieval period. In an area that was comparatively poor, available wealth and constructive effort were used for the building of castles and towers. The great barons had lands in other parts of the country and ecclesiastical wealth was concentrated on Durham. The monastic institutions depended on local endowment and did not channel wealth from elsewhere into 'depressed' areas. It has been stated 'except for Hexham and Tynemouth, a history of English medieval church architecture might well be written without a single Northumbrian example'. Here Pevsner is obviously misusing the word 'Northumbrian' for Northumberland. The former would include the wealth of both Durham and York; their churches would have to be included.

However, this does not mean that Northumberland churches must be neglected in the study of local history. The nature of the evidence provided should be far more stimulating, because it involves research in the strictest sense. Very often the visitor has no guide book or guide and so is compelled to observe and ponder. A whole series of problems will be presented in stark reality—often the cover of decent

Victorian plasterwork is lacking and the old tower was too much for the hand of demolition. There was always a need to use existing stonework, perhaps in an entirely different context. At Chollerton the pillars of the nave of the church were taken from Roman Chesters and a Roman altar stone was converted into a font. A font may have been made from a stone of a column, surmounted by a capital that has been scooped out to provide a basin. Grave-stones are built into walls and odd bits of masonry here and there provide surprises. It is sometimes forgotten in enumerating the churches of Northumberland that chapels existed within the walls of castles also.

A number of Saxon church towers still exist, tall and thin walled. The high walled naves have often disappeared, but sometimes the single stone window heads have been embedded in the masonry. It is not till the twelfth century that Norman churches are apparent and these are comparatively unambitious. The exceptions are Holy Island and Norham, both connected with Durham: Hexham, connected with York, and Tynemouth, first connected with Durham and then St Albans. These connections meant that the architecture of these places was influenced by the parent organizations. Both Durham and Tynemouth were Benedictine. The monastery of Holy Island was being constructed at the same time as Durham Cathedral and this is obvious in the architecture. Holy Island like Durham had rib-vaulting—one has to imagine what the rainbow arch carried—and also the circular columns of the nave were incised in the same fashion. The original church of Holy Island Priory had an apsidal east end, and it is interesting to compare it with the parish church, which is outside the monastic precint. The apsidal end of the priory church was eliminated by the extension of the chancel, which was given a straight east end. Tynemouth also had an apsidal east end, with an ambulatory and three chapels radiating from it.

The best parish church of the Norman period is Norham-on-Tweed. It is a comparatively large church and the nave contains an array of substantial circular piers with richly moulded arches. The chancel arch is very impressive. The south side of the chancel has five round headed windows with colonettes and decoration. They are set high up in the walls. The pilasters which provide a framework are non-functional, the walls being sufficiently strong. Mitford church also has a Norman nave. There were a number of chapels that have disappeared or have been reduced to ruins. The best known are St Cross, Wallsend: St Mary's, Jesmond; West Lilburn and Tuggal.

A good example of a Norman church is at Throckrington, now in a lonely and exposed situation. Here lies buried Lord Beveridge, the father of the modern Welfare State. A village that is almost deserted, it was once a substantial settlement. The church stands on rock and to realize its Norman appearance the south porch has to go. The bell cote is probably seventeenth century, but replacing one of the same kind. The church is heavily buttressed. One or two Norman windows remain and the simple chancel arch. The chancel is small and tunnel vaulted, probably with an apse at the east end originally. Old Bewick has similarities. It is here possible to distinguish the old stone work of nave and chancel externally. The church has an apsidal east end to take the altar and it must have caused difficulties for local builders. In the fourteenth century it was made square at the higher level. Within the church, the Norman chancel arch leads the eye to apsidal arch and gives an impression of greater length than the exterior. The church is some distance from the small present-day village.

Other churches with strong Norman emphasis are Warkworth, a large church, and Seaton Delaval chapel. Seaton Delaval is almost completely Norman—the porch is modern and within this is the original doorway. Possibly the chancel extension is fourteenth century replacing a Norman apse. The chancel and apsidal arches have characteristic zig zag pattern. The small Norman windows to the north are blocked. Warkworth has a vaulted chancel and so does Heddon on the Wall.

Other churches with elements of Norman architecture are Longframlington and Loughoughton (chancel arches). The interiors of both Bolam and Edlingham give an impression of being predominantly Norman. The nave and chancel of Ancroft are Norman with a good deal of restoration. The tower is fourteenth century and that of Edlingham too was added at a later date. The tower of Ponteland church and the west door are Norman. Some of the stonework seems to have come from the Roman Wall. Newburn also has a Norman tower. Norman architecture persists into the late twelfth century, though over a century there were considerable developments and differences. Brinkburn Priory in particular illustrates a period of transition. Building was begun in 1135 in a loop of the Coquet and like Hexham it was a priory for Augustinian canons. There are similarities in building, but Brinkburn is very much of a period—late twelfth century and this style was kept in the restoration of 1858. The old stonework is readily recognized and the amount of restoration (mainly the roof and upper levels) can be seen by comparing the present building with old prints. It combines an appearance of Norman solidity with a lightness obtained by the inclusion of lancet windows. There are still rounded Norman windows on the north side. The low chancel arch is not there and there is an impression of great spaciousness in the interior. There are both pointed structural arches and decorated round ones. There is a good deal of blank arcading. The north aisle retains springers for vaults and the north doorway is a curious combination of styles. It is one of the most interesting pieces of architecture in the county and can easily be overlooked, especially since there are two more entrances, one on the south side and the other into the south transept. The north doorway is very elaborately carved in four orders, showing different types of ornament. Above is a plain arcade of three trefoil-pointed arches.

Both Hexham and Tynemouth have great lancet windows, which became more common in the thirteenth century when there was much rebuilding. Mitford is another example and Ovingham with its Saxon tower emerges as a large church with aisled transepts and long lancet windows. Other churches increased in size by the addition of aisles as at Ford. The tower was not a common feature and Ford had a bell cote. At Stamfordham, the tower lost its prominence with the increasing size of the church. Bamburgh church too is mainly a development of the thirteenth century. Both churches at Bywell received alterations at this period—perhaps the best for church development. It was comparatively prosperous and the Border strife was not yet stirred. Other churches giving the impression of this period are Corbridge, Simonburn and Haltwhistle. Yet tunnel vaulting with thick transverse ribs was still used in churches as well as for bridges and the basements of towers. Two churches in particular show development in length—namely Kirkwhelpington and Newbiggin. Kirkwhelpington has a low buttressed tower and a long aisless nave and chancel. Newbiggin church is in a most impressive situation, overlooking the sea and obviously a well known landmark to sailors. It was an early thirteenth-century church with aisles and chancel. The tower, comparatively tall and slender was added in the same century. The spire was added in the fourteenth century. This and Warkworth are the only medieval spires in the county. The church contains both lancet and later traceried windows. Its length and size indicate the importance of the port of Newbiggin in the thirteenth century. There are some very fine grave covers and the eastern window of the chancel has five lancets without tracery.

In the county, bell cotes were more characteristic than towers. These express the Spartan nature of the countryside. There are examples at Ford, Bothal, Felton, Thockrington and Holy Island. The bells might serve as a warning as well as the summons to a service.

The fourteenth century was not entirely devoid of church building or improvements, especially in the towns. Felton church was extended and Morpeth St Mary's mostly rebuilt with a fine Jesse window to the east and sedilia which have a certain amount of decorative carving. There are indications on the pillars of the nave of mural painting. At St Nicholas, Newcastle the emphasis is mainly fourteenth century in the interior. The tower and steeple are of the following century. These are the result of substantial wealth from trade and the protection afforded by the castle and town walls. Widdrington church, associated with a famous border family and near by castle, was extensively altered in the fourteenth century. Elsdon church, too, is mainly fourteenth century. It was the chief church of a very large parish and border warfare does not seem to have completely stopped development. Some 1,000 corpses were buried to the north of the church after the battle of Otterburn 1388. Some thirteenth-century windows were retained in the fourteenth-century rebuilding. It has aisles that are comparatively narrow and so there is greater space for the nave. There are a whole number of problems about this church that remain unsettled and it is not certain that the half vaulting over the aisles was medieval. The church contains an interesting collection of monuments, including an incised slab with a shadowy figure and another with crude lettering cramped in the top of the slab with a vacant space beneath. There are horse skulls which once provided resonance for the bells. Two very fine stone coffins stand outside beneath the bell cote and a fine collection of tomb-stones have been gathered into the churchyard.

The last stage of medieval architecture is usually termed perpendicular with emphasis on height and vertical lines. In Northumberland apart from Newcastle, there is a strong Percy emphasis in this period. At Tynemouth a small but attractive Chantry Chapel was added to the east end of the priory church. At Warkworth in addition to two chapels within the castle a Collegiate church was started. The south front of the Warkworth parish church indicates what the style might have been—it contrasts with the Norman work of the north wall. At Alnwick Abbey and Hulne Priory the best preserved work dates to the fifteenth century, but most important of all is the church of St Michael, Alnwick. It stands in a prominent position to the west of the castle overlooking the Aln. The abbey and priory are both to the north of the river, the church and castle immediately to the south of it. St Michael's presents itself as a large completely perpendicular church. The tower, to the south-west angle of the church is strongly built and has stepped buttresses. It looks as if it could have supported a spire. There are aisles on both sides of the church, including nave and chancel. The chancel arch has been retained. The large windows have three lights with panel tracery and the bays are separated by stepped buttresses with pinnacles. Inside there is a maxi-

Chesters.

[illegible] Castle by E. Swinburne

A keelman on the Quayside at Newcastle.
Reconstruction, see "Geordie Pride" for picture in colour.

Drawn by A. Carse

Engraved by R. Scott

mum of space and light: the church is well furnished. Particularly attractive are the richly carved capitals of the columns of the chancel aisles or chapels. At the south-east angle of the church, a stair leads to the remains of a turret on the roof. It has been suggested that this may have been a guardroom or a small room for the priest.

The religious changes of the sixteenth century and in particular the dissolution of the monasteries in the reign of Henry VIII, have deprived the area of a good deal of its best architecture and sculpture. Only the gatehouse at Alnwick remains, at Brinkburn there is little but the church and one is left to wonder about Newminster. This being a daughter of Fountains, what was it like? The existing ruins are completely misleading and a good deal of them were re-erected for landscape purposes in the eighteenth and nineteenth centuries. But a series of excavations have revealed the size and the plan of the abbey church with its adjacent buildings. The church is situated to the north of the site, but to the south of the Wansbeck which afforded some protection from attack. The valley situation provided shelter, but reduced the length of daylight. The church in size was similar to Hexham and Tynemouth. Roughly it measures 260 feet in length and 70 feet in width for the nave which was comparatively long. The transepts had three chapels each and there was a tower at the crossing. A Galilee chapel was added at the west end. The cloister was 120 feet square with the usual range of buildings about it. It was not possible to investigate these fully because the excavation was confined within the present wire fence. There would be a range of offices, accommodation for guests and an array of farm buildings. Water was brought to the site from further up the Wansbeck by means of an aqueduct. The large culverts beneath the abbey are the supposed 'secret' tunnels.

Newminster was endowed with extensive lands and a number of distant 'granges' were attached to it. A Cistercian house would go in for sheep farming on a large scale.

Hulne Priory, in Alnwick Park, was established in the middle of the thirteenth century for Carmelite Friars. It is situated in a secluded spot overlooking the River Aln and retains a complete walled enclosure. This and the fifteenth-century square tower are indications of the great insecurity of the border lands. The priory is two miles to the north of Alnwick town. Besides the priory tower and external walls, there are very substantial remains. The church is 120 feet long with nave and chancel separated by a cross wall. There are remains of the Chapter House on the east side of the cloister. The buildings, at the dissolution of the monasteries, remained in the hands of the Percies and in the eighteenth century the area was developed into an attractive retreat within the park. There are the carved figures of friars standing at the eastern entrance and, though relating to the Gothic Revival of the eighteenth century, they indicate the medieval atmosphere of the place.

The sixteenth century is illustrated by the destruction of monasteries, friaries, chantries, and hospitals. There was also destruction of ornaments, images and monuments within churches. Wall paintings could be covered and stained glass destroyed. In the period of the Civil War and Commonwealth, this continued, but between 1648 and 1652 Colonel George Fenwick had the church of Holy Trinity built at Berwick. Very few churches were built at this period and another exists at Staunton Harold in Leicestershire. Existing churches often suffered further desecration, since Puritans and Presbyterians believed that the House of God should be as simple as an ordinary dwelling and there was no need for ceremony.

After the Restoration of the Monarchy (1660), the Church of England became triumphant and Nonconformists suffered persecution. For a generation their meetings were forbidden and the only legal places of assembly were Church of England. Nonconformists met in private places, but early Nonconformist churches emerge at the end of the seventeenth century, as at Great Bavington. The old Presbyterian Chapel in Cottingwood Lane, Morpeth dates to 1732 and the Friends Meeting House at Coanwood to 1760. Catholic meetings were for long enough held in private houses with the priests in secret service. Harnham Hall, near Belsay and Stanton Hall, west of Morpeth were Nonconformist meeting and burial places. Kate Babington of Harnham was not allowed in consecrated ground at Bolam and was buried in a rock-tomb cut in the hillside in the grounds of the house.

A new Anglican church was built at North Shields early in the reign of Charles II and extensive repairs were carried out at Bellingham, Elsdon and Eglingham. Generally the main changes were internal refittings with the restoration of the font. A number of new fonts date from this period—old ones were often lost or destroyed. A big font from old All Saints church, Newcastle is now at Kirkharle.

In the eighteenth century there were no striking developments. Catholic families were involved in the Jacobite Rebellions and the strength of Nonconformity meant that new wealth did not lead to church building. The Church of England could not contain the Methodist movement and the journeys of John Wesley from about 1740, led to the establishment of Methodist chapels in towns and in mining areas. The chapel becomes a regular feature of the colliery village and at Kirkheaton, where mines existed in the late eighteenth century, there is a chapel as well as an Anglican church. Other religions play a more important part in English life and the combinations of squire and parson found that domination was not so easy to maintain.

The Non-Anglican sects were sometimes weakened by their own divisions. Sometimes there are two Baptist or Methodist chapels in an area. There may be Congregationalists and Quakers also, besides Catholics. In the nineteenth century Catholics were at last able to build their own churches and to establish their own schools. All these add to the interest and complexity of an area. The type of building will indicate the status of the church, with the Anglican church occupying a central and dominant position. The Nonconformist congregations kept their own records and ran their own schools. Ministers were chosen by the community and eked out a living by keeping shops or perhaps schools. Although debarred from public office, they could exercise considerable influence and some were involved in the early Trade Unions.

In the nineteenth century faced with the growing menace of Nonconformity and Revolution, the authorities in Church and State were forced to fight back. The Government made grants to the cost of rebuilding churches. Some of the churches of Northumberland were in a very bad state of repair. Examples of these rebuilt churches are at Earsdon (near Whitley Bay) and Horton (near Blyth). A number of churches were built on the estates of Greenwick Naval Hospital (forfeited Derwentwater estates) at Greystead, Thorneyburn, Humshaugh and Wark on Tyne.

Newcastle All Saints and Gosforth parish church date their rebuilding to the end of the nineteenth century. The church of St Thomas, Newcastle was designed by John Dobson (1825-1830). In the Victorian period there was a great deal of building and rebuilding. There is no single characteristic style and Victorian churches in Northumberland can be in Norman style (as St James's, Morpeth) or Gothic (as at Cambo) or Italian (as at Milbourne). Towers and spires as at Matfen and Mitford are more characteristic of Midland England. St George's, Cullercoats is one of the few that achieve distinction. But churches are eloquent of the period and Nonconformist churches appear much more substantially, if not artistically.

A mixture of styles may be attempted in the same church and experiments with new materials. A great deal of coloured glass was placed in the windows and some of it is good. Interiors were renovated and old pews were removed. Refurnishings were often not in the best of taste, having over elaborate ornamentation.

In 1837 by Act of Parliament tithes were commuted to a money rent. The information collected for tithe awards and the plans that were compiled for the occasion, provide an interesting picture of the land allocation and the housing of the village.

The Church continued to play an important part, exercising a powerful influence in education and providing schools. It also provided a form of local government, the Vestry being the forerunner of the Parish Council. The Electoral Register is still kept in the Parish church and it is a ready way of obtaining information about population.

Books

BETJEMAN, JOHN. *Collins guide to English Churches*. Some 30 listed in Northumberland.
Churches. Studio Vista.
NEEDHAM, A. *How to Study an old church*. Batsford.
THOMPSON HAMILTON, A. *Historical Growth of the English Parish Church*. Cambridge U.P.
COX, J. C. and FORD, C. B. *Parish Churches*. Batsford.
COOK, G. H. *The English Medieval Parish Church*. Phoenix House.
Medieval Chantries and Chantry Chapels. Phoenix House.
ANDERSON, M. D. *Imagery of British Churches*. Murray.
Looking for History in British Churches. Murray.
Observer's Book of Churches (Warne).
Churches and Cathedrals. Ladybird Book.
PEVSNER, N. *Buildings of Northumberland*. Penguin.
DAVIS, C. D. *The Great Parish of Simonburn*. 1972.
DONNELLY, F. *Hartburn Church*.

The church in Local History

The church is of primary importance in the study of Local History.

1. It is often the oldest building in the village and has been in continuous use for centuries. Even if recently restored, it may retain some features of an older building. Its dedication may be of some interest.

2. It can be used to illustrate the history of architecture. Old windows may be re-used in different places in the same church. Good carved stone was not thrown away and stones from an older church might be used to mark graves. Grave-stone covers may have been built into the church walls.

3. All kinds of features can be investigated. There is much more stone carving in churches than supposed and there are small quan-

tities of medieval glass to be examined. Nineteenth-century glass is now found to be more attractive than formerly.

4. There are sundials and the old scratch dials for telling the time of day when no clocks existed. Time could be the unknown quantity, especially on a wet or cloudy day.

5. The font indicates that the church was responsible for baptism, a ceremonial beginning of Christian life. The church also recorded marriages and death. From 1538 compulsory records by the church were necessary and for 300 years this was the only method of public registration.

6. The church therefore is a local repository or records and parish records are valuable sources of information.

7. The church kept its own financial accounts and sometimes records of the misbehaviour of individuals followed by public penance.

8. Tomb-stones are social records and can give names, ages, and particulars of residence. Sometimes occupations are indicated. On the incised slabs the sword is the symbol of a warrior. The scissors or shears are said to symbolize women, but it may be occupational —the sign of a tailor. The horn is the symbol for the huntsman. It has to be remembered that in the eighteenth century the skull and crossbones was a symbol of time or death. It had nothing to do with piracy, nor were crossed legged knights Crusaders.

9. At a time when graveyards were plundered for newly interred bodies for dissection, guardhouses had to be established, as at Morpeth, and Doddington to protect the dead from the living.

10. There are reminders of old entertainment. At Mitford are still holes in the stonework of the church that were said to take medieval staging for plays. The Easter scene and other Biblical episodes could be re-enacted. Sometimes there is a place for the Easter sepulchre within the church.

11. A cylinder of stone with a central hole might serve as the support for a maypole. Dancing on the village green or in the churchyard was a feature of May Day. (There is one at Bothal.) The church provided entertainment including church ales, the equivalent of modern garden fetes.

12. The church in medieval times was a place of sanctuary and also a general place of meeting. Fire fighting apparatus might be kept in the church and business transacted at the porch.

13. Changes brought about by the Reformation in the sixteenth and seventeenth centuries can be traced. The rood screen, separating the chancel from the nave, might be removed, but its position in the stonework of the chancel arch can be seen. So also may that of

timberwork removed from side chapels. There may be empty niches where images one stood and the altar may be seen through a squint hole. This was once used for communication between chancel and nave, when the rood screen was in position. The priest's door provided him with a separate entrance and sedilia show that several clerics would take part in services. The pulpit is eloquent and the seating within the church is evidence of social status.

14. The date and style of the font may be of interest. Fonts were removed in Cromwellian times and very often new ones appeared when they were again required after 1660. Old ones can still be found.

15. Monuments within the churchyard and church are a study in themselves. The medieval monuments can be used for an enquiry into arms and armour, dress, heraldry and elements of architecture and sculpture. There are very fine alabaster monuments at Chillingham and Bothal. Warkworth has an impressive effigy of a knight. These can be brought to life to illustrate the medieval scene.

The artistic style of the monuments can be studied and it may be found that some head-stones have been re-used. Some have strange little carvings on the other side. These may or may not be contemporary with the inscription. The development of lettering may be considered and some of the inscriptions are crudely cut by workmen who were copying letters, but were unable to read. Students can copy or make rubbings of inscriptions. There are examples of fashion and style: they also give the common Christian names of a period. Surnames are also given and some strange names emerge. One may be prompted to try and discover details of a life so briefly recorded.

Epitaphs are a fascinating study and show that the churchyard is not without its humour.

16. It should be possible for a group to make a complete survey of a churchyard. Unfortunately at the present time many tomb-stones are being laid low by vandals, eroded by smoke and the weather, or even removed to provide pavements. The survey would number the tomb-stones in position and details of each could be recorded on cards. Then the information could be recorded graphically—surnames on one axis and times on the other. With a long time-life scale lives could be plotted to give a picture of life sequence in the village. Although only a fraction of the total population of the area would be recorded it might be regarded as a statistical sample. The number of grave-stones could be compared with the number of recorded deaths over a period. It also has to be remembered that one tombstone may carry the names of several members of the same family.

(For those unrecorded on tomb-stones the memorials are the ridge and furrow of the fields, the bell pits, the quarries, the hedges, ditches and field walls, the buildings and the machinery.)

Gray's 'Elegy written in a Country Churchyard' provides essential reading.

METHODS OF RECORDING

1. Copy of inscriptions.

2. Rubbings of inscriptions.

3. Sketches of churches, church furniture, tombs, sculpture. Window heads and tracery, pillars and capitals, gargoyles, sedilia, piscina, cupboards, brackets. Ironwork, woodwork, seating. Arms and hatchments. Porches and lychgates. Funeral equipment, biers and hearses.

4. Photography in black and white or colour.

5. Plans and architectural drawings.

6. Brass-rubbings or rubbings of incised slabs.

In Northumberland there is one existing old brass in All Saints' (now in Cathedral). This is of Roger Thornton, mayor of Newcastle and his wife. It is protected under glass and cannot be rubbed, but it is well worth seeing. The monument is in a very fine eighteenth-century church of classical style, contrasting with that of St Mary's in Gateshead across the Tyne. There are, however, a number of matrices in grave slabs from which brasses have been removed. The metal was valuable and religious change or war was an excuse for appropriation. The local history enthusiast is justified in extending his interest in brasses beyond the confines of the county to Northumbria or to persons from Northumberland with brasses elsewhere. The Reverend Goode of Ponteland has a brass at Odiham (Hants) and Prior de la Mare of Tynemouth has a magnificent brass at St Albans, where he became Abbot. There are no doubt others of this kind. In the other northern counties—Durham, Yorkshire, Cumberland, Westmorland and Lancashire there are brasses to be rubbed. Brass rubbings are of great value in the study of history over three and a half centuries. Like photographs, their study can be more rewarding than the study of the actual object. The position of the brass, time available and lighting may make detailed study very difficult. A number of persons can study a brass rubbing, which is raised to the vertical and to that extent 'brought to life'. All kinds of details can be picked out at leisure—matters of armour, equipment, dress and artistic motifs. Clerics, merchants and scholars can be studied as well as armoured knights. Wives and families of laymen are often included.

The canopies give details of church architecture and sculpture. The rise, decline and fall of the monumental brass is both a social and religious study. Originally it had a practical and spiritual purpose. It recorded the life of the deceased, but also called upon visitors 'to pray for his soul'. There was fear of purgatory and hell fire. Prayers for the dead were regarded as effective. With increase in numbers the quality of brasses tended to deteriorate. In the later part of the sixteenth century the brass became merely a memorial.

Brasses can also be used to trace changes in language and styles of lettering. The fashions of the period are also depicted.

There is a strong similarity in technique between the incising of stone slabs and of the brass plate. Craftsmen in England tended to favour the deep incisions and sweeping curves. There was not an elaboration of detail. It is possible to get something of the same effect as brass rubbing, by using the same technique for incised stones. The difficulty is that the stones tend to be badly chipped over a long period of time and the rubbings need a certain amount of touching up. The geology of the stones can be considered. The finest and most durable slabs were of marble or of Swithland slate. These materials were used for other purposes including fire places. Tombstones could be regarded as a form of Industrial Archaeology.

There is a project for a Graveyard Monument Survey, sponsored by the Northumberland Local History Society. Particulars, advice and cards for recording can be obtained from: Mr R. A. S. Cowper, 'Donwal', 1, Kings Road, Wallsend, or The Northumberland Rural Community Council, 24, The Grove, Gosforth, Newcastle upon Tyne, NE3 1NE.

The parsonage also comes into the picture. After 1660 when the Church of England re-emerged, the status of the clergy and increased value of their livings was shown in the development of finer houses. The neat Georgian residence becomes a characteristic of the eighteenth century. The parson depended on rents from land, his own farming activities, tithes, fees and gifts. Poorer parsons might eke out a living by teaching. Well-to-do clerics might have several livings, and use poorly paid curates. The clergy often enjoyed the life of the country —hunting and shooting in preference to fishing that might appear more appropriate. They might also be involved in justice and local administration. The parson and squire dominated the village. Some had time to pursue antiquarian studies and become writers of local history.

In the nineteenth century many parsonages tended to increase in size. The parson might well be a member of the dominant family of the area, son or brother of the squire. The Reverend Francis Grey of

Morpeth is a good example, and there was a titled cleric at Alnham. The rectory or parsonage was the residence of a man of property, who had to entertain his peers. It had a large garden, a gazebo or summer house, stables, coach-house and within well filled pantries and cellars. The parson and his family had their own cushioned pews in the church, and their deaths were duly recorded with suitable monuments.

In our time with alteration of circumstances and the decline of incomes from property, the parsonage is no longer a suitable residence for the parson. Some are left to decay or are demolished. Others may be taken over by persons of greater wealth. The new parsonage is often a small modern villa.

THE STUDY OF FARMS

The study of farms is of the greatest importance in discovering changes in village life. At present agriculture tends to occupy a smaller sector of the economy, while its products tend to be for non-local consumption. There is a tendency to specialization and the building up of bigger agricultural units. The decline in the number of farms is evident and quite a number of farmhouses become derelict or are used only for animals. It is difficult for the smallholder to survive. Very often he has to combine his farm work with some other occupation. It is of interest to trace changes of occupations within families. The larger farms tend to be some distance from the village, each in the midst of its own fields.

1. The name of the farm may be the oldest thing about it. Names of farms and fields tell something of their history, e.g. Nightfolds, Shortflatt or Unthank.

2. The number of acres of the farm and the type of land have to be considered—pasture, ploughland, woodland, etc.

3. It has to be discovered whether the farmer is the owner of the land as well as the occupier or whether the farm belongs to a big estate.

4. The next considerations are how long the farm was of the present size. How much has been taken away or added?

5. The farmhouse may next be studied to determine its date. It has to be noticed if there are several periods of construction or whether there are two or more farmhouses of different periods on the same

site. Building materials have to be noted, stone, bricks, timber, slates and pantiles.

6. The farm buildings are recorded in detail. The barn, an all-purpose building, is often the oldest. The dovecote may also be very old. Other buildings serve different purposes and it can be discovered how many horses could be used and how many milking cows could be tied. Shelter for other animals in covered yards or special apartments has to be considered. It is possible to discover how many horse wagons would be needed in the pre-tractor age. It is possible to compare things past with the present situation on the farm.

CHERRYBURN HOUSE.

FROM THE ENGRAVING BY JOHN BEWICK.

It will be found that buildings have served different purposes and the arches of the wagon-shed may have been blocked to give a continuous wall. Stables may have been turned into cattle-sheds, but the hay-racks and mangers are still in use. The old farmhouse itself may have been turned into a shelter for animals and hens, after a new one has been built.

7. There may be indications of older farm practices such as butter or cheese making. Little of these are now done locally but some of the old equipment may still be there. Cheese presses had huge stones and churns, used for butter making, may still be discovered.

8. It is possible to discover different processes of feeding animals at different periods of time. Also methods of hay-making, harvesting corn and harvesting roots and potatoes have changed. How were these products stored or used?

There was a period when practically everything was done by hand but there has been an increasing use of power and mechanical contrivances. Hay was once put into large piles which were hauled on to flat-bottomed carts. Mowing machines have replaced the scythe and sickle. The threshing machine has replaced the flail. The combine harvester has replaced the self binder and corn stooks have disappeared from the scene. The threshing machine provides a long and interesting story.

9. The use of power can be traced on the farm. A characteristic building of the Northumberland farm was the round-house or horse track or gingang. This provided shelter for a horse or horses that went round and round providing the power for the threshing machine and mill. These have now been converted to all kinds of purposes but the construction of the round-house was ingenious. They date from about 1800 and in due course, by the 1850s were being replaced by powerful stationary steam engines. Many farms still retain the huge factory-like chimneys. There are interesting variations on the same pattern. They can be round or square and built of brick or stone.

10. Other things that may occur are evidence of field drainage and perhaps the remains of dams, channels and sluices for irrigation purposes. The water meadows could have their fertility improved by periodic floodings of streams which deposited fertile silt and returned the spoils of erosion.

11. Plantations, rabbit warrens and deer parks have a story to tell. There are also coverts for the shelter of game.

12. The account can be brought completely up to date by making a survey of the present situation. This involves the acreage of land used for different purposes. The yields of the different crops over a period of rotation have to be considered. Then the different types of animals have to be enumerated and their purposes. Cows may be used to provide milk for the market or for the rearing of calves. Horses are now kept mainly for riding purposes—the hill farmer may need a horse to round up or to inspect his stock. Other animals and birds have to be recorded—pigs and poultry.

13. Machinery too has to be considered together with tractors and lorries used for haulage nowadays.

14. Mechanical means are now used for ditching, draining, hedge cutting, fencing and lifting. The farm can be organized on a factory basis.

15. Water supply is a matter of great importance and the earlier provision can be considered with ponds, wells, springs, pumps and reservoirs (wind pumps).

16. Houses and provision for workers has to be considered. The large farms had a range of cottages, few of which are now used by farm workers.

17. Problems of sanitation and drainage also have to be noticed.

18. The farm may be a unit in a large landed estate, which may have to be considered. This will have been an important factor in determining the course of change. It may illustrate the Agrarian Revolution, together with improvements in estate management, landscape and the building of both farms and cottages.

19. Associated with farming are a large number of skills and crafts. These include the construction and maintenance of field walls. Northumberland has hedges as well as walls. These had to be planted and maintained though now are often neglected. By regular cutting or layering when overgrown, a strong barrier can be maintained. Hedges also provide shelter. Hedgerow plants and trees are a study in themselves. There is also the art of timber fencing, associated with the sawmill and the production of posts, stakes, palings and gates of various types. These all have to be considered. The five barred wooden gate was of standard width, but now it is often replaced by a wider metal construction or even a grid. The old stone gate posts, that may last for centuries, have often been removed. Wattle hurdles may still be used for the protection of sheep. Stone stells (circular enclosures for protection against the weather), and collecting places for dipping, shearing, branding and medical attention also have to be noticed.

20. Plants, trees and shrubs were grown for various purposes. Some bushes were deliberately grown. Such were elder, crab apple and wild damson. Certain plants had medical qualities for man or beast. Dock leaves were used for wrapping butter. Some plants were aromatic and rushes were used both for lights and matting. Gorse was used for fuel in baking ovens and at times (as Bewick records) it was beaten in a stone trough to make it palatable for cattle in winter. Heather was used to provide roof covering for cottages.

21. The dovecote served the special purpose of providing fresh food. Until the agricultural changes in the eighteenth century there was a shortage of food for animals in winter and many were killed in the late autumn to be preserved in salt for the winter. Pigeons provided relief from salt meat and the dovecotes with proverbial holes in the walls could harbour hundreds of birds. Unlike those who

infest our public buildings, they could be caught whenever they were needed.

Associated Crafts. (See industrial archaeology.)

Quarries: Brick and tile works, drainage and roofing.

Smithy: Wheelwright's shop.

The Mill: lime kilns and coal pits: The sandpit.

Detailed investigations may be made into:

1. Soils, fertility, manures and fertilizers.
2. Experiments in the breeding and feeding of animals.
3. Modern methods of food production.
4. Effects of modern methods of cultivation, harvesting, breeding, fattening, fertilizing, draining and irrigation on the land.
5. The loss of the best land for roads and housing.

Books

BAILEY, J. and CULLEY, G. *A General View of Agriculture in the County of Northumberland.* 1805. Frank Graham Reprint.

BATES, C. J. *The Brothers Colling.* Journal of Agricultural Society of England. 1899.

CULLEY, G. *Livestock.* 1794.

WHITHAM

A Cheviot Ram; belonging to Mr. Thos. Smith of Woodhall

Taken in April 1798, when 7 Years Old.

LORD ERNLE. *English Farming Past and Present.* 1936.
FUSSEL, G. E. *The Story of Farming.* Pergamon Press.
The Farmers Tools 1500-1900.
MARSHALL, G. *Review of reports to Board of Agriculture from the North. 1808.* Reprint by David & Charles.
ORWIN, C. S. *A History of English Farming.* Nelson.
The Open Fields. Cambridge U.P.
PAWSON, H. C. *Survey of Agriculture in Northumberland.* 1961.
WINTER, G. *A Country Camera. 1844-1944.*
Country Life 1966.
YOUNG, A. *Six Months Fair through the North of England.* Vol. III, pp. 1-116.
HIGGS, *The Land.* Studio Vista.
LOBBAN, R. D. *Farming.* Batsford 1973.

Young Farmers Club Booklets
No. 22. *The Story of our Cattle.*
No. 24. *The Story of Farm Tools.*
No. 27. *The Story of Farm Buildings.*

SPECIAL STUDIES

THE SMITHY

The blacksmith's shop once existed in most villages and the craft persisted for centuries. The directories of the last century and the early twentieth century, indicate large numbers of them. With the advent of the motor-car and the decline of the horse, they have tended to turn to matters mechanical—repairing tractors and farm machinery.

The smith was a special craftsman in the old village. In medieval times his activities extended to the repair of armour and weapons as well as the provision of ploughshares and horse shoes. He was involved in both peace and war. The smiths were one of the most important craft guilds. The anvil, hammer and tongs have become proverbial. Tomb-stones carry the blacksmith's epitaph. The craft was handed on from father to son and there may still be generations of blacksmiths of the same family in a particular area. Some of them carried their skills to the making of railways and the building of iron ships.

Other crafts depended on his skill for making metal tools and fittings for machinery. Iron grills and gates would also be his work. The great days of the smith were the times of increasing horse traffic on the roads with the mail and stage-coaches as well as the carrying traffic. The smith might also make ornamental iron work for windows and gateways. There was a good deal of this from the eighteenth century onwards.

The local smithy can be located from maps—the building may still be there, if not still in use. A study may still be made of the craft.

The Carpenter, Joiner or Wheelwright

The other great craftsmen of the village was the man who worked in timber. There has been increasing specialization with craftsmen confining themselves to particular aspects of work in wood—whether furniture, housebuilding or vehicles. But at one time the village carpenter fitted or joined door frames, house frames or furniture. He attended to wooden vehicles and implements. Wooden coffins were also made by him. He would make ladders and shafts for tools. Gates

and timber fences would be included in his work. He might employ apprentices and store and cut his own timber. There was a sawpit with a top and bottom position for each of the sawyers. The bottom sawyer was in the pit and suffered more from dust. The carpenter would 'know' his timber and work it accordingly. He probably had his plans intimately in his mind and had no need to commit anything to paper. The work was done with great skill.

Carpenters' shops can still be found with the old equipment including the old lathe. A great deal of information can be obtained about the old country crafts. The carpenter would be responsible for the timberwork of the mill and its water wheel. Craftsmen in timber constructed many of the old mills and maintained the water wheels. The wheelwright provided all kinds of wheels in timber with iron rims for different types of wagons, carts and carriages.

THE SCHOOL

Another important institution to study in village or town is the school. We have reached the centenary of Forsters' Education Act, which provided for the establishment of schools from money raised by local rates. Education had not been considered a matter for the State and till then schools had been provided by private persons or voluntary bodies. The government did make small grants by way of assistance and inspectors saw that these were well and truly earned. The school is likely to be later than 1870 and much more likely to be later than 1902. Educational re-organization at various times, especially at present, may make educational inheritance difficult to trace in a particular building. The old school may now be an ordinary dwelling place.

It has to be remembered that education in a school in olden times was for selected persons—selection depended on their intended occupations and in medieval times these were mainly in the church. Teachers and civil servants of those days were inevitably trained as clerics. For other occupations training was in the actual profession, craft or trade. Apprenticeship was the form of training and in addition to this the intending farmer learnt in the field and the housewife in the house. The knight and foot soldier received their own special training.

Many of the early schools were 'chantry' schools, in or attached to

THE Royal William COACH, BETWEEN NEWCASTLE AND BERWICK.

The Public are respectfully informed that, on and after

MONDAY, THE 19th MARCH,

The above COACH will leave

BERWICK every Morning, (Sundays excepted,) at Six o'Clock,

Belford, at a Quarter before Eight,

And, after Breakfasting at Alnwick, will leave at 10 o'Clock,

And arrive at

MR. DODSWORTH'S,

QUEEN'S HEAD, NEWCASTLE, AT TWO O'CLOCK;

And leave the Queen's Head, Newcastle, at ½-past 11 o'Clock, A.M ;

AND AFTER DINING AT ALNWICK,

Will leave at Four o'Clock,

And arrive at Berwick at 8 o'Clock.

Fares from Newcastle to Berwick, 13s. Insides, 7s. Outside.
Do. Do. to Alnwick, 7s. Do. 4s. Do.

CHARLES HENRY COOK, PRINTER, PILGRIM STREET, NEWCASTLE.

An old coaching bill.

Previous page: Aerial view of Berwick.

Grainger Street, Newcastle.

THE PITMAN'S COMPLAINT.

O Lord hear the poor pitmen's cry
Look down on us with pitying eye;
With heavy bondage are opprest,
And all our families are distrest.

Thou heard the Isrealites of old,
And led them to a blessed fold;
Deliver us from slavery
And set the Sons of Britain free.

In the dark pit where we are bound,
The iron hand of oppression's found;
Our labour's hard, our wages small,
Some days we work for nought at all.

As lions greedy of their prey,
They take our rights from us away;
To starvation we are driven,
Pale and wan we are ill thriven.

Our masters pinch us very sore,
We never felt such smart before,
They have us so completely bet,
Not one in fifty's out of debt.

The Indian slaves for freedom groan,
We have a greater cause to moan,
You often pity slaves abroad,
But we have now a greater load.

Come, O ye rulers of our land,
Pray take our cause into your hand,
Then let us have fair Britain's law,
And save us from proud Pharoah's paw.

Beneath the harrow we are crush'd,
Our blood lies mangled with the dust;
Regardless of our cries and groans,
They suck the marrow from our bones.

As cannibals they have eat our flesh,
Their bellies swell to great excess,
To quench their thirst have drunk our blood,
And left us wallowing in the mud.

Does not the trumpet sound reform,
And are we not free Britons born;
We want to have a jubilee,
The slavish pitmen now set free.

Our flesh pots now are stained with rust,
Our cup-boards now without a crust,
The tears run from the mothers' eyes,
They can not bear their children's cries.

Arise my brethren from the dust,
And in the Lord let's put our trust,
Then all our foes he will confound,
And in the sea proud Pharoah dround.

Printed for the Author, by W. Fordyce, 48, Dean Street, Newcastle.
May 13th 1831

Broadsheet issued during the Miners Strike of 1844.

churches. The priest appointed had the task of reciting masses for the souls of the founder and his family. He often found it convenient to train boys in 'song' and 'grammar'. Some little knowledge of Latin was necessary for the boys to 'chant' in a form of service that was in the Latin tongue till nearly the middle of the sixteenth century. Some attempt was made by local people to save local endowments from confiscation after the Dissolution of the Monasteries (1536-9), but the Dissolution of the Chantries followed in the reign of Edward VI (1547).

In the second half of the sixteenth century many Grammar Schools were founded or re-founded. A local example is Morpeth, where a charter of Edward VI gave proprietary rights to the corporation and protected the lands of the former chantry. The school continued in the same building for nearly 300 years. At Hexham was also a 'chantry' school. Educational provision in Northumberland was comparatively poor and only Newcastle was reasonably well provided. Education was strictly controlled by the authorities in the interests of the Church of England, but there was a good deal of 'unofficial' instruction in Catholic houses and the Protestant Nonconformists developed their own academies with a wider curriculum.

Grammar Schools varied greatly in their history and also in numbers of pupils attending. There was always provision for 'petty' *or* lower schools and very often the high ambitions of founders could not be achieved. The ebb and flow of success depended on the abilities of schoolmasters. Sometimes the endowment was misappropriated.

In 1698 the Society for the Promotion of Christian Knowledge was established. Gentry and religious bodies were encouraged to subscribe money for the maintenance of 'Charity' Schools. By 1800 something like a hundred of these had been founded in Northumberland. A difficulty was fluctuating population and a school might be left completely stranded beyond any reasonable walking limit for pupils. Schools might well fall into disuse: apathy and religious divisions were other negative factors.

On the other hand with the development of industries and coal mining other centres of population developed, at first with no church or educational provision. Attempts were made to establish Sunday Schools. The Church of England and the parochial system were insufficient and a great deal was done by Methodists and Dissenting bodies. Further still by 1812 the British and Foreign School Society (Noncomformist) and the National Society for promoting the Education of the Poor in the Principles of the Established Church had been formed. Both societies made rapid progress and many schools were established. These were run on the monitorial system by which selected pupils helped to hand on the information. One teacher could supervise very large groups.

In addition to these, all kinds of schools were attempted. There were a number of 'Dames Schools' and local newspapers of the time carry advertisements about all kinds of schools. The old directories also give particulars. Often the teachers had few or no qualifications. But with increasing population and the restriction of hours of work for children as well as imposing age limits on employment more and more children lacked any educational provision. The result of a Commission of Enquiry was the Education Act of 1870. From this time new schools were established called 'Board Schools' since they were provided by Local Boards of Education. In course of time County Councils were established and they took over the local control of education in 1902. But many Church of England and Catholic Schools remained as well as the Council Schools. Changes took place in the Free Grammar Schools also and some became the equivalent of elementary. Country schools were often all age schools taking pupils to the statutory leaving age. Pupils had to obtain a certificate of competence if they wanted to leave school at an earlier age for work. There is a good deal of interesting information to be gathered about the old schools and it is important that this should be collected in larger centres.

1. The first thing that has to be considered is the building. Some church schools were modelled on churches and had a bell turret at the west end. Like the church bell, this was necessary to summon people from a distance. The accommodation was limited and the classes were not separated; the windows were deliberately placed high to prevent pupils from looking out.

2. Then seating has to be fitted in; the old schools had forms, but the educational authorities required 'standards' which depended on achievements in tests carried out by school inspectors. The types of forms or heavy desks still entered into consideration. A standard might be confined to one form.

3. Then comes the problem of heating and various types of coke stoves heated, or partly heated, churches and schools. One brand of stove gained the motto 'slow but sure' with the tortoise as a trade mark.

4. The pupils themselves can be recalled from old photographs, prints, sketches and reminiscences. How were they dressed? Uniform if anything was lacking. Boys had an assortment of jerseys and jackets. Often cord trousers were worn, including father's cut downs. Some wore knee breeches and leggings or farm attire. The girls wore long dresses—replicas of adult dress. Much of the clothing was tattered.

It is interesting to compare hair styles of different periods.

5. Lessons next have to be considered and in the first place the type of timetable. The 3 Rs and Religious Knowledge took up most of the time. All kinds of activities have to be recalled—the forms of art and craft or physical education at one time called 'drill'. It was not uncommon for children to be marched round and round the school yard.

6. An interesting survey could be made of all kinds of unorganized games from marbles to skipping. Small boys of a previous era played at trains—one being a locomotive and the others attached. Present day children could be motor traffic and act as cars. There is a wealth of songs and ditties attached to these games. (Opie. Language and lore of schoolchildren.) Nursery rhymes and traditional verses may have an entirely different meaning from what is currently thought about them.

7. The equipment has to be considered. The old slates have gone but the blackboard still remains as does the perennial piano. Children's books have changed a great deal and it is rather amusing to read the chap-books of the eighteenth century. Tales usually had a moral intention. Some critics objected to stories in which birds and animals talked. There may be still some very old horn books around and task cards were used for all kinds of purposes. Some of the books used as examples of penmanship are very illuminating. Great attention was paid to these matters and the pupil was expected 'to copy letters in a big round hand'.

8. 'Objects' were retained in cupboards for lesson purposes—birds' eggs and stuffed birds, samples of cotton and wool.

9. Teachers themselves provide an interesting study. Some were described as 'real' characters and exercised a good deal of influence within and without the school. In Goldsmith's *Deserted Village*, the schoolmaster had been one of the leading figures 'and e'en through vanquished he could still argue'. To be successful he had to be a general factotum.

Like the parson, the schoolmaster is a source of local history.

10. Other matters of interest are the provision of meals or any form of refreshment. In this connection, too, toilet facilities have to be considered.

11. The school was part of a community and has to be considered in connection with village life. It became a meeting place, a place for 'night' school and talks, a library centre and even an extra sleeping place. School attendance was intimately connected with outside activities and holidays were intended to coincide with periods of harvesting. In the 1860s government commissioners, making an

educational survey, thoughtlessly started in summer time and found that there was no attendance and schools were closed. Information had to be obtained by private enquiry. Attendance registers reflected the pressure of agricultural activities.

12. The lives of various pupils can be traced and the forms of employment that were taken may be determined. Many moved to other parts or emigrated to the dominions.

13. Evidence of various great occasions can be recalled from village celebrations, pageants or processions. It might be Empire Day, the relief of Mafeking, the news of Waterloo, a Coronation or a Jubilee. These great occasions provide monuments, fountains, wells, parts of memorial halls.

14. The school can show several stages of educational history and information can be obtained from public records as well as local sources.

Sources of Information

1. Reminiscences of teachers, pupils, parents and governors. These have to be checked and correlated.

2. Old reports, records and registers.

3. Log books were kept at schools, briefly recording activities.

4. Minutes of governors' or managers' meetings.

5. Information collected by the School Board or Council.

6. Report made by visitors whether ecclesiastical or H.M. Inspectors.

7. Reports by Government Commissioners on various types of education. Information was collected from all parts of the country.

8. Diocesan records—at one time all education was under ecclesiastical control and schoolmasters needed the Bishop's licence.

9. Diaries and letters contain educational information.

10. Biographies and autobiographies. Thomas Bewick writes of his own education and his woodcuts show scenes from all aspects of life.

11. Newspapers and magazines, including school magazines.

12. County Directories such as those by Parson and White (1827) and Bulmer (1886-7) provide information about schools.

13. The *Northumberland County History* (15 vols.), Hodgson and D. D. Dixon provide information on education in the country. Welford's *Men of Mark 'twixt Tyne and Tweed* gives some information.

14. Nonconformist Church often keep their own records.

15. Novels may provide some highly coloured information.

16. Estate papers at the County Record Office provide educational material.

17. The *Journal* and the *Research Review* of the Institutes of Education of the Universities of Durham and Newcastle provide a great deal of useful information.

Some Books

ALLASON, F. *Hayton C. of E. School. 1818-1968* (from the school near Carlisle).

BEWICK, T. *Autobiography*. Various versions.

BARNARD, H. C. *History of English Education.* Uvst. of London Press 1964.

CURTIS, S. J. *History of Education in Britain* (5th edn.) University Tutorial Press 1963.

GRAY, R. *St Andrews C. of E. School, Newcastle*. Newcastle Ed. Journal Mch. 1969.

GOSDEN, P. *How they were taught*. Basil Blackwell.

HUGHES, E. *North Country life in 18th century*. O.U.P. 1952.

HART, C. *Story of St Cuthbert's G.S. Newcastle*. Burns & Oates.

JONES, M. G. *The Charity School Movement*. Cass 1964.

KENNEDY, G. *The Story of Morpeth Grammar School*. 1952.

MAW, R. *Rutherford Grammar School*. Northumberland Press 1964.

LAWS, A. R. *Schola Novacastrensis*. (R.G.S. Newcastle) 1923.

LEACH, A. F. *Schools of Medieval England*. Methuen 1915.

MASON, M. G. *History of Elementary Education on Tyneside before 1870*. M.Ed. 1951 & Durham Research Review 1951.

MACLURE, J. S. *Educational Documents*. Chapman and Hall.

POCOCK, J. *Materials available for the History of Education in the North East (1500-1800)*. Univ. of Durham.

Schools and Schoolmasters. Durham Research Review. 1952.

REED, A. *Bruce's School*. W. Scott 1903.

RICHARDSON, W. *History of Wallsend.*

SIMON, B. *Education of the Labour Party Movement*. Laurence and Wishart 1965.

SIMON, J. & B. *Education in Leicestershire* (An example of a local survey).

SMITH, F, *A History of England's Elementary Education*. University of London 1931.

SPEED, P. F. *Learning and Teaching in Victorian Times*. Longmans.

TYSON, C. & HOGG, G. *Archive Unit on Popular Education in the North East*. No. 4.

THOMPSON, S. *Materials for the History of Hexham Schools*. Record Office.

WOOD, R. *Children: a collection of documents.* Evans.
WADE, H. *Voluntary Schools in Northumberland.* M.Ed. Thesis 1959.

Stamfordham Schoolmasters

At the west end of Stamfordham Church on either side of the tower arch are two memorials to two priests, who were also schoolmasters.

To the Memory of the
Revd. Richd. Baxter
Curate of this parish 46 years
& Master of the Free School
49 yrs. He died June 21 1808
Aged 78. He discharged the
Sacred Duties of his cure
with zeal and exemplary
diligence & his liberal &
assiduous attention to the office
of Schoolmaster will be long
revered by his numerous pupils
& Parishioners.

Nigh this place lieth ye
Body of Mr George Salkeld
the late worthy & indefatigable
Master 52 years of the Free
School in Stamfordham.

1744 Aged 72 years.

George Salkeld was born in 1672 and took up his post at the age of 20, remaining there for 52 years. Richard Baxter, born in 1730 and taking over some 15 years after Salkeld's death, remained master for 49 years. The two of them covered a period of 101 years, and one would like to know something of the progress of the school. The master who came between them was Benjamin Scorsbie, who died in 1759, and seems to have been a very unsatisfactory character. 'For some years it (the school) has been shamefully neglected by the headmaster who does not reside—was born blind and in some respects is not quite unexceptional.' *N.C.H.* Vol. XII, p. 299.

Richard Baxter, bearer of a famous name, could not but improve the situation and he was followed after nearly half a century of service by another bearer of a famous name, Walter Scott M.D., doctor and son of a doctor. 'Walter Scott of Stamfordham had the misfortune to possess a free and easy disposition, which brought him to the verge of impoverishment and compelled him, although an M.D. and a Justice of the Peace, to accept the office of master of Stamfordham Free School.' This was not good for the school and in 1829 he had been confined to his house for two years and his son, only 18, had taken charge. The Charity Commissioners were much concerned and found the properties providing the endowment had been much neglected.

'There was a school, school house, garden, close and stable with a farm of 76 acres. 'The farm buildings, as well as the school premises, are in bad condition. There is a lime kiln on the estate, from which no profit is now derived and a shaft for winning coals. The colliery is let to Messrs. Hawthorn & Co., who have agreed to give 2d. a fother for all the coals raised. There is also some clay, which is used for making crucibles for glass houses, and the same parties have agreed to pay 1s. 6d. per ton for the quantity taken. Nothing yet has been received for the working of the coals or clay. The management and letting of the property has been entirely left to the master himself.' The property was at Heugh and signs of old workings can be seen.

The school, which was founded in 1663, became a Public Elementary School after 1870 and was rebuilt in 1879. The stories of both schools could be interesting. There is also established a direct connection between schools and Industrial Archaeology.

INDUSTRIAL ARCHAEOLOGY

Books

BIRSTALL, A. F. *A History of Mechanical Engineering*. Faber 1963.

CHALONER, W. H. & MUSSON, A. E. *Industry & Technology*. Studio Vista 1963.

DERRY & WILLIAMS. *A Short History of Technology*. O.U.P.

HUDSON, K. Ed. *Industrial Archaeology* (Annual). David & Charles.

Introduction to Industrial Archaeology. Methuen 1966.

Handbook for Industrial Archaeologists. J. Baker 1967.

PANNELL, J. P. M. *Techniques of Industrial Archaeology*. 1966.

Illustrated History of Civil Engineering. Thames & Hudson 1964.

RICHARDS, J. M. *The functional tradition of Early Industrial Building*. Architectural Press 1958.

RIX, B. *Industrial Archaeology*. Historical Association.

CHAPMAN, S. D. & CHAMBERS, J. D. *The beginnings of Industrial Britain*. University Tutorial Press.

Industrial Archaeology has become both respectable and fashionable within the last decade or so. In 1948 recording and photographing collieries and pit heaps might have seemed quite ridiculous, and was it then realized that the steam engine was doomed? Specialist engineering and preservation societies have added to the interest in these matters and so Industrial Archaeology thrives.

Industrial Archaeology was a section of General Archaeology, some people turning their attention to things mechanical. However, it has now emerged as a study in its own right and the terms of definition are 'matters relating to Industry from the Industrial Revolution onwards' or perhaps more accurately from the 'first' Industrial Revolution onwards. Terms and dates both provide difficulties, but the essential elements are new forms of power and transport together with a great deal of re-organization. One tends to think in terms of a period from 1750 onwards, although the changes that became evident had a long ancestry.

The industrial archaeologist records the remains of these earlier industrial activities, since other processes and methods, other forms of transport and power have been developed, and the earlier ones have become obsolete. The changes tend to become increasingly rapid and things have a much shorter length of useful life, before being condemned for scrap or to the rubbish tip. The industrial archaeologist concerns himself with small pieces of equipment as well as the greater achievements of engineering and construction. The ramifications are so great that the limits are difficult to define. But these things can be included:

I. FORMS OF TRANSPORT

Roads and trackways

In prehistoric times trackways linked up settlements and trysting places that have long been abandoned. They followed natural courses, depending on the nature of the land, and made detours to avoid obstacles. Sheep walks are made in the same way, and the sheep continue to follow their own fixed paths over the moorland. Their local knowledge is handed on from one generation to another, and the sheep are far from being the foolish creatures that their critics imagine. The Bible is full of lore of this kind. 'We have erred ... like lost sheep.' It was most important to follow a leader in difficult country. Walking in open country, it is possible to see how the tracks emerged. They were used by both animals and human beings. Loads were carried by pack animals. Sometimes stones were laid in wet places. It is quite likely that there were considerable stretches of trackway made of logs in corduroy fashion. Tracks of this kind have been found through meres or mosses in the south-west of England. Very often on slopes these tracks become hollow ways as the result of erosion and a great deal of traffic. In places there are parallel lines where one difficult trackway has been abandoned for another.

By way of contrast (and this is like the present programme of building motor-ways) the Roman conquerors of Britain imposed their system of roads as a means of facilitating troop movements and main-

Pack Horse Bridge, Ovingham.

taining control. The roads are characteristic of a military conquest—direct from place to place and able to ignore any objections on the part of landowners. The Roman road builders chose the route that suited them and roads were well and truly laid in a style that was not repeated till the time of Telford and Macadam in the late eighteenth century.

In Saxon and Medieval times Roman roads and some of the old trackways continued in use, but more were developed, depending upon new centres of population and the location of fords or bridges. These factors help to explain the pattern of roads and while some develop others are lost, but are still recognizable. It also has to be remembered that there was much coast and river traffic and that the roads fitted in with this. Again the development of churches, monasteries and the shrines of saints, visited by pilgrims, meant that further routes would be developed. Holy Island was an important religious centre and there was constant traffic between the English and Scottish monasteries. Also the monasteries had remote granges or sheep-farms that had to be linked with the parent house. There were 'summer' pastures and also 'summer' roads with a certain amount of seasonal migration. Cattle and sheep were often on the move legitimately and otherwise. Routes were used by pedlars, gypsies and cattle thieves as well as pilgrims. Military men also had to be aware of the routes, frequented and otherwise. Old routes had the name of Gemmel's path and Clennel Street: there are also salter's ways and pedlar's ways. Some of these have been traced; others have not. Footpaths, farm tracks and bridleways often follow very old trackways.

For nearly 300 years during the long period of Border warfare and lawlessness, these tracks and routes were of the greatest importance. The raiders tended to pursue the strategy of moving in by means of hidden or less frequented ways. Then they collected the cattle on a returning drive, and pushed them as rapidly as possible from point to point.

The cattle needed food and water and for the defenders river crossings were the most important checking points. They might hope to recover some of their losses. Attempts to cross ridges and valleys could cause trouble for both raiders and defenders. Men were posted to keep watch at strategic points. One has to think of a network of ways sometimes coinciding with prehistoric tracks, sometimes moving differently, and always connected with the current use of the land—the roads from outside the village joining the routes through the common fields. Routes might well be aligned by means of standing stones, and there exist numerous sockets that carried stone crosses. Roads were also connected with watering places and wells, holy and otherwise.

There were recognized meeting places for the settlement of problems between the English and Scots—on the Solway for Cumberland, for the West March at Lamyford and for the East March at Ridingburn, while there was a meeting place on 'Gamelspeth' for the men of Coquetdale and Redesdale. At times these meetings might not be peaceful, even late in the reign of Elizabeth. At that time a number of Scots were settling in Northumberland and the movement southwards continued in the reign of James I. It is possible that there was some infiltration of Scottish Catholics into Northumberland encouraged by Catholic landlords.

From 1603 there was some development of trade also and Scotland tended to supply an increasing number of cattle for the meat markets of the south of England. (This was restricted to some extent by tolls, but developed immensely after 1707, the Act of Union.) The main drove route was on the eastern side of the country via the Solway, but there were considerable numbers of Scottish cattle coming into Northumberland for the markets of Newcastle, Hexham and Morpeth. These routes remained in use for a very considerable period, a good deal depending upon the time of enclosure of open fields. Large areas were not enclosed and here there was no difficulty. The drove roads depended on pasture available—the roads were often wide enough to provide some feeding, but other wider areas would be needed for resting places and periodic watering places would be necessary. The animals would only cover a limited distance, 10-12 miles in a day, and it is sometimes forgotten that all kinds of animals would have to walk to market. Railways later provided a method of transport for long distances and deprived the drovers on the long routes, but they were still needed for the shorter distances and it is the cattle truck of the twentieth century that has put an end to this.

It is possible to pick out these drove routes. Generally speaking the grass is very good. It was frequently grazed, but not over-grazed, and the soil had the advantage of plenty of manure, so that drove roads may appear as 'green' ways across barren moorland. Other indications are parallel banks, enclosing an area much wider than an ordinary road. There are banked roads of this kind on either side of Elsdon, crossed by the later turnpike. The night resting places were larger enclosed areas: a careful watch had to be kept on the cattle. Comparatively thin Highland beasts could be fattened on the way and overdriving was undesirable. When roads were made to some extent, they still required wide grass verges and in stony places the cattle had to be shod each with eight metal plates, since for cloven-footed animals the horse shoe was unsuitable. Some of the cattle bound for the meat market had no doubt served several years at the plough. Sheep were also driven along these routes to the local markets.

In due course the drove roads were reduced to serve local needs only and declined. But well within living memory cattle were driven to market. Near Rothley, a collecting area was at Donkinrigg near the cross roads. Cattle stayed there a night and were driven to the outskirts of Newcastle to remain another night before they were sold in the market. Some remote taverns depended on the drove routes. There was a well known site at Catcherside, north of Kirkwhelpington, where inebriated cattlemen got involved in affrays. Toll roads and enclosures made it difficult for the drovers and their routes tended to go out of general use.

General Wade was responsible for opening up the Highlands of Scotland with many miles of road—250 miles from 1723 to 1740. After the 1745 rebellion, when an English army found it impossible to proceed much beyond Hexham on account of the bad condition of the roads, plans were made for the Military Road from Newcastle to Carlisle. (Reproductions of the plan by the Society of Antiquaries, Newcastle, show the route and the Roman Wall in great detail.)

This was followed by a good deal of road building in the form of turnpikes. It might involve taking over and improving an existing route or parish road. It might mean alterations to suit the requirements of landlords, who were likely to be members of the Turnpike Trust, or to appease opponents. The road might have to follow the perimeter of an estate, and this could account for right-angled bends. If there were full co-operation of all concerned the route could be direct.

There is no published work on the drove roads or turnpikes of Northumberland, but there is a good deal of evidence available in the field and in the County Records Office at Gosforth, where many of the papers of Turnpike Trusts are deposited. The turnpikes are a monument to private enterprise and local self help. The local landlords played an important part—combining public spirit and private profit. Their quarries might provide stone and transport as well as benefits obtained from the improvement of routes. They also wanted to confine public traffic to certain channels only.

The turnpikes were of predetermined width with soft edges for animals, drained by ditches and built up of compacted stones. They were able to stand the pressure of vehicular traffic. Previously roads were often unsteady tracks, beset with pot holes and mud and deeply rutted. Stone pickings from the fields were deposited in the holes, but the routes were never satisfactory. Users of the old way, free of charge, now found that tolls were imposed by the Trustees for the use of the new way. The investors wanted some return for their capital outlay, and toll bars or gates were placed at strategic points for the collection of dues. Toll houses were built to provide accommodation for toll-gate keepers. Toll bars can be traced on the old maps and a number of toll houses are still in existence.

The improvement of road transport helped the development of local industries including quarries, brickworks, tileries, coal pits and lime kilns. It meant that agricultural produce could be conveyed more widely, even for an export market. It had some curious consequences. Hodgson noted the decline of agriculture in the Elsdon area at a time when one would have thought it prosperous. It was not good cornland, but ridge and furrow show that wide areas were cultivated. However with the development of coalmining and the improvement of roads it was more profitable to send coal to the Scottish Lowlands from local mines and receive corn in return. The fields about Elsdon reverted to pasture and of a dozen water mills in the area, hardly one could be found working.

A good deal of research is still necessary on turnpikes.

(There is a thesis by G. Dodds in the Records Office on this.) Maps are needed showing turnpike provision and the use of these roads at particular places. The increase and decline of profitability could be traced with eventually the local authority taking over. The rivalry of the railways was the main cause of diminishing returns from local tolls.

An imagined Route (All basic facts can be substantiated)

It can be an interesting study to trace the course of a turnpike, recording evidence of things past on the way. An example is the 19 mile stretch from Morpeth to Elsdon. People travelled from Elsdon to Morpeth market and malefactors were brought through for trial. The big new courthouse has been mentioned, approached from 1831 by the new Telford Bridge, the pride of the town. The visitor would observe the market activities as shown on the old prints, with the congregated cattle and stalls and the horseless gigs and carts lining the streets. The hotels, inns and alehouses would be well frequented, the local craftsmen well patronized.

We leave by Newgate Street, well lined with prosperous looking dwellings and turn down Dogger Bank, noticing the entrances to coach houses and reaching the tree covered stretch of the Wansbeck with the romantic ruins of Newminster to the left. Between Morpeth and Mitford the road uses three comparatively new bridges replacing old constructions or fords—this had been a difficult route. We also pass three water mills and Spittal House, Mitford, on an eminence overlooking the junction of Font and Wansbeck. (It was a medieval hospital and skeletons have been found.) Our first stop is the three storeyed Plough Inn (so well recorded about 1900 on Canon Macleod's photograph and now replaced). The smithy is just beyond for use of travellers and the Mitford Estates.

As we ascend the hill we notice the old mill on the Wansbeck and the ruins of Mitford Castle. Old Mitford Hall has been abandoned and a magnificent new hall has been built to the designs of Mr Dobson. The quarry is still visible. The church is in a ruinous condition, and only the chancel carries a roof.

Our route passes Lightwater which has one of Raistrick's newfangled threshing machines. Newton Underwood is a village on the decline and next we pass 'Red House' Farm, partly built in brick.

The road here winds a good deal and Throphill lies to the north. In the distance we see the Horse and Hounds (now the Dyke Neuk), where we stop again. We can see Meldon Park to the south, and here too is a smithy. Our road continues due north and then west: we move smoothly along an even stretch of road between the hawthorn hedges, and after several miles of steady travel we reach Longwitton. We make another stop at the east end of this straggling colliery village. There are derelict bell pits on either side and double rows of miner's cottages. Each miner is a small holder, and has a large croft attached to his house. Pigs, poultry and the odd cow wander about. The carrier drops some of his packages and proceeds. It is a long pull to Rothley cross roads. Here our road joins the Hexham to Rothbury turnpike. To the south we can see Rothley Castle, a home-made ruin on the crags, and in the other direction is Codger's or Cadger's Castle looking over the lake. (This is said to have been a place for cannon.)

Moving along the Hexham route westwards we see smoke to the north from the lime kilns and to the south is Donkinrigg where the cattle are collected. We are able to pick off the milestones as we move along. There is another long pull towards Gallowshill, and here is another smoky area. There are kilns for the making of tiles and pipes for field draining. A lot of the timber has been cut, but coal is available for these kilns and the lime kilns to the south.

At Gallowshill our route leaves the Hexham route, and though Morpeth is 14 miles behind it is still a long haul to Steng Cross. This length of the way is a bit boring, but we pass one or two houses including that of the blacksmith near Harwoodhead. He makes shoes for cattle as well as horses, and is usually kept busy. Always he hails us and the horses are not unwilling to stop.

Moving off, we are soon able to see in the distance, the remains of the villain Winter on his gibbet. This is usually passed in silence, but now we can see the magnificent view in the north—our route down to Elsdon. Since the gradient is with us and the horses have their heads for home, we make good speed, passing Pearson's House where we do not have to stop. The old drove road lies to the east of us. We have a zig-zag to get the slope down to the Elsdonburn past Starmyer's cottage. We pass over the bridge in style—the old ford is still visible—and clatter into Elsdon. It is industrious in its way, for here also we have collieries and kilns providing a good deal of smoke.

The route down to Elsdon provides a rewarding study and should be continued to Otterburn.

1. It is possible to pick out the old drove road which came upon

the turnpike beyond Elsdon. The toll house is still there with little windows on the alert. The banked sides of the drove road can be seen to the north, getting lost in the military area.

2. The house at Overacres belonged to the Howard family.

3. At Monkridge another route came in from the south at a later date. Monkridge was one of the stages on the later Otterburn to Newcastle route. (See Archive Unit No. 2.)

4. Hereabouts is another fine example of a toll house. There are obvious older routes to north and south that here came in and users of the turnpike had to pay. To the north is yet another lime kiln.

5. In Otterburn itself is a fine piece of Industrial Archaeology—if the term can be properly used for it. The water mill established in the early nineteenth century is still in use, and over the Rede near it is an old single line traffic bridge. Otterburn tweeds are famous.

6. Bridges should be checked for dates, but the date may be of restoration and not the original. Often too there is evidence of previous crossing by ford.

At a later stage a more direct link was made between Otterburn

and Newcastle. A plan exists showing proposed improvements in 1829. The final route, the modern A696 differs from this and it is interesting to compare plan and final alignment. A letter of protest exists from James Ellis of Otterburn—it has a modern ring about it. (Detailed information on this is contained in Archive Teaching Unit No. 2 *Travel in the Turnpike Age*. University of Newcastle Department of Education.)

This road makes an excellent study since there are a number of interesting hostelries. It joins the old Roman road of Dere Street (A68) just beyond Elishaw, which was also improved in the Turnpike Age. A serious attempt was made to open this route to Scotland in rivalry to A1. (Dere Street has milestones.)

Yet another interesting route developed in the eighteenth century is the turnpike from Hexham via Rothbury and Alnwick to Alnmouth, one of the grain ports. It was used by carriers and coaches. Many of the milestones are still in position. Of these stones two types may be discovered—one a type of squared pillar with Roman numerals and the other rounded with the Arabic type of numeral. Measuring will show that they are approximately a mile apart, but some miles are longer than others. The best way to explore these is on bicycle or on foot—pacing or a meter on a bicycle will give the approximate position. (They are given on 1 inch O.S. Maps.) It gives some interest to a walk—the motorist passes by, unheeding. Observation of milestones was intended at a much slower pace. It is also of interest to calculate convenient stopping places on the route. It is possible to study gradients that are minimized by a casual glance at the map or the speed of the motor vehicle. The way was much more intimate and personal. A profile can be made of a route.

On such a route, by walking or otherwise at selected stops, it is possible to make a section of the route giving dimensions of the hard core of the road and the extent of the grass verges. Notice should be taken of the walls and ditches. It is possible to use visible evidence for dating purposes. Attempts can be made to date hedgerows, trees in the hedge and avenues of trees. A lot of these go back to the eighteenth century. In parklands, trees growing upon ridge and furrow, put back the date of the ploughing of the land. The road cuts across country and sometimes the road coincides with field boundaries, or the field has been ploughed to fit the alignment of the road. In other areas the road cuts across ridge and furrow with their former continuity shown. This ploughing predates the road. Sometimes the turnpike took the line of a previous track.

All kinds of details can be collected about vegetation along the route and observations made upon the landscape. The road can be

(Victoria and Albert Museum).

Beilby Glass.

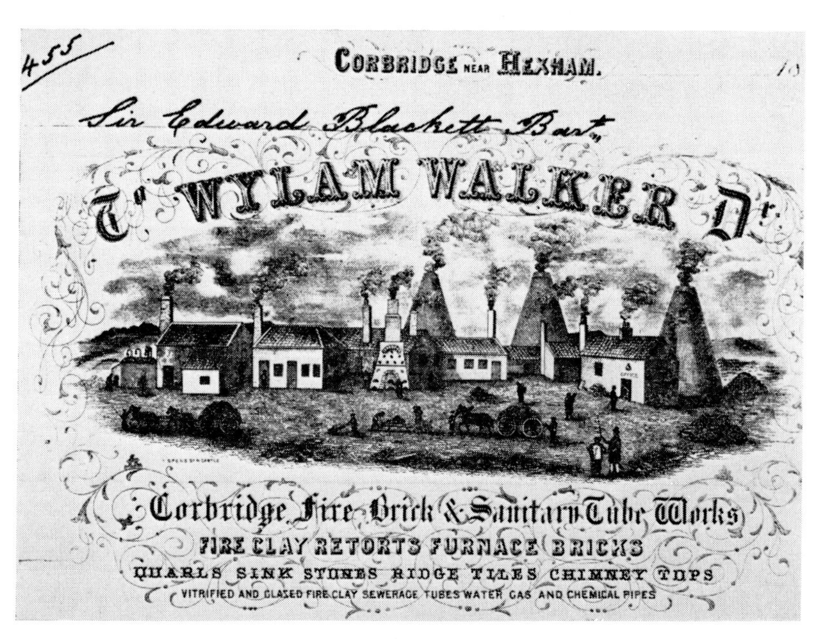

Corbridge Works.

Bewick's Workshop, Newcastle.

[illegible] A 19th-century castellated mansion

made the basis of a general study. (Two ash trees recently cut down near Rothley cross roads gave ring counts (years of growth) of 191 years and 231 years. On the basis of rings per inch of wood the results were 200 and 240 respectively.)

One might start from Hexham, an attractive market town from a description of Dibdin (1838). He saw the abbey, tower and grammar school. Then he went to the market place.

'I do not remember to have seen a market place—even in my own town of Normandy—exhibit a more lively picture than did this of Hexham, on the day of our visit. Rival vendors, pitted against each other, in carts, made the air ring with their vociferations. Hardware glittered here: crockery was spread out there: hats maintained a sable phalanx in a third place; while, in a fourth, a stentorian orator appeared to be almost splitting his cheeks, as well as almost bursting his lungs, in an elaborate eulogy upon a pair of corduroy small clothes. The audience, collected in pretty good numbers, seemed to look on in silent wonder; but no purchase was made during my observation of the motley scene. There was a man in a cart, hard by, who ever and anon, kept thrusting forward knives, razors, hatchets and axes; displaying an agility and an escape from accident, in a manner that perfectly astonished me. He should be hired for Astley's or Sadler's Wells. A bell tolled at the hour of one and every vendor and orator became silent—at his dinner meal.'

Dibdin had travelled from Newcastle by train to Hexham, but he travelled along our road towards Chesters, crossing the Tyne to the north of Hexham by a fine eighteenth-century bridge. The road follows the east bank of the North Tyne with the church of St John Lee standing far above. (1818, a Dobson design.) The Fallowfield area was noted for its leadmines, but Dibdin was making for Chesters, the home of Mr Clayton. He describes it.

'A delightful mansion, delightfully situated—based upon a slice of Severus's Wall—cellars, where barley and the grape held alternate dominion—drawing rooms, where good breeding and good pictures unite to make your heart buoyant—a dining room, replenished and adorned with all the rites of hospitality—quick interchange of lively and winning discourse—all this was only a portion of the accompaniments of our reception at Chesters.'

He continued afterwards along the military road towards Naworth Castle, the residence of the Earl of Carlisle. There were some 20 miles to a change of horses.

Our road crosses the Military Road east of Chollerford. Then the Newcastle-Carlisle Railway had a station at Humshaugh—it is now converted into a riverside house and the metals have gone. The road passes a farm called Dunkirk, and then is crossed by the railway on a fine bridge which has angled arches. There was a station at Chollerton which has disappeared, and the stable for the church has been converted to a Post Office. The farm opposite has a windmill-like tower for a granary as well as the chimney of a steam engine. Swinburne Castle is in process of demolition. The quarries of the neighbourhood continue to supply roadstone as they did for turnpikes. Hereabouts the Hexham road crosses Dere Street and passes through Colwell. There are reservoirs on either hand to supply Newcastle and Gateshead with water.

A castle-like dovecote crowns the hill and in the trees, a mile further on, is Bavington Hall—built for Delavals and now inhabited by Shaftoes.

Great Bavington, to the west, was a Nonconformist centre and further on the parklands of Kirkharle show the influence of Capability Brown. The road now crosses the Newcastle-Otterburn route. New Deanham, to the east, was built in 1669-70 and has not been much altered. Wallington is seen over the Wansbeck and is approached by Paine's fine eighteenth-century bridge. Here the road joins the Newcastle-Cambo route, which comes in from the east. Cambo, north of Wallington Hall, is another estate village. The milestones are now clearly marked and the road makes its way past Hartington Hall to Gallows hill, where the milestone shows 21 miles from Hexham. Here the road joins the Elsdon-Morpeth route. They part company at Rothley cross roads and the route is scenically beautiful. Here are visible artificial lakes and fortifications. The Rothley lime works have recently closed, but the large kilns are still visible and the line of a tramway to the quarries. The quarries were able to make use of the Rothbury Railway. The line has gone but the bridges remain. The road passes over the railway here and under it at Ewesley. From this point can be seen the arches of the Fontburn viaduct and the reservoir beyond.

At Forestburngate is an inn, the Crown and Thistle, depending upon travellers and here again the road crosses the railway. There is a long open stretch of road climbing towards Garleigh with the hills on the one hand and the green pastures, showing signs of the earlier plough, to the south.

There is also evidence of intermittent mining and the Wardshill coal mine still functions.

The landscape of Cragside can be seen from the height and the road descends into Rothbury, past the disused station and over the old bridge. The distance from Hexham is 31 miles.

On leaving Rothbury the road follows the north bank of the Coquet eastwards, before turning sharply northwards through the trees of Cragside. There is a steep ascent to the open moors, but even here one passes pit houses. This must have been a hard stretch for horses —a rise of something like 700 feet in four miles.

The eighth milestone from Alnwick is near Wellhope Knowe, and there is a steep descent to Newmoor House. Here the route crosses the Wooler way and the old coach road can be seen taking a higher route to the south above the present roadway. Rimside was a notorious place to travellers and was considered the worst part of the route. The cross roads today have a bad reputation for accidents. Having crossed the Wooler way, the Alnwick road crosses the Roman Devil's Causeway. Hereabouts can be found both types of milestone. Edlingham lies to the north and the rectory was the place of a robbery that reached the level of national importance and a Parliamentary enquiry into police action in the late nineteenth century. Also evident from here are the windings and disappearance of the Coldstream-Alnwick Railway. It was probably the most expensive piece of railway construction in Northumberland, and was built for prestige, not profit. Bridges, tunnels, viaducts and great cuttings were involved. By contrast the roadway to Alnwick is almost contemptuously straight and a distance of some 12 miles from Rothbury is completed.

The final stretch of the roadway ran eastwards from Alnwick between mills at Allerdean and Bilton. There were further mills at Lesbury and the way came to an end at Alnmouth, keeping on the north side of the river. The bridge over the Aln to the south was constructed in the middle of the last century and named after the Duchess of Northumberland. By then Alnmouth was more a seaside pleasure place than a port.

In dealing with these journeys information can be obtained from newspapers, magazines and the writings of travellers. There was a good deal of travelling for pleasure or curiosity in the eighteenth century and early nineteenth century. Contributions were made to periodicals. Defoe can be regarded as a journalist, so can Cobbett. Boswell took Dr Johnson on a Scottish tour and Sir Walter Scott travelled a great deal.

Various types of maps can be used in conjunction to discover the changes that have taken place over periods of time. The most recent 1 inch Ordnance Survey maps of Northumberland indicate very considerable changes since 1948. The changes can be traced back further still through a century of changing maps. Estate plans and maps for turnpikes indicate further developments. A turnpike might be imposed on a pre-existing system of farm tracks and by-ways. All kinds of little changes have taken place with corners of a winding way chopped off. Hedges may indicate the old track. The line of the North Road can be seen rising over the hill at Helm between Morpeth and Felton. All kinds of relics of horse transport can be observed. Some coal merchants, tinkers and gypsies still use horses. Breweries, too, keep horses together with drays and vans. Ponies are still used in mines and by hauliers of sea coal. There are numerous mounting blocks that can be noted and also rings for tethering. Inns often retain the old stables converted to other uses. A number of smiths are still at work, though shoeing horses now tends to be a side line and they are concerned with repairs to mechanical things. Cobbled streets, still existing in towns, are a reminder of the age of horse transport.

There is a good deal of harness still lying about in farm buildings, and it needs to be rescued for Museum purposes. Horse brasses have become collector's pieces and so have authentic post-horns. (Replicas are readily available.)

Toll houses are rapidly disappearing. The one at Knowesgate has been demolished (A696) and so has the one at Rudchester (B6318). The attractive little house at Cowden is derelict and the one at Bewclay is in a precarious position. A few should have preservation orders, even if it means extending the road the other way rather than at the cost of the toll house. They would make ideal observation points for R.A.C. or A.A. Scouts.

Bridges too can be measured, sketched, photographed and recorded, since many of these are being rendered unsafe by heavy wagons. It is possible to see the old and new bridge side by side, as at Felton and Warkworth.

A grave-stone in Matfen churchyard reads as follows:

ERECTED
TO THE MEMORY
OF
JOSEPH FRASER
ROAD SURVEYOR
OF
MATFEN BURNSIDE
who died on the 11th of May 1846.
Aged 40 years.

THE INN AND THE INNKEEPER

'There can be little that inspires the reminiscent imagination more than the history of the old inns of England, which through centuries have waved their signs of open welcome to all who passed their way: and wherein men of all classes have met to pass the time of day and to exchange views on matters of immediate interest: great names perhaps unwitting each of the other's identity.' (Sir Edwin Lutyens.)

The inn is the social centre of the village and an important source of information. The affairs of the village are here discussed and made known: news is received here. The inn itself as a building may be of considerable age—it may have been an ordinary house converted into a hostelry. The inn sign and name may be of very considerable interest. It may carry the name of a great local or national character or King. This can often indicate the period and the sign of 'White Hart' or 'Black Bull' may have heraldic significance. Inns like the Masons' or Joiners' Arms may be associated with early trade unions or Friendly Societies. Some have religious significance and the 'Angel' may well be of medieval date originally. 'The Lamb and Flag' is another. There were many ale-houses in medieval times with the sign of the evergreen bush. These were managed often by women and open to all. Inns were not very common, since full hospitality was provided by monasteries. Inns were however established to provide extra accommodation for pilgrims and a sign might be the medieval equivalent of A.A. or R.A.C. approval.

In the fifteenth century more inns were built and in the sixteenth century still more. In Shakespeare's time inns were meeting places for poets and plays might be performed in inn yards.

The Church in the later sixteenth century did not concern itself so much with these matters and Puritans condemned both drinking and play acting. But more accommodation was needed for travelling people and the number of inns increased. They were particularly associated with the development of roads and the increasing number of coaches as well as the usual riders. The inns were at strategic positions on the coach routes and the traveller had time for refreshments while the horses were changed. 'Click-em In' refers to the quick turn about. The inns provided the necessary space for travellers and also food and drink. Good stabling was essential with a plentiful supply of corn and hay for the horses. Remote inns depended upon travelling people and occasional visits from isolated farmers. Increasing motor traffic in modern times has brought back custom to them. Inns often retain momentoes of the old coaching days. In the eighteenth and early nineteenth centuries some of them were associated with cock-fighting and the popular bare-fist contests. Others were directly associated with smuggling of foreign spirits and the circulation of whisky distilled in the remote valleys or dales of the north. The ruined inn on Rimside Moor near the crossing of the Morpeth-Cornhill and Rothbury-Alnwick roads had a notorious reputation.

The Olde Cross Inn, Alnwick.

Inn names reflect social history—The Fat Ox may refer to the eighteenth-century monster of the Agrarian revolution, when breeders competed in producing massive cattle. The Dun Cow however is a reference to St Cuthbert of Durham. The 'Old Hundredth' at North Shields and the 'Sun' at Morpeth are ready to welcome visitors from church. The 'Four Alls' at Ovington (Yorks.) refers to the Queen (Victoria) 'I govern All': the soldier 'I fight for all': the clergyman 'I pray for all': and the farmer or John Bull 'I pay for all'.

The Wellington Hotel - Riding Mill

The 'Travellers Rest' was inviting, but the 'Three Horse Shoes' meant a compulsory stay! The 'Ship' welcomed the sailor home from sea, as well as others. The Engine and Railway Inns indicate a new form of power or transport that was to lead to the decline of the stagecoach. Hotels may also illustrate the concern in the middle of the last century about the evils of drink. The 'Two Queens' of Cambo was closed by Sir Walter Trevelyan and a Temperance Hotel appeared at Scots Gap on the new railway. At Matfen the Temperance Hotel and the Black Bull co-exist, overlooking the full flow of drinking water in the aqueduct of the Whittledean Waterworks. At Elsdon John Gallon's house of 1729, once called the Crown, has become a farm-house only and Bacchus sits on his barrel humorously above the door of the neighbouring house. The 'Bird And Bush' is still there:

a variation of the 'Bird In Hand'. The 'Cock and Bull' anywhere is a reminder of the telling of tall stories, not of cock-fighting or bear-baiting. The 'Royal French Arms' at Throckley is a reminder of French refugees in this county during the period of the revolution. Lord Nelson and the Duke of Wellington had their names honoured many times as did the great men of the neighbourhood. The Marquis of Granby, in the middle of the eighteenth century, was concerned about the welfare of sailors and soldiers and innkeepers (sometimes ex-sailors) remembered him. Collingwood, Delaval, Ridley and Percy are remembered by name as well as by sign. The Queen's Head often referred to Elizabeth I and the 'Crown and Thistle' (Forestburngate), or the 'Rose and Thistle' (Alwinton), were intended to appeal to the loyalty of Englishmen and Scots alike.

It can be of great interest to use inns and taverns for the study of communications as well as of particular locality. Their numbers in an area over a period of time can be an indication of growth or decline of certain elements of population. For example, mining or factory communities would require extra provision, whereas scattered farming communities might have to be content with home brewed ale. The Directories of Parson and White in the 1820s and those of Bulmer 1887-8 give lists of hotels, inns and ale-houses together with the names of the proprietors. This information can be compared with information obtained about the provision for religion and education in the same areas.

RICHARDSON, A. *English Inns*. Batsford.
ANDERSON, M. D. *History on the Highway*. Faber.
GRAHAM, F. *North Country Inn Signs*. F. Graham.
Old Inns and Taverns of Northumberland. F. Graham.
BACHELOR, D. *Old English Inns*. Batsford.

Scottish & Newcastle Breweries: Vaux Breweries provide information and produce brochures and booklets.

The Brewers' Society have published a booklet on Inns and a History of the Scottish & Newcastle Breweries is being written.

Travellers through time

Reminiscences or reports by travellers are one method of obtaining information. Travellers may be well informed or superficial, but their impressions may be worth considering as a basis for correction. Also they do reveal difficulties experienced in travelling and these can be compared with modern problems. Again what did they look for and what discover? Some of the travellers in Northumberland have been—

BOGG, EDMUND. *One Thousand Miles of Wandering in the Border Country*. 1898.

CAMDEN, WILLIAM. *Britannia*. London 1586 in Latin. Translated into English by Philemon Holland. London 1610. David & Charles reprint.

COBBETT, WILLIAM. *Rural Rides*. London 1830. Published in 2 vols. by Dent in Everyman Edition.

DEFOE, DANIEL. *A Tour thro' the whole Island of Britain*. 3 vols. 1724-7. Everyman Edition 2 vols.

DIBDIN, T. F. *Bibliographical Tour of England and Scotland*. 1838.

FIENNES, CELIA. *Journeys of Celia Fiennes 1685 to 1703*. Edition by C. Morris. Cresset Press 1947.

GARDINER, L. *Stage-Coach to John O'Groats*. Hollis and Carter 1961.

GRAHAM, P. ANDERSON. *Highways and Byways in Northumbria*. Macmillan 1921.

JAMIESON, M. *Coaching in the North Country*. F. Graham 1969.

LAWSON. *The Military Road. Archaeologia Aeliana* 1966.

LELAND, JOHN. *Itinerary c. 1540*. Published in 9 vols. Oxford 1710-12.

MOOREHOUSE, G. *Companion to Northumberland*. Methuen 1953.

MORLEY, F. *Great North Road*. Hutchinson 1962.

MORRIS, J. E. *Northumberland*. Methuen 1917.

Murray's Handbooks—1864, 1873, 1890.

TOMLINSON. *Comprehensive Guide to Northumberland*.

VALE, E. *North Country*. Batsford 1937.

Ward's North of England Directory 1851.

WESLEY, J. *Journals*. He was very much in the North.

YOUNG, ARTHUR. *A Six Months' Tour thro' the North of England*. 4 vols. 1770-1.

RAILWAYS, WAGONWAYS AND TRAMWAYS

Railways, wagonways and tramways belong to the same family. Great difficulties were experienced in conveying heavy loads by wheeled vehicles or sledges over old tracks or roads. The wagonway consisted of supports or sleepers carrying parallel rails on which carts or trucks could be retained by means of flanged wheels. The invention is said to be Northumbrian, but there is some reason to believe that Huntington Beaumont of Leicestershire introduced the wagonway in the Cowpen-Bebside area when a group of Midland mining magnates attempted to win coal cheaply in this area in the early seventeenth century. The attempt was a costly failure, but the wagonway seems to have developed. It was found to be the best way of bringing coals from the pit-head to the place of loading on to ships.

One of the early wagonways is that leading from the Plessey Mines to the port of Blyth, and this can still be traced for the greater part of the route. The very steady descent to the sea meant that hauling a large wagon was little trouble for a horse and the empty wagon was easily brought back. This wagonway existed in the early eighteenth century and its line was altered later. John Gibson's Map of the Collieries on the Rivers Tyne and Wear (1787) shows the wagonways also. Furthermore it gives interesting information about the land-owners and their seats. The roads are also included, showing very considerable differences from the present day. It also shows the centres of population. The map is reproduced in Archive Unit No. 3 (Railways in the Making) which is strongly recommended for a study of early wagonways. They are directly connected with the development of mining. The use of coal depended upon facilities that were available for transportation. Canals were not developed in North-umberland, and wagonways provided the method of moving heavy loads. Horses provided the power, by means of the gin, for raising coal from mines.

The other essential development was that of the steam engine—originally used for pumping water from mines, but converted to other purposes. Stationary steam engines were used in mills and also to haul loads up inclines. Some of the wagonways had these steam engines installed at strategic points for the steeper gradients. On self acting inclines the loaded wagons, descending, hauled up the empties on an endless rope system—the empty wagons had a braking effect too.

A Cornishman, Richard Trevithick, is credited with the first loco-motive and Christopher Blackett had one constructed for Wylam colliery, but it proved too heavy for the wagonway. In 1813 William Hedley built his Puffing Billy and Wylam Dilly, which were smooth wheeled engines (no rack was necessary). However, they proved heavy for the rails and for a time, till stronger rails were invented, they were each given eight wheels instead of four, in order to spread the load.

George Stephenson invented his Blucher in 1814, copying the ideas of others, but his great success was the construction of the Stockton-Darlington line which was opened in 1825. His Locomotion was here triumphant and showed its advantage over the stationary steam engine. The problem of providing sufficiently strong iron rails was solved by John Birkinshaw at the Bedlington Ironworks on the banks of the Blyth, not far from Huntington Beaumont's original wooden way.

In 1829 Stephenson built the locomotive that won the Rainhill Trials for the Liverpool to Manchester Railway. This was an event of national importance and the Prime Minister, the Duke of Wellington, attended the ceremonial opening in 1830. On this occasion William Huskisson, ex-President of the Board of Trade and one time MP for Morpeth, was killed. But the Railway Age had begun. The building of railways became an epic struggle against physical features, the elements and determined opposition. It involved the greatest changes to the landscape that man had seen—crossing morasses, bridging of rivers and ravines, the excavation of great cuttings, the piling of great embankments and the driving of lengthy tunnels. This was done mainly by man power and horse power, and involved great efforts of organization. Railway building became almost a mania, and the north played a leading part in this.

Railways were originally devised for the carrying of heavy loads and a complicated network developed between various collieries and the ports or staithes. There was no rationalization about this and railways appeared as chaotic as our present day jumble of pipes and power lines. Some lines had a very short life and others were projected, but remained undeveloped. With the growth of passenger traffic (which was not originally intended) and the increasing speed of locomotives (Stephenson's 30 m.p.h. was breath-taking), some co-ordination was needed and various points were linked, making use of colliery lines. Here information comes by comparing maps of different dates, showing the development of main and branch lines. A great deal of capital was involved. The Newcastle-Carlisle Railway was approved by Act of Parliament in 1829, but was not fully open till 1839.

Dibdin, in 1838, travelled from Newcastle to Hexham by rail. Of Newcastle he declared 'The very spirit of steam may be said to take up its permanent abode. The marvellous manufactory of Mr Stephenson alone occupies 400 workmen, for the supply of steam engines to all parts of the world. It would follow that, while the breast of the River Tyne was bearing up countless steamers that are ploughing its yielding surface, the land would also bear evidence of the same propelling power; and accordingly a Rail Road to Hexham, Haydon Bridge and Carlisle, was no sooner planned than executed. The success has been complete and the pencil of the artist has been called in aid to illustrate and confirm the talents of the engineer.'

The artist was Carmichael and a reprint of the illustrated book is now available.

Dibdin went to the station by horse vehicle 'and in about half an hour we saw the mighty train prepared to receive us. We were off at a tangent. Horses, dogs, sheep and pigs—coal, wood, pitch, tar, hemp and tallow—carriages, carts and gigs were all picturesquely arranged, as the electrical shock took place, which told us that we were in movement. The whizzing steam and trailing smoke denoted everything to be in full play. At first we seemed to be shot through the air, but the pace slackened a little, giving us time not only to notice the several stages or stations, but breath to express our admiration at the elegance of their structure in stone. It should still seem to be the region of chaste architecture ... Now we stopped to take up a sportsman, upon his cob, with his double barrelled gun and a brace of pointers; and now to eject a miller with sundry sacks of flour. The party in the particular machine which we occupied was rather select, well dressed and disposed not only to be happy among themselves, but with everything about and around them. There was female elegance and beauty. A passenger secretly remarked to me "'twas a bridal party and the happy pair were to spend the day in Hexham".'

Here Dibdin left the train and, after looking round Hexham, went by carriage to Chesters. He has left a delightful picture of early travel by train.

Sykes—Local Records Vol. III p. 92—gives this account for June 18th, 1838. 'The Newcastle and Carlisle Railway was opened through its whole extent from Redheugh, a little to the west of Gateshead, to the city of Carlisle. The vast number of ladies and gentlemen who had assembled for the purpose of travelling to the other end of the line, the countless spectators and the numerous bands of music, made up a scene of great animation and gaiety. At half past twelve o'clock the signal was given for the engines to start, when the Rapid was despatched as an advanced guard, without any train and was followed by 13 other engines, drawing 120 well filled carriages. The aggregate number of passengers in all the trains was estimated at nearly 4,000 and the trains when close together, above half a mile in length. The gay procession was received with great enthusiasm along the route, particularly at Corbridge, Hexham and Haydon Bridge, and the whole party reached Carlisle between 5 and 6 o'clock. The shades of night had set in before the trains commenced their homeward journey and the first did not arrive at Redheugh until between 2 and 3 o'clock in the morning and many of them at a much later hour.'

June 18th, the anniversary of Waterloo, was a favourite date for these celebrations, and ten years later (1844) the Newcastle to Darlington

Railway was opened, thus connecting Newcastle with London. Three trains from Newcastle reached York and were joined by a train from London. All proceeded to Newcastle.

On July 1st 1847. 'The remaining portion of the Newcastle and Berwick Railway, namely from Morpeth to Chathill, was opened for public traffic, thus completing the great line of railway communications between London and Edinburgh. On July 5th the mail coach between Newcastle and Edinburgh arrived in the former town for the last time, after being established for 61 years.'

Now we witness the closure of the railways and significantly to passenger traffic before goods. There are similar scenes for 'last' trains.

The Newcastle-Edinburgh line at first used temporary bridges and along this route some magnificent viaducts were built. The Royal Border Bridge was begun in 1847 by Robert Stephenson and completed in 1850. On August 29th it was formally opened by Queen Victoria. On July 29th, 1850 occurred the ceremonial opening of Dobson's impressive Central Station—a very fine piece of railway architecture with a classical stone portico and a large enclosure roofed in great curves of iron and glass.

Another development was that of the Blyth and Tyne Railway. The local ports of Blyth and Seaton Sluice had insufficient water for any but small vessels, and coal shipping could be seriously limited. The coal owners were anxious to obtain direct access to the Tyne and use was made of the Seghill Railway (1847).

An extension was made to Bedlington, crossing the Blyth on a timber viaduct 80 feet in height and 770 feet in length, very near to the site of the ironworks, which made rails and locomotives for a considerable period, but the location proved unsuitable in face of strong competition and the ironworks that played an important part in early railway development were closed by 1867.

The longer railway routes were brought about by the larger Railway Companies who were in competition, especially for traffic between England and Scotland. In the north there was the NER Company, based on York, and the North British, based on Edinburgh. The former controlled the Edinburgh to Newcastle route and the latter had a main route from Edinburgh to Carlisle. In 1862 the North British took over the Border Counties Railway from Riccarton to Hexham. By agreement with the NER the NBR obtained the right to use the line from Hexham to Newcastle. They also hoped to take over the Blyth and Tyne Railway from Newcastle to Morpeth opened in 1857.

In 1865 was opened the so-called 'Wannie' line from Morpeth to Redesmouth, providing an independent route to Scotland. The railway was expected to provide transport from the Ridsdale iron mines and for other products. There would be transport for passengers and also for farm animals. Yet another route was provided from Newcastle to Edinburgh. The North British also prompted the establishment of a Northumberland Central Railway Company (from 1863) to construct a line from Scots Gap through Rothbury, Thropton and Hartburn to join the Edinburgh-Carlisle route at St Boswell's. A branch line was in fact constructed to Rothbury and opened in 1870. In 1872 it was taken over by the North British.

The North Eastern Railway Company was forced by public pressure, especially in the Alnwick area, to construct a competing line. This linked Alnwick with Wooler and thence to Cornhill. It was a difficult line to construct and never an economic proposition. It provided travellers with a rather picturesque route. Closure was forced by the floods of 1948 that swept away a number of bridges and also weakened the bridge over the Tyne at Hexham for the Riccarton route.

These routes in construction extended railways to the maximum limits and in the twentieth century closures have been characteristic of the period of decline. The same applies to collieries and many lines were intended to serve collieries only. It is an interesting essay in detection to trace them in the field and to obtain supplementary information from relevant maps. Another example of a railway that did not survive is the mineral line from Tongues Pit near Kirkheaton to Ponteland. It was intended to convey coal direct to Newcastle, but the attempt was a costly fiasco. Water took over the mine and the railway became derelict. It was removed for scrap metal at the beginning of the war (1940).

Railway lines were extremely dangerous to intruders and iron notices still exist in various parts, threatening trespassers with a £2 fine. These notices have enormous strength for survival and are eloquent of the Railway Age. They now overlook forgotten stretches of embankment and it is now possible to explore railways without peril, though, depending on the situation, there may still be trespass. These routes should be public routes for walking and riding, since they pass through particularly attractive country. At one time British Railways ran Scenic Excursions calling at the little station gardens. These are now mostly derelict and the buildings often in a ruinous state. Some might have been retained as hostels.

The railway provides a good subject for local study covering a fairly extensive area and dealing with territory that is different from that of the road. This comes from the very nature of the railway, which has to avoid steep inclines. It provides part of the interest for the lines from Morpeth to West Woodburn, or Rothbury, from Alnwick to Wooler and the route from Hexham to Riccarton. The line between Riccarton and Carlisle has been closed, though some attempt is being made to restore the route by a Railway Preservation Society.

The railway enthusiast can see the problems of the route—Stephenson walked the route he intended to use for a railway. The embankments, cuttings, viaducts and bridges can be recorded. Some are preserved for farm purposes and the unusual viaduct at Kielder, constructed to harmonize with the Duke of Northumberland's Gothic castle, has now been preserved by the National Trust.

Notice may be taken of the communities and the industries that the line was constructed to serve. It is now perhaps strange that the railway, disliked as bringing noise and smoke into a quiet landscape, is now accepted as a general part of it. Vegetation takes advantage of the situation and plant growth on the abandoned trackway can be a study in itself. Some plants have a temporary lease, before others take over and a great deal depends on the growth of tree cover.

It is possible to visualize the route as if from a train window by walking along the abandoned track. A brief look at the Wannie may serve as an example.

The Wansbeck Valley Railway was opened on May 1st, 1865 and the distance from Morpeth to Redesmouth is 25 miles. The timetable shows three trains a day each way and providing for three classes. The time taken either way was approximately one hour, twenty-five minutes. The full journey from Newcastle (New Bridge) to Edinburgh took 5 hours and 10 minutes. The full life span of the railway has been 101 years. The closure in the autumn of 1966, was followed by the complete removal of the metals and the fittings. It is now a piece of 'Industrial Archaeology'.

Starting at Morpeth, there can be seen the Old Station Buildings, now used for goods purposes. The Blyth line comes in from the south and some of the old equipment remains. The present Morpeth Station with a canopy of iron and glass over the platforms has been partly demolished. There is a map of coloured tiles set in the wall, showing the railways of the north-east in the early twentieth century. The old water tank has gone, and some damage was done by the recent accident. The remains of the Wannie line, retained as a siding, were torn up. The old line passed the hospital and crossed the A1 over a bridge, wide enough for a double track. On either side the land, partly a golf course, shows the ridge and furrow of the common fields. Operations are in progress on the Morpeth by-pass and the pharmaceutical factory has been completed. All this should have been east of the town. The neglected route follows through the lush pastures of Mitford and Meldon, divided by hawthorn hedges. The cornfields reveal their 'native sites' to the camera of the air photographer.

The trains, when running, could be used to tell the time, since on a single track railway, the whole line from Morpeth to Scots Gap, Scots Gap to Rothbury or Redesmouth, had to be clear before a train could enter. The men of the fields about Mitford and Meldon would tell the time of day from the trains and they would be able to tell the difference in tone of the locomotive in each direction. Outwards it was imperious and on its return much more complacent.

Some of the scenes would make Constable landscapes with buildings of rich stone and red pantiles, fields of buttercups and hedges of may. The browsing cattle were used to the trains and the driver had to be aware of stray sheep. Meldon has a small church and a large rectory. Raine, the historian of North Durham and friend of Hodgson, was once here. The only signs of steam now are the blackening of the bridge by the station and the large chimney of a farm steam engine. Meldon station, once a depot for cattle trucks, is now ruinous, the station house having suffered from fire. Beyond Meldon views are obtained of both Meldon and Angerton Halls, north of the Wansbeck, both built by Dobson. South of the line in the trees can be seen the Saxon tower of Bolam Church.

The next station is Angerton where there is a level crossing and beyond this the railway crosses the Wansbeck. For the rest of the way the line is north of the river. It crosses Devil's Causeway near Marlish and Huckhoe Hill, a British fortified site can be seen to the south. Middleton Station is at the east end of a long village and only the broom covered platforms remain. The railway passes between defensive sites (one called Villain's Bog) to Scots Gap Junction. Here the Rothbury line branched north and here was a turntable as well as a water tank. Scots Gap was and still is a collecting centre for cattle. Formerly many came by train—now all travel by road. Wallington Hall lies at a respectable distance from Scots Gap, where a Temperance Hotel was permitted. Sir Walter Trevelyan was a strong advocate of the railway, but he did not want it too near.

'Just after passing Scots Gap, a newly erected lime kiln of large size is seen. It has been put up by Sir Walter Trevelyan, Bart, one of the most earnest promoters of the line. This will be a great boon to agriculturalists, as placing within their reach a valuable fertilizing agent, hitherto almost unobtainable in many parts of the district through which the line runs.' (From *Newcastle Journal* May 1st, 1865.)

THE KEELMEN'S STRIKE, 1822.

A Victorian Public House on Scotswood Road, Newcastle.

Northumbrian Pitmen, *c.* 1890.

This was a commercial proposition. Now the masonry has been removed, but a long wagonway leads through the trees towards the quarries near Knowesgate. The railway, after passing under the Rothbury-Hexham turnpike, crosses the Knowesgate road by a finely constructed bridge. It rises a hundred feet between Scots Gap and Knowesgate. This was a war-time store and the station house is occupied. It was once the terminus for Armstrong guns on their way to be tested on the range. The railway crosses the Otterburn road and approaches Ray, once the country seat of Sir Charles Parsons. The house was demolished after the war and only cottages and stables remain. The pele tower is in the midst of a pheasantry. The whole of the area was landscaped. Hodgson traversed the old tracks by horse and on foot, making accurate observations on native encampments. He lived for a time at Kirkwhelpington, where fate was hard to him, but he continued his historical work. South of the railway on the Wansbeck is the deserted village of West Whelpington, now being quarried away. It was deserted in Hodgson's time. The country now presents a much wilder aspect as the railway winds over the moorland. In autumn it is colourful with heather and there is the sound of bees and grouse. In winter the aspect is often black and white. The snows of 1963-4 saw an engine with a snow plough stuck for two days (this was back near Catcherside). The highest point of the line is at Summit Cottages, where the train was reduced to walking pace and employees could drop off, when returning from Morpeth Market.

From this point the line descends to West Woodburn, an area of much quarrying. The account of the 1865 opening continues—'Between Woodburn and the terminus at Redesmouth, a loop line connects the new railway with the Ridsdale mines; and from this promising undertaking will proceed the mineral traffic to which we have already referred, there being every probability that it will constitute an important source of revenue to the company.' Large areas were in fact exploited for iron ore by open cast methods and coal seams were also exploited as far as Bellingham and Plashetts. All these are now derelict. Spoil heaps remain and the masonry of the furnaces at Ridsdale. There was also a school and there remain the houses of the employees. The branch line can still be traced and the railway crossed the Rede over a magnificent angled viaduct. This has been demolished. Here is the station of Redesmouth, where the engine sheds remain and a signal cabin. At this junction, one train waited for another to come up or down. One way went by Bellingham and the North Tyne Valley to Riccarton and the other by Barrasford and Humshaugh to Hexham. Both directions present possibilities of exploration and a good deal of railway archaeology.

Other possibilities are individual mineral lines or quarry tramways. Yet another allied subject is that of the electric tramways of Newcastle and Gateshead, developed and completely defunct within half a century.

Visits

1. Newcastle Museum of Science and Industry.
2. York Railway Museum.
3. County Records Office, Melton Park. (See Guide: Appendix C.) Railway plans deposited here.
4. The railway journey, and particularly interesting are the routes from Newcastle to Edinburgh (or Berwick), Newcastle to Carlisle, Newcastle to Alston.
5. A complete expedition by rail.

Investigations can be made into special aspects of railway development—the 'milk' train or the 'fish' train, the excursion train and the effects of the railway upon the life of a community.

Refer to:

GARD, R. M. & HARTLEY, J. R. *Archive Unit No. 3 Railways in the Making*. University of Newcastle.
ABC of the LNER 1947 Re-numbering Edition (nationalization).
ALLEN, C. J. *The LNER*. Ian Allan 1966.
NE Railway. Ian Allan 1964.
BAXTER, B. *Stone Blocks and Iron Rails*. David & Charles 1966.
Bradshaw's *Railway Guides*.
FOWKES, E. H. *Railway History & the Local Historian*. (E. Yorks. Local History Society.)
HAMILTON ELLIS, C. *The Engines that passed*. Allen & Unwin.
The Trains we loved. Allen & Unwin.
British Railway History Vol. 1 1830-76. Vol. 2 1876-1947. Allen & Unwin.
HOOLE, K. *Regional History of British Railways*. Vol. IV North-East England. David & Charles.
Railway History in Pictures. The North East. David & Charles.
HEARSE, C. S. *The Tramways of Northumberland*. Andrew Reed 1961.
LEE, C. F. 'Wagonways of Tyneside'. *Archaeologia Aeliana* 1951.
MARSHALL, C. F. D. *History of British Railways to 1830*. 1938.

MACLEAN, J. S. *Newcastle and Carlisle Railway. 1825-62.* Robinson 1948.

Northumberland County Records Office. Catalogue to Railway Exhibition.

PAINE, E. M. S. *The Two James's and the Two Stephensons.* 1861. New Ed. 1961. Phoenix.

ROLT, L. T. C. *George and Robert Stephenson.* Longmans 1960.

ROBBINS, M. *Points and Signals.* Allen & Unwin 1967.

Scott's *Railway Companion.* 1837.

SIMMONS, J. *Railways of Britain.* Kegan & Paul 1961. *Reprinted.* Macmillan 1968.

Stephenson Exhibition 1948. Lang Gallery Catalogue.

TOMLINSON, W. W. *The North Eastern Railway: its Rise and Development.* (1914, reprinted 1967.)

VALLANCE, H. A. *British Branch Lines.* Batsford.

WARREN, J. G. H. *A century of Locomotive Building by Robert Stephenson & Co. 1823-1923.* A. Reid 1923.

Newcastle and Carlisle Railway. Views by Carmichael. Reprint F. Graham.

COAL MINING AND IRONWORKS

In 1895 Cadwalder J. Bates in the last paragraph of his *History of Northumberland* wrote—'Agriculture has suffered comparatively less in Northumberland than in many other counties: still, the problem of how to keep any population on the land is none the less pressing. It is harrowing to see in many districts the ruins of what until recently were smiling homesteads, where stalwart families were brought up in health and happiness. What will occur in the not distant future, when the coalfields will be exhausted, it is difficult to foresee.'

He noted as remarkable the changes made at Blyth Harbour, the result being that whereas in 1883 146,264 tons of coal were shipped, in 1894 the quantity had risen to 2,643,778 tons. The output of Northumberland collieries had risen from 1,053,274 tons in 1794 to 6,463,550 tons in 1874 and in 1894 the total was 9,541,199 tons. Coal was a great source of wealth for the neighbourhood. The effects of coal winning were the development of collieries, spoil heaps, wagonways and miners' houses. The coal owners had improved residences at a distance, and smoke rose from the funnels of steamers and locomotives, from factory chimneys and from those of the ever-growing spread of houses.

Now other forms of power have replaced steam, but coal is still an important basic material. It has been used from prehistoric times, but the most remarkable developments have been from the time of Elizabeth I. An expanding London had to depend increasingly for fuel on supplies of Newcastle coal—'sea coal' because this was the method of transport that gave Newcastle the advantage.

There were growing demands for coal for house-heating (which involved the construction of enclosed chimneys) and for industrial purposes.

A lot of the old coal workings are unrecorded, revealed only by a collapse of the land surface or by modern opencast mining that lays bare the old pillar and stall system. Pillars of coal were left in place to prevent subsidence. There were numerous bell pits, which consist each of a circular deposit of spoil with a central depression. The coal was reached by digging a large well-like hole and this provided the centre for workings that were extended to the limits of safety. Regulations to prevent these pits becoming dangerously close were formulated. Coal was raised from the depths by windlass. A plan in the Public Record Office shows the situation at Cowpen in 1597. The lands were Crown lands (the result of the confiscation of monastic property) and mining rights were leased. On this occasion a freeholder demanded compensation. The plan shows some 15 pits or holes at strategic distances, several are shown with windlasses. The strips of the open fields are also shown. A lot of this mining went on unrecorded, and it was to this area that Huntington Beaumont came to seek his fortune.

The comparatively small 'bell pits' can be discovered over wide areas, where local seams were used for local purposes. There are numerous examples to the north of Netherwitton and also near Elsdon and Monkridge. There is another series in the area of Ros Castle, near Chillingham. There are also pits in the area of the Lee, south of Rothbury. Larger developments here put an end to a projected Spa at Chirm, where there were mineral waters. Baths were projected at Blyth, but the sea itself had healthy effects and the place developed on ships and coal. Whitley Bay became the seaside resort. The development of the coal trade had the effect of ruining streams and the landscape for a considerable period in coal mining sectors of the county.

The growth of deeper mining was assisted by the development of the steam pump and the Davy Safety Lamp after the Felling Explosion of 1812. The Rev. John Hodgson, then incumbent of Heworth, played an important part in obtaining improvements. Ventilation of mines was obtained by a system of passages and blockings underground to bring the air where it was needed. For this purpose a fire was kept burning under the ventilation shaft. The air rising through this chimney brought fresh air into the mine through the other shaft. A number of these ventilation shafts can still be seen.

The form of power for a considerable period was the horse gin, working on the same principle as the farm machine. The horse went round and round, turning an upright shaft on which was a large revolving drum or wheel carrying the cable. In course of time the steam engine replaced the horse for its main task, but the horse gin was retained for emergency purposes. Wagonways have already been mentioned as a method of removing coals from the pit heads. The termini were often staithes of stout timber along which coal wagons could be hauled. Drops or spouts conveyed the coal into the holds of ships. On the Tyne there was considerable opposition from the keelmen, whose task had been to convey coals on their 'keels' to waiting ships. They were now threatened with redundancy.

The steam engine was originally developed for the pumping of water from mines. This was always a problem and limited the extent of early mining. The sump would retain a certain amount of water only and drifts or drainage channels were cut with difficulty. Buckets were also used—raised by horse power and designed to tip easily. The 'rag and chain' pump was another method that had long been used. The 'Fire Engine' perfected by Newcomen in the early eighteenth century was ideally suited for pumping. It operated by atmospheric pressure when steam was condensed in the cylinder and an up and down motion could be effected. The 'Fire Engine' was expensive on fuel but coal was there at hand. The water itself, pumped to a height, could provide further power through water wheels.

In the 1780s James Watt developed a steam engine with a rotary motion, which could be used for driving machinery. In turn from this came the locomotive which was developed for hauling coal along the wagonways. Steam engines of various kinds were intimately associated with coal mining, and it is only recently that they have been replaced. Steam engine boilers may now be seen to serve as storage tanks and the tall smoking chimneys of mines have often disappeared. These seemed to be the natural counterpart of the sunken shaft. It was the breaking of the great beam of the steam engine that led to the Hartley Colliery disaster of January 16th, 1862. This cost the lives of 204 men and boys—there is a common monument in Earsdon churchyard. Only after this calamity were two shafts for a colliery compulsory by law.

The development of a mine can often be traced in a particular area. 'Sinkers' Row' may indicate the beginning. These men would be there for a considerable time before the mine produced coal, the presence of which depended on local knowledge of the stratification or by boring. The growth of other rows of houses indicates the development of a mining community. The 'chapel' may be another factor, since Methodism appealed to miners and they were a race of men that moved a great deal. Men came into coal mining from tin or lead mines. Houses for miners by the standards of the day were comparatively well built, and some of the mining villages were built to plan. This is often obscured by decay and the growth of monstrous pit heaps. The mining village had a very distinct community spirit and all kinds of recreational activities were developed—with interest in dogs and pigeons, gardens and brass bands. There were Friendly Societies and the inevitable development of Trade Unions. A lot of information needs to be gathered on these activities, and the story of a mining community is as important to the study of social history as the development of the big estate or the big house. In fact these are two sides to the same picture, but it is more difficult to collect information about the men than the managers. A good deal still needs to be known about working conditions. The Report of the Commission on Mines (1842) cannot be accepted verbatim as applying to the whole country. There is evidence to suggest that although mining was a difficult and dangerous operation, the miner was better off than the farm or factory worker. He was certainly better fed and housed. How many made use of the Mechanics Institute when it was established? How many rose from the ranks? Some became Trade Union leaders and Members of Parliament. It was not unknown for a miner to enter the Church and become a priest. There is a lot of information waiting to be collected and danger that records may be dispersed or destroyed and recollections not recorded.

A river may be used to provide an element of continuity in story or research. The Blyth may be taken as an example. Its meaning is 'gentle' or 'merry' and except at the mouth, where the sea is responsible it is not liable to flooding. The source of the river is a hill beyond Kirkheaton called Blackhill; on this is a ruined stone farmhouse that was long occupied before being abandoned. It overlooks the Tyne valley and about it is a complex of obsolete field walls, but more than this, there are obvious effects of mining. Both coal and limestone were obtained here and some old tracks can be traced.

Kirkheaton, with an eighteenth-century church and a seventeenth-century manor house stands about a village green and is almost surrounded by the cavities of limestone quarries. Another surprising factor is the existence of a small Methodist chapel, now disused. This further suggests mining activities. There is field evidence of earlier mining activities, but recorded evidence of eighteenth-century developments. Borings were made to discover the nature of the local coal deposits and mines were developed. The population of the village in 1801 was 149 and by 1881 it had risen to 170. In 1951 it had fallen to 70 only.

The Bog Hall Colliery closed before the Great War, but after the war an attempt was made to revive the mining industry. It was intended to supply coal direct to ships upon the Tyne, and for this purpose a new railway was constructed at considerable expense, linking the new drift mine at Tongues with Ponteland Railway Station. The experiment was a costly failure. It seems that accurate information was not obtained in advance and the water was too much even for twentieth-century equipment. Cottages had been built at Wallridge, though it had been difficult to find workers. Remains of the colliery can still be seen with considerable spoil heaps and the railway can still be traced. Not far away can be discovered the line of Devil's Causeway on its north-east route. The railway runs approximately west to east. It is a reminder that mining always had its hazards for the speculator. In the last years of the seventeenth century Sir John Fenwick, financially embarrassed before getting involved in treason, had mortgaged his interests in this area to Sir William Blackett. A stone, overgrown with grass, carries the date 1695 and probably gives the time of the final take-over.

There can also be seen the limestone quarries and kilns that helped to improve the land of the surrounding estates. Local coal provided the fuel. To the north of the Blyth in this area lie the lands of the Swinburnes of Capheaton and yet another big estate was that of the Middletons of Belsay. They too were concerned in building country houses, improving farmsteads, constructing roads and using the mineral wealth of the area. Estate villages were developed at Capheaton and Belsay, while other places suffered decline. Bradford and Harnham are examples of this. Brick and tile kilns are noticeable at Capheaton, Belsay and Kirkley. There are corn mills at Bradford, Whalton, Ogle and Kirkley, but in the early nineteenth century gin-gans were being installed on many of the farms and this might mean milling at the farm itself.

A stream near Ogle, joining the Blyth, is called Pitman's syke. Ogle belonged at one time to the Duke of Newcastle, and in 1787, at the time of Gibson's Map, it belonged to the Duke of Portland. Dean Ogle lived at Kirkley with the main church at Ponteland. He was responsible for an obelisk, commemorating the Revolution of

1688 and was the author of a Latin poem, in which he praised the river Blyth. The Blyth is doubled in size by its junction with the Pont. It is surprising that the name of Blyth survived the marriage. The Pont has been used as a source of water from Roman times and Prestwick Carr, a shallow lake, was drained in the last century. At Bellasis the combined waters of Blyth and Pont pass beneath a hump backed bridge and after this 'beautiful seat' comes the 'dark valley' of Blagdon, so named because of the growth of trees. Blagdon Hall was the home of the Whites and then the Ridleys by marriage. The Ridleys acquired a good deal of property on the Blyth. There were coal pits at Downhill and at Plessey. Plessey has a windmill which dates back to 1749 and there is a water mill in the valley below. Plessey was once a thriving little mining community and John Wesley addressed a meeting in a quarry, which probably provided stone for old Hartford Hall. The mining village disappeared when the pits became derelict at the beginning of the nineteenth century. The miners were transferred further down the river to Cowpen. The wagonway ran from the pits of the Plessey area to the port of Blyth and it is plainly marked on Gibson's map.

Sir John Clark (1724) noted in his Journal a 'coalwork' (colliery) some five miles south of Morpeth and two miles east of the highway to Newcastle. There was a 'cassey way' (wagonway) of 4½ feet wide and four miles long carrying the coals to the sea. The coals 'are drawen on a kind of wagon with four thick wheels of solid timber unshod and by one horse'. A model of a wagon made at Blyth for the Great Exhibition of 1851 is one of the prize possessions of the Bowes Museum. Many of these wagons must have run on the Plessey Wagonway.

Hartford House was considered to be one of the great beauties of the River Blyth and the Burdons owed their wealth partly to coal. Hodgson describes it 'like a jewel in the diadem of enchantment, glitters among beautiful woods and grounds on the northern banks of the Blyth'. Mackenzie is a little more restrained. 'There is a large old mansion house and some good farmsteads on this estate. The woody declivities of the river at this place afford some very rich scenery. Hartford House, the seat of the late William Burdon Esq., appears to advantage, seated on the summit of the opposite bank. A neat cottage on the one hand and the stables and coach house on the other, add much to the beauty of the scene.' There was once a hospital in this area, and it is perhaps fitting that Hartford House should be used as a Miners' Convalescent Home.

William Burdon, born in Newcastle in 1764, was educated at the Royal Grammar School and Emmanuel College, Cambridge. He was a brilliant scholar and disappointed his parents by not taking Holy Orders. They were staunch Tories, while he tended to Liberalism. (The Liberals were out of office from 1782-1830.) He obtained a reputation as a philosopher, and among other things wrote a *Life of Napoleon* (1804), of which later he became critical. His most famous work was entitled *Materials for Thinking*. He had Hartford House rebuilt and here spent the last years of his life trying to illustrate the superiority of the mind over the ailments of the body. He died in 1818, and his son followed him politically being a supporter of Earl Grey. By this time mining activities had ceased in the Plessey area, but developments were taking place further down the river. In recent years coal deposits have been exploited on both sides of the Blyth by open cast methods and the whole area is undergoing change. Reference might be made in passing to the Cramlington airship hangar, recently demolished, as an example of remarkable developments.

In the eighteenth century the remarkable area was below Bedlington. 'The seclusion and loveliness of the spot have long been despoiled of their charms and the noise and smoke of trade have usurped their place.' Bedlington was famous for its nailers, for whom iron had to be provided locally. Hence the development of the ironworks. Water power was used for the bellows and hammers of the forges. There was local ironstone (supplemented by scrap from ballast), limestone and timber, when coal could not yet be used in smelting. In 1736 the premises were leased by Wm. Tomlinson of Newcastle, then Malings of Sunderland and later by Hawks and Longridge of Gateshead. A note of sale in a Newcastle Newspaper of 1782 mentions a slitting mill, warehouses, smiths' shops and a dwelling house at Watson's quay. It was said to be capable of producing 500 tons of rod and hoop iron per annum. The sea was a mile away and iron could easily be brought in as ballast.

At a time when the output of pig iron in Northumberland and Durham was not more than 2,000 tons a year, this was considerable even if optimistic. It explains the importance of Bedlington Ironworks for a period, since it was not until 1850 that there was a rapid increase in the output of iron elsewhere. Then Bedlington Ironworks were doomed. By the early nineteenth century the works extended to both sides of the Blyth. Ironwork and chains were made for ships being built in the area and from 1820 iron rails were made for railways.

In 1821 Mr William Jones wrote 'Light has at length shone from the north and I pronounce as my decided opinion that the malleable Iron rail road at Bleddington Works is by far the best I have ever seen both in respect of its material and its form.' (Tomlinson, p. 16.)

Robert Stephenson also testifies to its success. 'But perhaps the best example of this kind of railroad is to be found at Bedlington Ironworks in Northumberland where Mr Longridge has laid about 3 miles of it.' This was for the purpose of bringing coals to the river.

Locomotives were also built here and Daniel Gooch gained his first experience in these works. Joseph Locke, also of Bedlington, gained his first experience of steam traction by seeing a steam engine travelling on the turnpike near Morpeth, in 1829. The engine was built by Messrs R. and W. Hawthorn for a Mr Robson of Alnwick. It was to work and draw a threshing machine. These locomotives were not dissimilar in appearance.

The proprietors of Bedlington Ironworks undertook to provide 1,200 tons of malleable iron rails at £12 10s. per ton for the Stockton to Darlington Railway. A set of spare wheels was made for the engine 'Locomotion', which ran on that railway.

Something like 140 locomotives were made here and some of them were exported. By 1850 a climax had been reached. Old prints show a weir, extensive works and twelve large smoking chimneys or furnaces. There were a number of houses in the valley and on the top of the banks both on the Bedlington and Bebside situations. There were quays on either side and wagonways, but prosperity did not continue. The situation, ideal for the beginning, was too difficult for large scale developments. Access by water was limited and by land it was extremely difficult because of the steep banks. By 1855 the works were closed temporarily and after fitful progress for a few years after 1861, closed finally in 1867. A hundred years later shipbuilding and repair work at Blyth also ceased.

In the *County History* (1909) the site is described thus—'A considerable number of cottages remain at the Bankhead, but the furnaces and buildings of the works have long since fallen into decay.' Now the situation is very much worse. Under a broken bandstand is a stone which once stood proudly over the office door—

Vivitur igne et acqua	We live by fire and water
et ferro, Deo favente	and iron, God willing
G. & B. 1829.	

The site awaits recognition and some rehabilitation at the hands of the industrial archaeologist as a place of national importance comparable with Coalbrookdale. There are still quite a lot of Cyclopean remains in the area, and it could be made attractive to visitors. The port of Blyth has received a new lease of life with the proposed development of aluminium. Its past has been based on iron, coal and ship building. There are traditions both in timber and iron. Iron ships took the place of those of timber: an iron viaduct took the place of a timber one. The mouth of the river is now dominated by the four tall chimneys of Cambois Power Station, but coal still provides the primary impulse. The river Blyth begins and ends on coal.

Another industry on the river that has been discontinued should be briefly mentioned. This is the making of salt: salt was an essential product for preservation purposes. When animals had to be slaughtered in the late autumn they had to be preserved in salt. Up to and including the last war, the family pig was preserved in this way after slaughter. Large quantities of salt in earlier times were needed by the great houses and monasteries. The Bishop of Durham and the Abbot of Newminster had salt pans on the tidal estuary of the Blyth and on the coast. After the Dissolution of the Monasteries, salt making continued under lay proprietors and South Shields also was well known as a place of salt.

The method of salt-making was to construct large iron pans about 20 feet by 12 feet and 14 inches deep. They were made from riveted iron plates and supported from above as well as beneath. Fires of timber or coal below them evaporated the brine and the salt was scraped into wicker containers to dry out. Salt was used among many purposes for curing fish for use on ships. With the development of transport and other methods of preservation, the local salt industry declined. For long enough salt meat was the main item in any diet. Attempts to develop a chemical industry (Alkali works) at Blyth were not successful, nor did the Baths make much impact.

Ship and boat building were begun at Blyth in the middle of the eighteenth century by Edmund Hannay. This industry has a history of 200 years and has not been adequately recorded. It was not mentioned in the recently produced *History of Ship Building in the North East.* (D. Dougan.)

Books

ATKINSON, F. *Some Northumberland Collieries 1824.* Vol. XI Transactions of Arch. & Ant. Society of Northumberland and Durham.
The Great Northern Coalfield 1700-1900. Durham Local History Society.

ASHTON, T. S. *The Industrial Revolution.* O.U.P.

ASHTON, T. S. and SYKES, J. *Coal Industry in the Eighteenth Century.*

BELL, J. T. W. *Plans of the Great Northern Coalfield 1843-61.*

BUDDLE, J. *First Report on Accidents in Coal Mines.*

C.J. *The Compleat Collier*. Reprinted by F. Graham.

GALLOWAY, R. L. *History of Coalmining in Britain*. Reprint David and Charles 1968.

GIBSON, J. *Plans of the Collieries of Tyne and Wear*. 1787.

GREENWELL, G. C. *Glossary of Terms used in the Coal Trade of Northumberland and Durham. 1888*. Reprint Frank Graham.

HAIR, T. H. *Coal Mines of N.E. England 1844*. Reprinted by F. Graham 1969.

HUGHES, E. *North Country Life in the Eighteenth Century*. Oxford 1952.

MOTT, R. A. *History of Coke Making*. 1936.

'London and Newcastle Chaldrons'. *Archaeologia Aeliana* 1962. pp. 227-239.

NEF, J. U. *The Rise of the British Coal Industry*. 1932. 2 vols. (recently reprinted).

SMAILES, A. E. *North England*. Nelson 1960. Reprint 1968.

TOMALIN, M. *Coal Mines and Miners*. 1960.

TYSON, J. C. and TURNBULL, L. *Coals from Newcastle*. Archive Unit No. 1 University of Newcastle.

Visit the Museum at Beamish Hall, Co. Durham. This is an Open Air Museum including all kinds of relics.

LIMESTONE BURNING

Travellers in the north in the eighteenth century mention the building of stone walls and the construction of lime kilns, which were soon active. They were often associated; the better stone went for construction, the smaller and more easily broken pieces went to the kilns. The walls are accepted as part of the landscape: the kilns are forgotten, but were responsible for greatly improving the land.

Lime kilns vary in detail from area to area, but the basic structure is the same.

Limestone could be burnt in a single process in a 'pye' kiln or continuously in a running kiln. The commonest form of kiln is a square or semi-circular tower, built into a hillside or a ramp. Common dimensions are 15-20 feet across and a similar height. Within the structure is an oval or circular bowl some 10 feet in diameter and lined with brick. The sides are parallel internally for 6-8 feet downwards from the top and then taper towards the bottom where there are grates each with two flues. Here after firing, the ash and lime could be raked out. Each grate was within an arched tunnel, and there could be two, three or four of these within one kiln. They were to channel the draught into the fires and to provide a place for filling carts with the burnt lime.

Lime was used both for building purposes and spreading on the fields. It was also used for lime-washing sheds and farmhouses and was regarded as a cleansing agent. Cowsheds had an annual lime wash, and the same was laid down by law for factories after 1800.

Kilns have a fairly long history and for building purposes they were constructed temporarily on a site. Kilns of the eighteenth century were for continuous use. All kinds of fuel were burnt in them—wood, coal, turf or fern. Harder stones took longer to burn but made better lime. Chalk took twenty-four hours to burn, while limestone took some sixty hours.

Arthur Young in 1770 noted near Belford that 'discoveries of coal led to the burning of lime for the purposes of agriculture, as a manure, in a much larger way than had been usual: and for this work three new lime kilns were erected, in a most substantial manner and at great expense.'

He also noticed a good deal of 'intake' land, especially in the lead mining areas. The miners were encouraged to make small holdings, and their little wall-enclosed fields can still be seen near houses that are now derelict.

A great deal depended on transport for the distribution of lime. Beyond the immediate area, pack animals might be used. There also had to be the supplies of fuel, but coal and limestone were often found in association. The kiln was so situated that all the carrying of coal and limestone was downhill. Poor coal could be used for lime burning and about 1800 prices quoted were 1/- per load of smithy coal, 11d. a load for house coal and 7d. a load for lime coal.

Lime kilns and quarries are not immediately recognizable, especially if they have been abandoned for a century or so. The tendency was for concentration in bigger units for commercial purposes and strictly local kilns became disused. Then again with the immediate area about the kiln quarried, it might be advisable to set up a new kiln nearer the source of supply. Very often the quarries and kilns are hidden by a rich growth of grass or vegetation. Trees and hawthorn bushes may have grown in the shelter of a quarry wall.

Kilns as well as quarries may be shown on the 6 inch O.S. survey maps, but when one searches a surprising number may be revealed in the field—as for example at Alwinton near the church and overlooking the Coquet. There are several in the Elsdon area and one at

Tosson near Rothbury. They can be casually mistaken for old fortifications and even called 'peles'—some have rounded arches and others pointed. Exploration will show whether the various factors fit together. Bell pits reveal the source of coal supply and a series of these will generally emerge. Timber was used for lighting the kiln, but all kinds of fuel could be used—bracken, whin (gorse), peat or turf as well as coal. Tramways or cart tracks can be detected leading down to the kiln and away from it. The quarry face was stepped backwards for working and there had to be no dangerous overhang. The stone was systematically removed by first clearing the surface vegetation to prevent any fall and then stone would be brought down by blasting. This was put into carts to be carted to the kiln or for use in field walls. For larger and later enterprises tramways and wagons were used as for coal.

There were also self-acting inclines whereby the loaded trucks descending hauled back the empties to the top of the incline. The tramways were comparatively narrow in gauge—30 inches.

The correct proportions of coal and limestone had to be periodically tipped into the kiln. The burnt lime and ash were raked out at the bottom and shovelled into carts after cooling somewhat.

Tramways could be linked with railways or with harbour jetties.

Lime, like coal, was exported and carried by sea in large quantities. There were lime kilns on a commercial scale at Whitley Bay and Scremerston: there still exist very large lime kilns on Holy Island, at Beadnell and at Seahouses. These must have produced very large quantities of lime and their smoking mouths must have been a feature of the coastline. They were well known as a place of warmth and light.

Large scale limestone-burning centres were near Cambo on the railway, at Chollerton and Longwitton, both on railways. The last two have only recently been discontinued. Although producing good lime, they could not compete with the large chemical combines. Lime carting and spreading was once an important part of farm routine. Now it is carried out by the contractor, who moves in with several great motor wagons and an automatic hopper. A cloud of white or yellow dust will indicate his operations.

A great deal could be written on the story of lime and it presents an interesting contrast to that of coal. Cottage and shed walls were lime washed periodically with brushes made from marram grass. The exterior whitewashing of farmhouses has never been a feature of the Northumberland landscape, in contrast with Cumberland and parts of Durham and Yorkshire. But lime has served to sweeten pastures and improve gardens. Large quantities of lime were used from the Dryburn Quarries at Lowick in 1892 after a serious outbreak of anthrax, before they were at last closed down.

(By burning calcium carbonate becomes calcium oxide, the 'quick' lime of the building trade. Lime was also used for the purification of water.)

LEAD MINING

Lead played an important part in the economy of the north for a very considerable period, and it is difficult to separate Durham and Northumberland. The industry was confined to the Northern Pennines —Upper Teesdale, Weardale, Derwent and Allendale. Another rich area was about Alston on the border between Northumberland and Cumberland. Veins of lead are very different from seams of coal. Coal is a deposition and its seams are horizontal or slightly tilted. Lead is a metallic intrusion that penetrated into the vertical cracks of existing rocks, so that lead deposits are much less predictable and a promising vein can suddenly fade out. These veins may also contain barytes or witherite. The methods of lead mining, therefore, differ from those of coal mining.

Lead mining has a long history, but in the eighteenth century there was intensified development to meet military, colonial and domestic needs. William Ramsay of Newcastle became the chief proprietor of lead mines at Haydon field and Settlington Groves. From 1787 he had old shafts repaired, a dam was built across the Terret Burn to ensure water and new shafts were excavated. He found it more advantageous to pay piece-rates to sinkers and ore getters, rather than a daily rate. Other workers were paid daily for making the dam, pulling and repairing threaves of ling or leading coal, timber or water. The man who 'kept the gin' (presumably worked the horse gin) was paid 2/6d. a week and £25 per annum was paid to the manager. Women were put on washing the ore and were paid 3/6d. per 'bing' (8 cwts.). The men refused less than 6/- per bing. The ore getters and sinkers were paid 15/- and 11/- per bing respectively. These mines were very profitable for a limited time and Ramsay then leased part of Sir William Blackett's mines.

Sir William had inherited substantial properties from his father and added to these some of the mortgaged Fenwick estates. These included Fallowfield, Ridley, Willimoteswick, Halton, Halton Shields and Aydon Castle. The rich veins of lead at Coalcleugh and Allenheads were worked. The London Lead Company at the turn of the century began mining on Alston Moor, about Blanchland and in Upper Weardale. Sometimes the landowners did not exploit the lead deposits themselves, but made leases to adventurers for rents and shares of the product. Greenwich Hospital, which acquired Derwentwater estates, adopted this method. The Blackett-Beaumont group worked their own properties, and made very considerable profits from lead mining. Smelting mills were erected at Langley and Acton near Blanchland. Fallowfield was the northern limit of the lead industry, although attempts to obtain ore were made unsuccessfully further north (e.g. Kirkwhelpington).

The most common method of mining was by a tunnel or level driven into the hillside, following a vein of lead. This tunnel was provided with an arched entrance and was constructed in stone. These levels provided ways along which the lead was hauled by ponies. Wagonways were made at first with timber rails and then of iron. There was not the danger of flooding that beset the coal mines. In fact lead was often revealed by water. A dam was made to build up a considerable head of water, and this was let loose down the hillside, tearing away as it did the top soil and revealing veins of lead in the rock below.

These were called 'hushes' and can still be traced. Lead mining leaves comparatively few surface remains, beyond the entrance to a shaft or level. The surface remains are the crushing and smelting apparatus. For this purpose the ore often had to be carried over difficult country by pack-horses. Hardy 'Galloways' were used carrying 2 or 3 hundredweights each. They used well-formed tracks with paving laid over wet places. Wagonways often could not be attempted in very hilly country.

The 'bouse' or mixed ore was first broken by hand and then passed beneath wood hammers or stamps. These consisted of three or four heavy timbers shod with iron. They were lifted by notches on the shaft of the water wheel and, in dropping, crushed the ore. (Later crushing rollers were used.) The crushed ore was stirred in streams of water running through troughs called buddles. These were at first of timber, but after 1825 were constructed in stone. The tendency was to concentrate on a number of large dressing floors. The dressed ore was reduced in smelt mills. At first these tended to be small in exposed places for draught, but with the use of bellows, driven by water power, they could be in much lower situations. One smelt mill would have several furnaces, since the ore had to be twice refined and silver extracted. One man could tend to a furnace smelting 5-6 cwts. of ore. In the later eighteenth century the big concerns like the London Lead Company and the Greenwich Hospital Estates were able to provide reverberatory furnaces. These were long oblong structures —some 15 feet long and 12 feet wide with a height of 7 or 8 feet. There was an iron grate at one end and a chimney at the other. With a high chimney bellows were unnecessary.

The danger of lead smelting was the highly poisonous fumes that were produced. Lead poisoning was a common occupational hazard for both miner and smelter. It could lead in time to debility, delirium and death. The tall chimneys and long flues were an attempt to take away the fumes, but there were also the possibilities of the recovery of lead from the vapour. The tall chimney became a feature of lead smelting—often two or three miles from the smelt mill and high on the hillside. The chimney and flue could provide an enormous draught and to limit this and to encourage condensation zig-zags were constructed in the flue tunnels. These were constructed of masonry and metallic deposits were brought about on the walls. The flues could be cleaned by water running in the reverse direction from the smoke into settling ponds. The other method of scraping could be dangerous to those taking part in the operation.

Sometimes a condenser house was used and the fumes had to make their way through water or water and brushwood.

All these remains need investigation. A look at Parson and White's Directory of 1828 gives a good idea of the development of the lead industry to that stage. Lead was used for roofing, the making of pipes and of pewter, but above all for the making of ammunition. During the Napoleonic Wars the price of lead rose to £40 per bing (21 cwts.). In 1776 it had been £12 and by 1825 was still fetching £25 per bing. The lead industry tended to go into a decline in the 1870s at the time of an agricultural recession also.

In 1828 the emphasis was on prosperity. 'The level of Nent force, from Old Hagg's engine shaft is a stupendous adit, more than four miles in length; strangers who wish to explore it, may be accommodated with boats and guides by applying at the Lowbyer Inn, Near Alston.' 'A strong vein is now worked near Fallowfield, that was drowned, but recovered about 15 years ago.'

There was some lead at Holy Island and Hartington, but there were great activities about Blanchland. There were smelting mills at Shildon and Beldon with others at Ramshaw and Whiteheaps. A lead mine at Thockrington was not successful, but at Langley it was different.

'Langley Mill is an extensive establishment for smelting and refining the lead ore belonging to Greenwich Hospital. There is another large establishment of the same kind occupied by the Hudgill Mining Company. Both these mills are the property of Greenwich Hospital and contain together 11 smelting hearths, six calcining furnaces, two slag hearths, one reverberatory and two reducing furnaces. The ore smelted here is brought from the mines of Alston Moor. Upwards of 70,000 pigs of lead of 1½ cwt. each are usually produced here yearly and about 50,000 ounces of silver.'

Colonel and Mrs Beaumont were estimated as having an income of £50,000 per annum from lead. Both the Ordnance Department of the Army and the East India Company were supplied. Seeing the danger from railways and improved communications, Colonel Beaumont invested in Spanish lead and reduced his interests in Northern England.

It was a tough life in the lead mining areas and the Wesleys found the men almost savages. They were hard drinkers, though intermittently, since they were paid monthly, but when the settlement of the annual account came there were great celebrations. To pay them £250,000 was brought in a coach protected by dragoons. This was in early summer and there would be terrific spending, including the settlement of debts. Leadminers were not allowed in Newcastle and so made merry in Blaydon. The mines were idle for a complete fortnight or more. The living conditions of the miners could be primitive and they even used rye bread. They depended a good deal on their small holdings and potato patches. These small holdings were not economic units in themselves, and were worked by the family, when the men were in the mines. The farmsteads were scattered because the mines were small. The only concentrations were at the smelt mills. Often the settlements had only a short life before the men moved on. It was not possible to subsist on agriculture alone, though one man might acquire a number of holdings and so continue.

The leadminers were affected by religious movements and, converted by evangelical priests, might become devoted Methodists or Baptists. At first they worshipped and sang in their homes. The chapels came at a later stage and the size is no indication of population. The local chapel might last two or three generations. The decay of lead mines was slow and by degrees the men left. Some might take up other forms of mining or be tempted by the prospects of gold in Australia, United States or elsewhere.

Most of the lead mines have been closed. In 1968 the mine at Settlingstones closed. It had been a lead mine, but was latterly used for the extraction of witherite. It gives a good impression of the working of a small mine and before closure was adequately recorded.

The Settlingstones Mine is situated on the Stanegate west of Newborough and not far from the Roman Wall.

Some of the most important remains of lead mining are at Allendale (NY 837560), where there is a smelt mill by the river to the south-east of the bridge. Below the church is the entrance to the Blackett level, begun in 1855 to drain and explore the valley. Allenheads (NY 860455) is a very good example of a former lead mining village, and here is a dressing floor with the bouse teams or store places for the ore. Each group of miners had a separate store since they were paid on production.

At Killhope (NY 827429) in Upper Weardale is the striking example of a water wheel, 30 feet in diameter, which provided power for a crushing plant. Ore was brought from a nearby level and tipped in the store places. Then it was taken by truck and tipped into a hopper above the iron crushing rollers. After crushing the ore was washed to clear the waste and the lead was taken to the Nenthead smelt mill.

Langley (NY 988414) also had a smelt mill and the flue can be traced over the old railway east of the station. It extends for nearly a mile to a high standing chimney. Coal was supplied to the smelt mill from the adjacent Stubblick Colliery. Both railway and mines have gone into disuse. The lead and coal mines prompted the development of both roads and railways. Railways were taken as far as Alston (which still remains) and to Catton (which has been closed).

The remains of the lead industry give some interest to the empty dales of the North Pennines and elsewhere. The abandoned small holdings can be seen with small green fields, some spoil heaps are still visible and the hushes. There are many mining shafts and a number of isolated tall chimneys. From Allenheads to Allendale is a good area to investigate. A long tour could include Shildon to the north of Blanchland and Ramshaw to the south, in County Durham. Then Rookhope can be reached and a course westwards reaches Allenheads. There is a large smelt mill near Rookhope and remains can be seen including the broken arches that carried the flue over the stream. These areas also provide coal and iron mines and the remains of wagonways. There is still a great deal of quarrying for the construction of roads. The derelict mining areas provide splendid examples of nature taking back her lost acres with coloured coverings of flowers.

Books

BOWLING, H. *The Land of the Three Rivers.* Macmillan 1958.
Beaumont Papers in Newcastle University Library.

CLOUGH, R. T. *Lead Smelting Mills of the Yorkshire Dales.* 1862. (A fine piece of Industrial Archaeology.)

COOMBES, L. C. 'Lead Mining in E. and W. Allendale.' *Archaeologia Aeliana* 1958.

Durham area—History Field Studies. Univ. of Durham 1966.

FORSTER, WESTGARTH. *Section of Strata from Newcastle to Cross Fell.* A. Reid 1883.

HUGHES, E. *North Country Life in the Eighteenth Century.* Oxford 1952.

RAISTRICK, A. *Lead Smelting in the North Pennines during the seventeenth and eighteenth centuries.* Proc. Univ. Durham Phil. Soc. 1966.

RAISTRICK, A and JENNINGS, B. *History of leadmining in the Pennines.* Longmans 1965.

SMAILES, A. E. *North England.* Nelson 1968.

SMITH, S. *Lead and Zinc Ores of Northumberland and Alston Moor.* H.M.S.O. 1923.

CHAPMAN & CHAMBERS. *The beginnings of Industrial Britain.* 1970.

GLASS

Another important industry in the north was glass making. Glass had been comparatively a luxury and windows were regarded as evidence of wealth—hence from 1697 the window tax. Ordinary people might have to be content with materials not transparent or use oiled paper to admit light. Bottles, too, were made of leather for a long time and glass bottles imitated the form of their predecessors. Table glass was very expensive. The establishment of glass manufacture on the Tyne owed a great deal to Huguenot refugees in the seventeenth century, especially from Lorraine. Names such as Henzell, Tysack and Dagnia are evidence of this. The main centres were at South Shields, Newcastle and Lemington. The Cooksons established glass works at South Shields for crown and plate glass. The materials of sand, clay and cheap coal were readily available. Not all the smoke in this area came from the evaporation of brine. Lemington was another centre of glass making, and in 1760 the Delavals established bottleworks at Hartley to make use of the small coal. Thomas Delaval had some experience of the glass industry in Germany. Many of these bottles were exported. Glass was also needed for glasshouses or what we should call 'green' houses. These were an important feature of the eighteenth-century country mansion. There was also a growing passion for plate glass. This was made by rolling molten glass into large flat sheets. Before this process window glass consisted of comparatively small pieces and size of panes can often be an indication of date. Crown glass (sometimes called bull's eye glass) which had a boss in the centre of each pane, became less popular, and tended to go out of production after 1850.

Crystal Palace which housed the Great Exhibition of 1851 expressed the triumph of glass, and in the same year the window tax was abolished. By that time Income Tax was firmly re-established. For a century and a half the Window Tax had provided the government with considerable revenue and the evidence of tax evasion during this period is still visible.

There are not many visible remains of the old glass industry. The huge cone at Lemington dates back to the eighteenth century and glass is still made in the same area. The smaller glass works have disappeared and little remains of the Seaton Sluice bottleworks. However, it is still possible to collect and study local products. These range from the commonplace green glass bottles to the products of Beilby, which may be worth thousands of pounds to collectors.

The glass industry illustrates the way in which several factors combine to bring about development—the availability of raw materials, a plentiful supply of coal and the opportunities of safe transport by sea. The return of ships in ballast also helped the development of the trade. Broken glass was brought back to Seaton Sluice.

It is also of interest to record that in 1880 the first glass bulbs for electrical lighting were blown on Tyneside. Sir Joseph Swan was responsible for the invention.

For a study of glass a visit to the Laing Gallery is necessary and there is a particularly good article by the late Lady Ridley in *Archaeologia Aeliana* Vol. XL (1962) pp. 145-162.

Mackenzie in *General Description of Northumberland* Vol. 1 pp. 167-9 gives a list of 31 glasshouses on Tyne c. 1810.

POTTERY

In the past all kinds of crafts and industries were widespread. This applies to the making of pottery in particular.

'Few places combine more conveniences for manufacturing every form of earthenware than the banks of the Tyne, where there are now about 20 Potteries. Flint and potters' clay are brought from the south of England, in ships coming for coals and the chief materials used for colouring and glazing are procured in the neighbourhood. These establishments, have, within the last 20 years, been considerably improved and several of the largest now produce ware equal in beauty and durability to that manufactured in Staffordshire, from which county large quantities were formerly sent to this port.' (Parson & White, p. cxxxii. 1828.)

References to potteries can be collected from the directories and from old newspapers in which sales of property and other business were advertised. Pottery is valuable for archaeological studies in helping to provide datable deposits, and this applies to all periods. It can help to determine the duration of the occupation of a site and the time of its desertion. It might also be possible to determine whether local pottery was used. This is certain to apply to coarser material, but quality pottery was also made locally. Sometimes the sources of local clay can be discovered.

In addition to the Tyneside potteries, others can be found in the county. In 1740 the *Newcastle Courant* mentions a Pottery at Rivergreen, some four miles to the west of Morpeth and close to the Wansbeck. It is advertised as 'a very good earthenware manufactory, the best in the north', and it was to be let. Later Matthew White of Blagdon advertised two farms at Rivergreen for sale with both lime and coal upon them. There is a house near Meldon still called Clay House, and Hodgson mentions (Pt. 2, Vol. 2, p. 22) that large quantities of blue clay had been taken thence to be worked at Gateshead. There is still some evidence of the pottery near Rivergreen Mill with overgrown mounds and holes.

Another pottery existed at Morpeth. In 1756 the *Newcastle Journal* carries an advertisement—'To be sold by George Ward & Company at their Manufactory at Cottingwood, nigh Morpeth, all sorts of Earthen Ware, glazed and unglazed.' The establishments now on the site are the Girls' and Boys' Grammar Schools, and the material is human 'clay'.

In the *Chronicle* of February 9th, 1793 there is mention of the Spile-Bank Pottery, Morpeth. This may be the same, but there seems no reason for a change of name, since Cottingwood was well known. The Partnership between Richard Austin, Robert Smith and William Green was dissolved and the business of the pottery was to be carried on by Robert Jackson & Company. The incline which takes the road to the north of Morpeth is called Pottery Bank and this may be the site.

Other newspaper references show the dangers of pot making. In the *Journal* of September 16th, 1758 is recorded 'On Wednesday night the pot house at the Skinner Burn was burnt down; and but for the timely assistance of the glassmen in all likelihood many of the adjacent buildings would have been consumed.'

The *Chronicle* of August 12th, 1775 gives some idea of the types of pottery made on the Tyne.

'P. Jackson, Pilgrim Street, Newcastle, having brought his different kinds of Earthenware to great perfection, hopes for Encouragement from his Friends. He sells wholesale and retail at his manufactory on Gateshead Common, adjoining the Turnpike Road and near the two-mile Stone, and at his shop on the Quay, Creamcoloured, enamelled, fine black, gilded, spotted and brown earthenware; also large Ware, as Milk, Cream, Butter and Beef Pots and Washing Mugs. Hawkers from Northumberland and Cumberland may be supplied at his shop.' The itinerant 'pot-man' was a well-known character in most areas.

Information is obtained from local newspapers and directories. Trade Directories or Catalogues illustrate the kind of products that were sold.

TOBACCO PIPES

Another local industry, interesting in itself, has the added advantage of providing datable material in the post medieval period. This is the making of clay tobacco pipes, which were used over a period of more than three centuries, and are still in limited use by smokers as well as by children blowing bubbles. Some old timers still tend to use 'clay-pipes' and the smoking of them was not unknown to women.

Tobacco smoking was a habit adopted by European travellers from American Indians in the later part of the sixteenth century. This became a fashion and caused much controversy. King James I wrote an article attacking the evil practice, but it was encouraged by inn-keepers who kept common pipes. The tobacco container had not to be combustible and metal was first used, but the clay pipe proved to be more suitable. Millions of these must have been produced over the centuries and untold man hours spent in smoking them. The remains are scattered around since the life of a clay pipe was not long. Fragments tend to accumulate on occupational sites, gardens and cultivated fields. They may also indicate the intrusion of stone robbers on archaeological sites.

The first English colony in North America, Virginia, provided tobacco and by 1625 Camden, the antiquary, noticed there were many tobacco shops. Tobacco was grown in this country as well as imported: it was a source of revenue for the Crown.

Since in the early stages of smoking, tobacco was very expensive, the bowls of clay tobacco pipes tended to be small. Very broadly speaking, the greater the length of the stem and the greater the size of the bowl, the later the date of the pipe. During the seventeenth century the habit of tobacco smoking increased, especially as it was considered that tobacco might be effective in warding off the plague. Pipe smoking was combined with coffee drinking, and from the time of Charles II snuff-taking became the fashion in certain elegant circles. A century later Dr Johnson condemned the pipe, but took snuff and drank tea copiously. In the early nineteenth century there was the development of cigar smoking, and from the time of the Crimean War (1854-6) the cigarette. This meant some decline in pipe smoking, and to some extent the briar pipe became a rival to the clay.

White clay was used for pipe making. It was worked to the right consistency and dummy lengths were made from it. Steel wire was threaded to provide an air-hole through the stem and a metal stopper formed the bowl. The moulds were placed under pressure. After drying and finishing the pipes were placed in earthenware firing pots inside furnaces and baked hard.

After being in use for some time the pipes were subjected to fire for cleansing purposes. They were made in quantity and were comparatively cheap to buy. In the eighteenth century a gross of pipes could be purchased for 2/6d. They were stamped with the maker's initials. Pipe clay hair curlers for wigs were also manufactured.

In the north-east clay pipes were probably being made at Gateshead as early as 1640—the supply of clay by sea fitted in with other trading activities, and it might well be carried for ballast. It was not unusual for an innkeeper to be also a pipe-maker.

Until the nineteenth century pipe-makers were confined to areas which were also ports, although there were individuals who moved about. It was a light industry and limited equipment was needed. Pipes were brought into the north from other areas, and one has to consider seamen as well as traders to be a source. Fragments also came in ballast. The disposal of night soil may also account for the distribution of fragments that are found in various places. J. Parsons in *Archaeologia Aeliana* XLII 1964 pp. 249-254 gives a list of 264 known north-eastern pipe-makers. The earliest find dates from about

1650. He also lists sources of information, the different styles for different periods and the variations in makers' marks.

Collecting fragments of clay pipes can add interest to the tedium of gardening. A number of fragments can be collected before ever a bowl is discovered. The fragments bearing makers' initials are only a small proportion of the total. It is possible to piece them together. The writer has collected hundreds of fragments from one Morpeth allotment patch with some 40 bowls. They cover something like 250 years and are the result of 'accidents' not deliberate disposal. The area is part of the north fields of the town, crossed by a footpath which passed close to the site of a mill. This was used for centuries and in the mid-nineteenth century was converted into a public house called the Prince Albert. One proprietor, Tommy Longstaffe, kept a small menagerie and the field is known as Tommy's Field. The archaeological evidence is explained by documentation.

There is a collection of pipes in the Bowes Museum, Barnard Castle, and another in the Black Gate, Newcastle. The firm W. D. and H. O. Wills also have a pipe collection which can be seen by visiting their factory on the Coast Road to Newcastle.

References

PARSONS, J. E. 'The Archaeology of the clay tobacco pipe in north-east England.' *Archaeologia Aeliana* 1964. pp. 231-254.

JARRET, M. G. 'West Whelpington.' *Archaeologia Aeliana* 1962. pp. 217-8. 'Makers of Clay Pipes.' *Archaeologia Aeliana* 1960. pp. 238-9. 'Makers of Clay Pipes.' *Archaeologia Aeliana* 1964. pp. 255-260.

DUNHILL, A. H. *The gentle art of smoking*. Max Reinhardt 1961.

There are some references to tobacco in

DAVIS, DOROTHY. *History of Shopping*. Routledge & Kegan Paul 1966.

About 1680 William Stout of Lancaster, a substantial shopkeeper brought tobacco at 2d. per lb. and sold it for 6d. It is likely that the tobacco (Virginian) had evaded the customs or benefited from the lower duty on colonial products. Colonial tobacco was said to be 'cheap and nasty'. Spanish tobacco on the other hand was good, but very expensive. There was a good deal of adulteration, i.e. other materials were mixed with tobacco. Coltsfoot was used a good deal for this purpose, and no doubt individual smokers made their own mixture.

THE CHEMICAL INDUSTRY

In 1827 Mackenzie, describing Newcastle's trade, wrote, 'Besides coal, the principal exports are glass of all kinds, silver bullion, pig lead, red and white lead, lead shot, butter, pickled salmon, bacon, hams, copperas, grindstones, flagstones, firestones, bricks and tiles, cinders and coke, cast and wrought iron and steel, ale, beer and porter, soap, litharge, earthenware, flour, painters' colours, Prussian blue, salammoniac, soda, oil of vitriol, paper, watch glasses, leather gloves, lamp black, whale oil, coal-tar, canvas, etc.'

This is rather a mixed lot and includes some chemicals. Salt and glass have already been mentioned. Salt was a source of other chemicals and the making of glass was in competition with them. Copperas was a basis for dyes, and in 1748 there was a copperas works at Hartley (the pyrites came from the coal mines).

With the growth of the textile industries bleach was needed, and with the development of dirt of engineering and clothing materials that required frequent washing, soap was in great demand. Alkali was necessary for the making of soap. A good deal of this came from wood ash and kelp, but this was limited in supply, and the most obvious source was natural salt. About 1791 Leblanc patented a process of obtaining soda from salt, and this was adopted by William Losh at Walker. Brine was heated with sulphuric acid to obtain salt cake. This was heated in a furnace with coal and limestone to produce 'black ash'. This needed further processing to form soda crystals and involved a lot of waste. Tall chimneys, characteristic of the chemical industry, were necessary to carry away fumes, but spoil heaps multiplied. About 1859, however, John Glover contrived a tower to recover oxides of nitrate normally lost in the making of sulphuric acid. Gossage towers helped in the recovery of hydrochloric acid gas, from which bleach could be made. Other processes helped the recovery of sulphur from waste. The processes became very complicated and much capital was needed. The authorities imposed all kinds of regulations for the abatement of nuisances, and the result was a tendency to amalgamation. Before 1891 there were something like two dozen factories on Tyneside, but with the formation of the United Alkali Company, they were reduced to four—St Bede at Jarrow, Tennants at Hebburn, Friars Goose and Allhusens. After

1920 only Allhusens remained, and in 1926 this was swallowed up in ICI. The chemical industry tended to move southwards and concentrate at Billingham because natural salts could be obtained directly from wells and not through the lengthy process of evaporation of sea water. The general development was towards concentration in industry.

In 1837 Thomas Hedley, son of a sheep farmer, came to Newcastle and started to make soap. He combined this with the making of candles, so as to be able to use all kinds of tallow. He prospered, but after his death the firm became a limited company (1897). In 1930 it was acquired by Procter and Gamble, but the old name of 'Thomas Hedley' remained for thirty years after this.

By way of contrast Christian Allhusen belonged to a family that left Kiel at the time of the occupation of a large part of Germany by Napoleon. He entered the grain and shipping business and was associated with Henry Bolckow, another German. About 1840 Allhusen's business sense took him into the chemical industry. He took over the moribund soap and alkali works of Doubleday and Easterly. This was turned eventually into the largest alkali works in Europe. Though not a chemist, he readily adopted the new process at the right time, and by the time of his death in 1890, he was a millionaire.

Another industry was the manufacture of chemical manure. Bones, charcoal and animal waste as well as imported chemicals were used for this. It illustrates the disadvantages of living in an industrial town. An inspector reported ... 'It not infrequently happens that in some of the works registered for the manufacture of chemical manure, some allied trade is also carried on which is of a nature to give rise to much complaint owing to its noxious or unpleasant character, such as that of horse slaughterer, bone boiler, blood drier, glue maker etc. ...

'The manure is made from carcases, shoddy leather, slaughter house refuse and some mineral phosphate. The method is as follows—a heap of 20 or 30 tons of shoddy is made in the shed and on this is poured blood and refuse from the slaughter houses. Any carcases that the owner may buy ... are, after being skinned, buried in this heap, the heap being allowed to stand and rot for five or six months.' It was later turned and mixed with bone, acid and chemicals. The stench was terrible.

Crushing machinery was needed in the first instance for bones, but later for crushing phosphate rocks.

The oldest superphosphate works on Tyneside was founded at Blaydon by William Richardson in 1844, and reconstituted as the Blaydon Alkali and Manure Works in 1877.

Langdale's factory started in 1849 and Fisons are still on this old site.

Other trades were concerned with the making of dyes, colours and paints. These were used in all kinds of other industries—ship building, engineering, decorating and printing. There was also a growth in the production of proprietary medicines and drugs to meet the ailments of a growing industrial society. In 1868 nearly a hundred of these are listed (Campbell pp. 47-9).

Industrial archaeology can involve the collection and study of the smaller remains, as well as the investigation of larger sites, where these have not been covered. Some of these products were made locally before the tendency to concentration on Tyneside. Much information can be obtained from newspapers, directories and the proceedings of various societies as well as the account books of defunct firms. For example, the mill on the Coquet at Guyzance Bridge was used for the production of aluminium hydroxide and its coloured lakes. The term 'Guyzance White' is still used in the printing industry.

COAL GAS

The production of coal gas for lighting purposes can be regarded as part of the chemical industry. The production of tars and coke are associated with the same process. Some firms provided their own gas lighting at an early stage. From January 1818 there was the first gas lighting in Newcastle in Moseley Street. This was extended and gas lamps began to replace the 1,000 oil lamps Newcastle had. By 1827 there were 269 gas lamps in the town centre. The gasworks were usually unable to provide all that was needed. There was no guarantee of quantity or quality and there were numerous accidents. It was not until 1838 that a number of small firms were bought out by the Newcastle and Gateshead Gas Company. Thirty years later the Redheugh Gas Works greatly increased the output of gas. Gaslight became the characteristic of an age, but gas was also used for industrial and heating purposes. There was a proliferation of gasworks in the smaller towns, and the cast iron lamp standards became a part of the environment. The incandescent gas mantle gave a yellowish light and the gas made a hissing sound. This in turn has been replaced by electricity—bright and silent.

Sir Joseph Swan played an important part in the process. Many houses still show signs of the gas light fittings that preceded electricity. The process continues and pipe lines are being laid across the countryside to carry the natural gas from the bed of the North Sea to various parts of the country.

CAMPBELL, W. A. *A Century of Chemistry on Tyneside.* p. 23 gives list of chemicals exported from Tyne 1893.

MAPS AND THEIR USES

For the study of an area a number of maps are necessary. For convenience of handling and containing most of the county on one sheet, the Bartholomew ½ inch map is very useful. It gives contours and places of historical interest as well as the roads of the area. For a more detailed investigation six 1 inch Ordnance Survey Maps are needed—O.S. 64 Berwick, O.S. 70 Jedburgh, O.S. 78 Alnwick, O.S. 76 Carlisle, O.S. 77 Hexham and O.S. 78 Newcastle. These are a necessary minimum for exploring in the field and preliminary investigation in the study. They are quite detailed and reveal a surprising amount of information.

For a more intensive study the 2½ inch Ordnance Survey Maps are very valuable and are needed for special areas. More detailed still are the 6 inch maps. These are kept at the County Library and County Record Office, but educational institutions usually have a supply and it is possible to get parts duplicated.

The 25 inch maps provide the detail necessary for the intensive study of urban areas.

Ordnance Survey Maps have now reached their centenary, and they have frequently been reproduced since the 1860s. David and Charles are now reproducing facsimiles of the first 1 inch O.S. maps. This makes it possible to compare the county as it was a century ago with the present situation. This is necessary to assess the changes, and it is particularly valuable in the study of roads and railways. One can trace missing villages or farmsteads and discover more modern settlements. There has been much change in the location of mining villages. Surprising changes are shown by comparing the 1948 maps with those of 1968, and in a few years hence great changes in the roads system will have taken place.

The older maps show the routes of now abandoned railways, isolated schools and unfrequented roads. It is rather important to preserve rights of way which may lapse with disuse. Milestones, mileposts and toll bars may be shown as well as mills and old coal pits. The comparison of new and old maps is a stimulus to investigation. The explorer is prompted to look into the old directories and records for further information.

The Ordnance Survey also supplies geological maps and maps showing land utilization. These are closely correlated and help to illuminate other maps. The Ordnance Survey produces Historical and Archaeological Maps. Here it is important to be up to date, since these maps record sites that have been investigated. Earlier ones can only serve to illustrate the process of archaeological research.

Ancient Britain covers the Pre-Roman period and Map 1 covers the North of Britain.

Roman Britain covers the period A.D. 43 to A.D. 410 and the map covers the whole country. There is a separate detailed map for Hadrian's Wall.

Britain in the Dark Ages covers the 500 years after the departure of the Romans.

Monastic Britain covers the country with two maps. The northern one covers Northern England and Scotland. Further maps are being done on Ancient Monuments, and the Department of the Environment and the National Trust both produce maps giving the location of ancient monuments and places of historical interest.

The Ordnance Survey still supply the Gough Map of Great Britain, reproduced from the fourteenth-century original in the Bodleian Library, at the remarkably low cost of 25p. The Department of the Environment supply facsimiles of the Saxton Maps of the sixteenth century, county by county. These are remarkably good value at 37½p. each.

Reproductions of the maps of Speed (c. 1610) are also available from Phoenix House or Frank Graham.

A Descriptive List of the Maps of Northumberland 1576-1900 has been compiled by Harold Whitaker and published for the Newcastle Society of Antiquaries in 1949. This gives details of all known maps of Northumberland.

In addition to those already mentioned, very valuable are Mercator's Maps from 1595, Hollar and Janson from 1644. John Ogilby produced a series of road maps in 1675, and Warburton a very useful map in 1716.

After the 1745 Rebellion a survey was made of the Roman Wall area for the purpose of constructing a Military Road from Newcastle to Carlisle. This has been reproduced by the Newcastle Society of Antiquaries.

Shortly after 1750 Kitchin produced an excellent map of Northumberland which gives roads, estates and industrial activities in some detail. Armstrong's Map of 1769 shows how far the making of turnpikes had proceeded in 20 years.

Cary produced another good map in 1787, and there were maps made to accompany the Agricultural Survey of 1794. The maps of Greenwood 1828-31 are of the greatest value. By way of contrast Cobbett in 1832 produced what is described as 'the crudest map of all' in a geographical survey. It is a not very accurate outline of Northumberland with fifteen dots upon it. Berwick, Coldstream, Wooler, Belford, Alnwick, Rothbury, Bellingham, Morpeth, Haltwhistle, Hexam (his spelling), Corbridge, Allendale, Blyth, North Shields and Newcastle are the only places he records.

There follows a fairly regular procession of maps after this, used in the directories. Special maps are compiled for railways. About 1850 detailed maps of the collieries were made by Bell, and these include the local estates with the big houses and their owners.

Estate maps provide additional information at various times. Other maps that are very valuable but varying in date are the Enclosure Awards of the Agrarian Revolution in the late eighteenth century and early nineteenth. After 1838 maps were drawn in connection with the Commutation of Tithes. These are listed with dates in the handbook to the Northumberland County Records Office (Appendix A) together with the Enclosure Awards (Appendix B). Railways' plans are listed in Appendix C.

Local authorities have plans of public works and buildings. There were also detailed surveys made following the Public Health Act 1848.

The continuous supply of maps during the century of Ordnance Survey has been indicated. Finally, the aeroplane has provided another method of land survey, revealing the past as well as recording the present. Air photographs can be used very profitably in connection with the relevant maps.

Maps also provide information about local government, poor law areas and political constituencies.

USE OF ARCHIVES

The student of local history is faced with a number of problems in seeking information about a family, person, place or industry. Questions may be put by others or they may arise from the course of enquiry. One may wonder why a place, road, or field has a particular name or why a road takes an unusual turn. A house may have some blocked windows (the result of window tax?). A field may have an uneven surface, or growths of denser vegetation in parts. This may be the signs of an abandoned settlement.

To look at a series of maps may explain names and changes. Place names disappear or a village name becomes the name of a farm. This has to be explained, and old prints or plans may provide some information. Information from local inhabitants may be valuable, but it has to be checked for accuracy. Archive material may provide the necessary additional information.

Directories will provide information about an area, including the names and occupations of the people. These, however, tend to be not earlier than 1801, the year of the first census. Before this Parish Registers have to be used in an attempt to gather vital statistics. Very few parishes have records dating to Tudor times, and there was much destruction in the Civil War. Registers were not kept during that period, and although they were resumed after 1660, many have decayed or disappeared. These registers may be still kept in the church itself or they may have been transferred to the Local Records Office. If the registers are not there, there may well be transcripts or microfilm copies for perusal. A good deal depends on the parochial centre—the Borough of Blyth lies within the limits of the parish of Earsdon and Bedlington was attached to the Palatinate of Durham. Records may be in the Diocesan Registry.

The church can provide information about the number of persons attending communion, the number of Protestant or Catholic Dissenters. There is also a good deal of information relating to schools and schoolmasters. From school records information about the community can be obtained, and this is first hand material.

Tithe Maps (c. 1840) provide valuable information. By Act of Parliament (1838) tithes, payable in produce from certain lands to the church or the lay appropriator, were converted into a money rental, based on the price of corn. For this purpose a comprehensive land survey was made and it is evident who held properties in a particular area at this time.

In a county of large estates a great deal of information is obtainable from family papers. These are often deposited at the County Records Office, and are available for inspection. The estates may cover a very wide area and surveys were periodically made. Good examples are obtainable from the Greenwich Hospital Estate Reports. Greenwich Hospital acquired a good deal of Derwentwater property after the 1715 Rebellion. Lord Beveridge, a Northumbrian, obtained much of his information for the study of prices from Greenwich Hospital records.

From estate records details can be obtained about agriculture—rents, rotation of crops, wages and prices. Particulars are obtained about stock and industrial activities—mining, limestone burning, the making of bricks and tiles. Details are provided concerning farms, cottages and fields, mills and smithies. Information may be acquired about transport, travel, food supply and the activities of servants within the household. Extensive surveys were made of the Percy estates at different periods. It is possible to see how and when enclosures were made. Villages present different aspects at different times. Some surveyors made detailed plans of roads as well as boundaries and buildings. Field names are also recorded.

Other surveys show the effects of landscaping, emparking and the planting of trees. Surveys of Capheaton of 1761 and 1799 show a remarkable development of trees during this period. The effects of drainage are also shown—a bog may be drained or converted into an ornamental lake. Plans may vary from those of a dovecote or school to a complete change in the layout of a big house or estate.

Farms may be separately detailed with rental, acreage and buildings, including the horse gin. Dovecotes tend to go into decay in the nineteenth century, and by chance unusual things can be recorded—a windmill used for threshing corn or raising coals from a mine. The surveyor may fancy the 'fire engine' for pumping purposes and includes a little illustration of it. Follies also occur, especially in the eighteenth century. Accounts give details of expenditure on different items.

Changes such as the enclosure of land, the development of roads and railways, the promotion of water works and gas works all required public approval through Act of Parliament. The terms of the Acts and development plans are very often deposited at the Local Record Office. These can be inspected.

Some of the problems that can be worked out are the effects of the development of a road, railway or reservoir in a particular area. One form of transport affects another and changes in the use of land influence the development or decline of communities. This can be traced in educational provision or the frequency of attendance at religious centres. (An isolated school or chapel indicated population in the area at one time.) One source of information supplements another, and estate records can detail the activities of an entire community.

Other types of Records deposited include those of mining. Mining activities went on for centuries by private enterprise until nationalization. There were successes and failures. Old maps show the widespread mining activities in hill country, where workings would not now be profitable. There are records of wages, hours and working conditions, questions of profitability and problems of safety.

There are fairly full records of the activities of various Railway Companies as well as the development of roads through Turnpike Trusts.

Other problems that can be investigated concern law and order, the administration of justice, charities and what might be termed social services. Modern changes make investigations all the more urgent. The activities of the Justices of the Peace can be studied from Quarter Sessions Records. The Justices were responsible for all kinds of matters besides the administration of justice. The establishment of County Councils did not come about till 1888 and a great deal of the work, now carried out by them, was a century ago the responsibility of other bodies.

Poor Law was a perennial problem, and the basis of the poor law system was established in the time of Elizabeth I. During the eighteenth and early nineteenth centuries it was under great pressure from social changes. In 1834 the Poor Law Amendment Act altered the organization. The parish ceased to be the unit; parishes were amalgamated into Poor Law Unions, each with a workhouse. Local Boards of Guardians were established for purposes of administration. Records are available of the administration of the Poor Law before and after 1834. There are Records in the County Archives Office relating to Alnwick, Belford, Bellingham, Berwick, Haltwhistle, Hexham and Morpeth. 'Poor Law' became 'Public Assistance' and finally 'Social Security' in the era of the Welfare State. National responsibility now makes it all the more necessary to investigate local responsibility of the past.

The police system is also subject to change and amalgamation of local forces occurs. Police Records have been deposited at the County Archives centre. Military service has also undergone great changes and here is a field for further investigation—the local regiments and their activities. Methods of recruitment provide material for an interesting study.

Particularly in towns, the study of matters like water supply and sanitation require investigation. Originally both of these were on a local, help yourself basis. There are springs, wells, pumps, pants, public fountains and horse troughs. With increasing population in urban areas, Town Councils had to take action. Good examples are the emergence of the Newcastle and Gateshead and the Tynemouth Water Companies, bringing water from a considerable distance to increasingly thirsty towns. Sanitation is the problem of the disposal of waste which tends to increase. Here again it became a more general responsibility of the government and local authorities to enforce cleanliness and a proper drainage system. Drainage is half the problem of housing. Houses, too, are a subject for study.

Other matters for investigation are prisons, hospitals and mental institutions. There is detailed material available about voluntary organizations and public bodies dealing with these matters.

Other organizations to be investigated are local Trade Unions, Co-operative Societies and Mechanics Institutes. These are all interconnected in the development of modern democracy.

A wider field for investigation is that of elections, both for Parliament and for local councils. A great deal of material is available in the form of public and private papers, posters, pamphlets and writings in local newspapers. Expenses for elections are often included in the accounts of the county families. Poll books are also available showing who voted for whom in a particular election. Parliamentary reform ended the open type of election.

Other sources of information are Window Tax, Hearth Tax and Land Tax assessments. Hair Powder Tax certificates may be an interesting side line.

There are all kinds of matters relating to borough administration, both before and after the Municipal Reform Act of 1835. Information includes Court Records, Council Minutes, Guild Records, the administration of the common fields or perhaps a river with port facilities.

From various sources information can be collected about sports, pastimes and entertainments. Local customs may also be included and the study of dialect or song. There are local artists and local craftsmen—makers of bagpipes or shepherds' crooks.

Local Archive Repositories

Cumberland. County Archives, Carlisle Castle.
Durham. County Archives, Shire Hall, Durham.
Also the Priors Kitchen, University of Durham.
Gateshead. Library.
Newcastle. City Archives, 7, Saville Place, Newcastle.
University Library.
Central Library.
Literary and Philosophical Society Library.
Mining Institute Library.
Northumberland County Record Office, Melton Park, Gosforth.
Northumberland County Library, Morpeth.

Useful Books

CELORIA, F. *Teach yourself Local History.*
DOUCH, R. *Local History and the Teacher.*
DIBBEN, A. D. *Title Deeds.* (Historical Association.)
EMMISON, F. G. *Introduction to Archives.* B.B.C.
Archives and Local History.
How to read Local Archives.
County Records. (Historical Association.)
GOODER, E. A. *Latin for Local History.*
GRIEVE, H. *Examples of English Handwriting.* (Essex Record Office.)
HECTOR, L. C. *Handwriting of English Documents.*
HOSKINS, W. G. *Local History in England.*
HUMPHREYS, D. W. *Local History for Students.* (Historical Association.)
KUHLICKE, F. W. *English Local History Handlist.* (Historical Association.)
POWELL, W. R. *Local History from Blue Books.* (Historical Association.)
TATE, W. E. *The Parish Chest.*
WEST, J. *Village Records.*
The *Local* (formerly *Amateur*) *Historian* is published by the National Council for Social Service, 26, Bedford Square, London, W.C.1.

PHOTOGRAPHS, PICTURES AND PRINTS

Photography is a remarkable development of the last century or so. Before its invention the artist recorded his impressions of persons, buildings and landscapes. An artist would paint, draw or engrave a representation of a horse, an ox or dog for the eighteenth-century aristocrat. My lord might have himself painted individually or with his family against the background of his mansion or hall. These can have their beauty enhanced by the skill of the artist. The camera, too, can mislead by cutting a scene from connection with its regular environment or by providing the most favourable light. But the photograph can be a piece of evidence and the camera a method of obtaining it.

A series of photographs or transparencies of a house or church can be used as a method of detailed study. The building can be reviewed in tranquillity and all kinds of details may emerge that were not apparent to the photographer. The photograph or transparency can show different stages of building from the texture of the mortar or stonework or the size of the bricks. An additional storey to a house may be shown; the positions of windows may have been altered and the photograph shows the changes.

Photographs or transparencies can be used to study the details of structure that are not obvious from the ground. Details of carving, vaulting and roof bosses can be seen from the transparency. Carved misericorde seats can be much more easily studied in this way, rather than crouching in the chancel of a church.

Whereas the artist or observer is selective and only sees what he wants to see, the camera records all that variations of light, shade and colour make apparent. This means that photographs and transparencies can be used for general study. A landscape can be a beautiful scene, a geological study, a piece of agriculture, or afforestation, a geographical study, or an example of rural sociology. The cloud formations might also be included. The photographer might be recording field patterns that he had not noticed. Sometimes one has to go back to see whether what the camera recorded was really there.

A selection of photographs or slides can be a necessary preparation for a field study. It can be indicated to members of a group, the features or details that are to be observed on the site. Since there is so much change in building and development, the landscape and the townscape need to be recorded periodically to indicate the extent of change.

Some photographs and slides should be purchased for a small collection. The ordinary photographer cannot compete with the professional, especially when photographing interiors and some Ministry of Works photographs or slides are an asset. The photographer can add to these others of personal interest.

Obviously the most valuable type of photograph or slide to buy is the aerial view, which is difficult to obtain even if one chartered an aircraft. The Ministry of Works provide excellent examples from the buildings under their care.

Aerial photographs are a special study in themselves. They provide general views of fairly wide areas. A photograph of this kind can cover a number of square miles and this technique has been used for mapping. It was also used a great deal in the last war for discovering enemy activities. The air photograph can reveal depressions in the ground and also mounds or structures. Disturbances of the soil are also revealed. Air photography has revealed all kinds of sites by differences of soil or crop cover. At ground level nothing whatsoever would be visible.

The air photograph is the best method of studying a prehistoric earthwork, a Roman camp, a Saxon palace, a motte and bailey site, a monastic plan, a deserted village or an inhabited town. It readily reveals methods of communication and one can see the interaction of roads, rivers and railways. Aerial photography provides endless possibilities.

Photography now has a history of more than a century and it is important that old photographs should be preserved for record purposes. They provide information on family groups, ceremonies, dress and social status. Postcards come into this category too and are a a method of recording the appearance of places at different times. In the early decades of the twentieth century there was a cult of the postcard and many of these were collected. In the era of the cine camera and coloured transparencies at least a selection of the old postcards should be preserved in every local museum. They are also suitable material for the County Records Office.

BOOKS

B. ALLSOP. *Historic Architecture of Northumberland.* Oriel Press 1969.

B. ALLSOPP. *Historical Architecture of Newcastle upon Tyne.* Oriel Press 1968.

A. A. CAESAR. *A Regional Survey of England and Wales—N.E. England.* G. Philip 1954.

D. DOUGAN. *Newcastle Past and Present.* Frank Graham 1971.

R. GARD. *Northumberland at the turn of the Century.* Oriel Press 1970. Old photographs reproduced with brief comment.

F. GRAHAM. *Northumberland & Durham 100 years ago.* F. Graham.

Picturesque Northumberland & Durham. F. Graham. Old prints faithfully reproduced.

Historic Newcastle. F. Graham 1970. Many illustrations in colour.

J. K. S. ST JOSEPH. *The use of Air Photography.* John Baker.

Medieval England. C.U.P. 1958.

Monastic Sites from the Air. C.U.P. 1952.

N. MCCORD. *Northumberland. History from the air.* F. Graham. 1972.

N. MCCORD and D. T. ROWE. *Northumberland and Durham. An Industrial Miscellany.* F. Graham 1971.

J. A. STEERS. *The English Coast.* Collins.

D. SIMPSON. *Castles from the Air. Country Life* 1949.

WINTER. *Country Camera. Country Life.*

H.M.S.O. *Border National Park.* H.M.S.O. 1969.

The Northumberland Record Office has a collection of slides.

Turners of Newcastle have local slides and air photographs.

There is a collection of Air Photographs at the Museum of Antiquities, Newcastle upon Tyne.

Aerofilms have a fine catalogue of air photographs.

Also Air Photos Unit, Ministry of Housing and Local Government, Whitehall, London, S.W.1.

LOCAL SONGS

Northumberland and Durham are famous for their local dialect songs. Well over five thousand have survived. The following list gives some of the best known collections.

T. G. ALLAN. *Allan's Illustrated Edition of Tyneside Songs.* 1891. Reprint, 1972. With important introduction by David Harker.

T. ARMSTRONG. *Tommy Armstrong Sings.* All the known songs of Stanley's pitman poet collected in one volume.

T. BELL. *Rhymes of Northern Bards.* 1812. Reprint, 1971. Introduction by David Harker. The classic collection of northern songs.

G. POLWARTH. *North Country Songs.* 1969.
Folk Songs of the North. 1970.
Come You not from Newcastle. 1972.

C. SHARP. *The Bishoprick Garland.* 1834. Reprint, 1969.

NORTH COUNTRY ARTISTS

From the monks who decorated the Lindisfarne Gospels and the Codex Amiatinus down to the twentieth-century Northumberland has had many fine artists. Unfortunately little has been written about them. The Catalogues of past Exhibitions at the Laing Art Gallery are of great importance. The following books are of interest.

B. ANDERSON. *Thomas Bewick, The Tyneside Engraver.* 1928.

G. BOYD. *Bewick Gleanings.* 1886. Reprint, 1973.

C. S. FELVER. *Joseph Crawhall. The Newcastle Wood Engraver.* (1821-1896). 1972.

C. E. HARDY. *John Bowes and the Bowes Museum.* 1971.

R. ROBINSON. *Thomas Bewick. His Life and Times.* 1887. Reprint, 1972.

W. B. SCOTT. *Scenes from Northumbrian History.* The Mural Paintings at Wallington Hall.

M. WEEKLEY. *Thomas Bewick.* 1953.

L. WILKES. *Tyneside Portraits.* 1971. Biographies of Robert Trollop, Charles Avison, Thomas Bewick, Beilby Family, T. M. Richardson (Senior), Richard Grainger, John Dobson, W. B. Scott, Jack Common.

ACKNOWLEDGEMENTS

This work was begun in 1968-9 during a Fellowship at Newcastle University, and I have to thank the Northumberland Education Committee for the opportunity, and the History and Education Departments of the University for providing a temporary abode. I am grateful to the Museum of Antiquities and University Library for services provided. The County Record Office and County Library have been very helpful. Numerous landowners, farmers and houseowners have kindly allowed me to inspect and photograph their properties. I have received encouragement from the growing number of Local History Societies and from my publisher, Mr. Frank Graham. Finally my wife did most of the typing.
Note—For Ministry of Works read Department of Environment.

INDEX

Brick tax, 87